SHIFTING SANDS

Links of Noltland, Westray: Interim Report on Neolithic and Bronze Age Excavations, 2007–09

Archaeology Report no 4

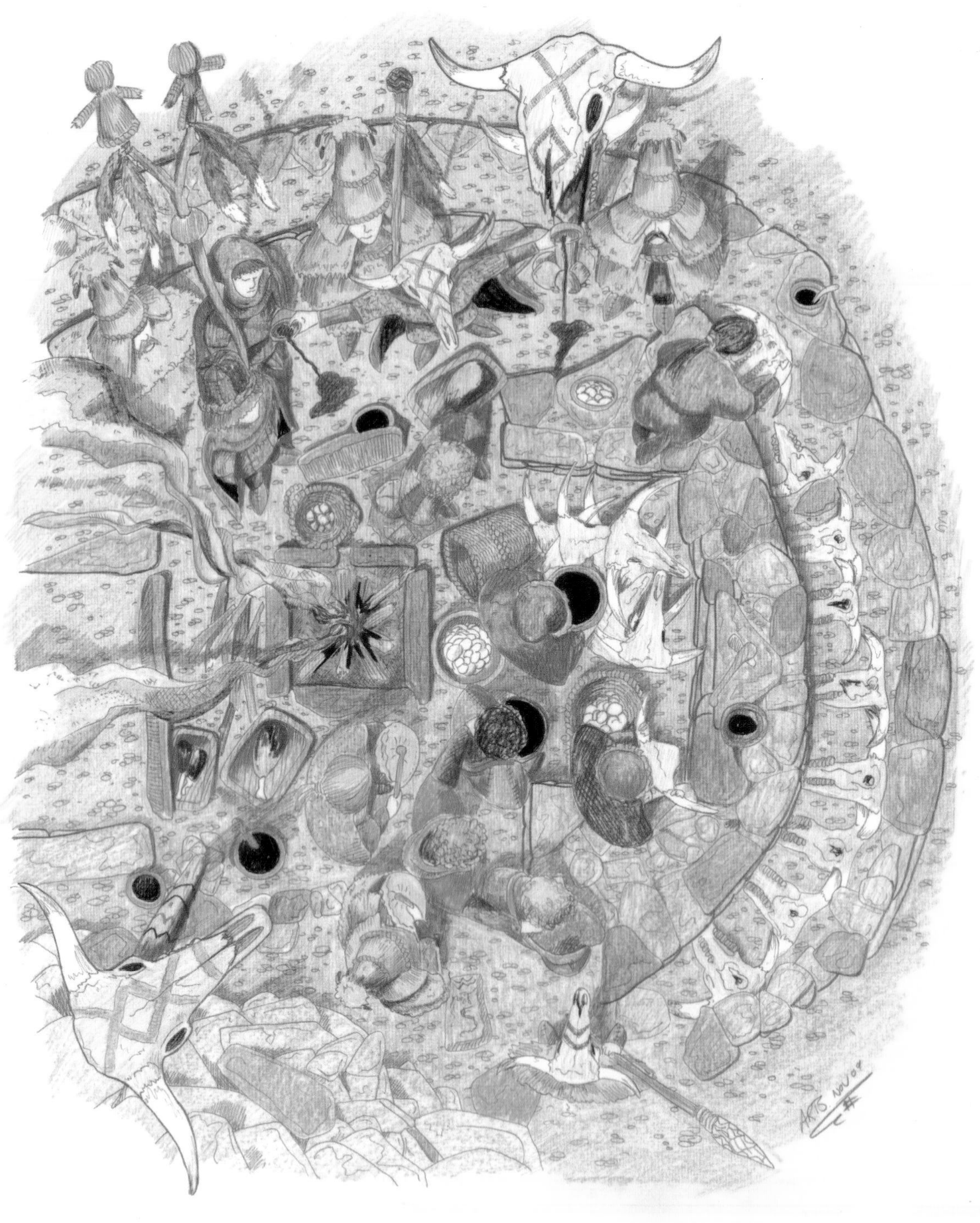

An imaginative reconstruction of a ceremony to deposit the cow skulls within the foundations of Structure 9. Illustration by Alan Braby.

SHIFTING SANDS

Links of Noltland, Westray: Interim Report on Neolithic and Bronze Age Excavations, 2007–09

Archaeology Report no 4

Hazel Moore and Graeme Wilson

With contributions by

John Carrott, Charlotte Crowston, Amanda Forster, Sheena Fraser, Dawn Gooney, Elizabeth Goring, Mhairi Hastie, Laura McKenna, Dawn McLaren, Sean Rice, Alan Saville, Alison Sheridan and Ian Simpson

Illustrations by

Alan Braby and Marion O'Neill

Contributors

John Carrott: Palaeoecology Research Services Ltd, Kingston upon Hull
Charlotte Crowston: Edinburgh
Amanda Forster: Birmingham
Sheena Fraser: Edinburgh
Dawn Gooney: Dept of Archaeology, University of Edinburgh
Elizabeth Goring: Edinburgh
Mhairi Hastie: Centre for Field Archaeolopgy (CFA), Musselburgh
Laura McKenna: School of Biological and Environmental Sciences, University of Stirling
Dawn McLaren: National Museum of Scotland, Edinburgh
Hazel Moore: EASE Archaeology, Edinburgh
Sean Rice: Cheltenham
Alan Saville: National Museum of Scotland, Edinburgh
Alison Sheridan: National Museum of Scotland, Edinburgh
Ian Simpson: School of Biological and Environmental Sciences, University of Stirling
Graeme Wilson: EASE Archaeology, Edinburgh

First published by Historic Scotland 2011

ISBN 978-1-84917-051-2

Cover photographs by Michael Brooks

CONTENTS

LIST OF ILLUSTRATIONS

ABSTRACT

Extensive archaeological remains lie in coastal machair at Links of Noltland, discovered and initially excavated by Dr David Clarke in the late 1970s. The site is designated as a Scheduled Ancient Monument and is managed by Historic Scotland as a Property in Care on behalf of Scottish Ministers. Over the past 20 years, the surrounding dune system has been depleted by natural forces, possibly linked to climate change. Traces of older landscapes and ancient human activity are being revealed as sand is stripped away. An ongoing campaign of monitoring and assessment, commissioned and sponsored by Historic Scotland, has recently been followed up with rescue excavation and more than a dozen stone buildings of Neolithic and Bronze Age date have so far been recorded: all are unusually well preserved.

This is the setting, richly endowed with fields, farms, houses and tombs, for several millennia of human endeavour through some of the most formative yet least known periods in Orkney's past. The exceptional significance of the site was already beyond question when, in 2009, a small stone figurine was recovered which is now recognised as representing the earliest depiction of the human form from Scotland; equally exceptional is a building with whole cattle skulls set into its foundations. This multiplicity of remains sets Links of Noltland apart: not only are the individual houses and fields of great interest in themselves, but the opportunities they offer to investigate the inter-relationships between settlements of contemporary date and over longer time frames are surely unique. This report brings together the findings of excavation with the preliminary specialist analyses to provide an interim summary of the results to a wider audience. It is hoped that this will generate discussion and interest which, in turn, will inform future work.

ACKNOWLEDGEMENTS

The authors would like to thank Lorna and Jim Brown, the landowners at Noltland, for their support and practical assistance; their interest in this project has been a great encouragement to us and their local knowledge has been invaluable. We would also like to thank William and Sandy McEwan who never failed to find room for us when it was needed and who have helped in so many ways with our work on Westray over the years. Isabelle and John Harcus have also supported and assisted us, for which we are very grateful. The support of the wider community of Westray, and especially the Westray Heritage Trust, has been a key factor in the project. At Historic Scotland, Peter Yeoman, Richard Strachan, Allan Rutherford and Rod McCullagh have all individually steered us along gently, offering advice and support when it was needed. And thanks to Andrew Burnet at Historic Scotland for managing this publication, with copy-editing by Jackie Henrie. Olly Owen, Caroline Wickham-Jones, Niall Sharples and David Clarke have contributed ideas and discussed past excavations, providing many useful insights. We would like to express our thanks to the project management board, which has broad representation including Doreen Grove and Peter Bromley from Historic Scotland, and Julie Gibson, the County Archaeologist. Thanks are also due to Historic Scotland's Monument Conservation Unit in Orkney, and to Lucy Vaughan and Stephen Watt from Historic Scotland's Regional Office at Fort George. Alan Braby is responsible for the wonderful illustrations with the exception of the figurine, for which we thank Marion O'Neill. Finally, we would like to thank all of our team members, past and present, for their enthusiasm, dynamism and fortitude, often in the face of appalling weather conditions. They are, in no particular order: Amanda Brend, Martin Carruthers, Charlotte Crowston, Ian Dudley-Channell, Patricia Edwards, Rebecca Enlander, Janine Ferguson, Eddie Fitzgerald Clarke, Sheena Fraser, Dawn Gooney, Sarah Hammond, Jakob Kainz, Maeve McCormick, Ellen McInnes, Laura McKenna, Finn Morris, Alexis Mosely, Hazel Mosely, Paul Neary, Mairead Ni Challanain, Dan O'Meara, Tessa Poller, Sean Rice, Claire Riley, Tudor Skinner, Sam Voake, Al Wright, and Duncan Wright.

1 INTRODUCTION

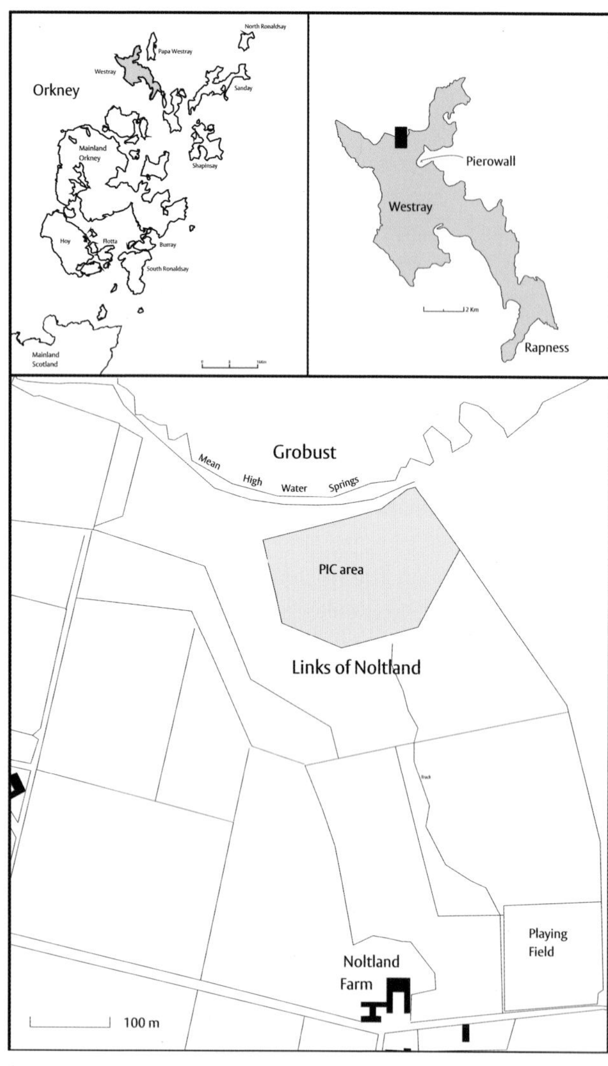

1 Location map

Archaeological remains sporadically exposed at Links of Noltland on the Orcadian island of Westray (HY 428 493) indicate that the area was a focus for human activity in the earlier prehistoric period. Neolithic and Bronze Age period settlement and agricultural remains are both abundant and well preserved. In recognition of its exceptional archaeological significance, a substantial percentage of the area was taken into state care as a Property in Care (PIC) in 1984 and a further portion was designated as a Scheduled Ancient Monument (HS Index 90337, HY44 NW33).

Geomorphologically, the area forms part of a high energy system which is subject to complex processes of erosion and deposition. In recent years, erosion has worsened considerably and hitherto unaffected areas have become vulnerable. In direct consequence, many more archaeological remains have been exposed and are at risk from destruction.

Historic Scotland responded to this risk by implementing an extensive programme of archaeological monitoring, together with a range of conservation measures. The latter have included reburial of individual sites, hard landscaping works, sowing marram grass and the erection of a protective fence. The evidence suggests that while such measures can provide short-term respite, they will not be sufficient to safeguard all of the remains currently at risk. The archaeological response has now moved on to a rescue footing, with attention directed towards the rapid recovery of information from the most threatened sites, rather than preservation *in situ*. The aim of this work is to increase our knowledge of this early settlement and, at the same time, to better define the priorities for longer-term protection.

Four seasons of rescue excavation have been completed since 2007 and further field seasons are programmed for summer 2010 and beyond. This work has already identified some 14 separate stone buildings, comprising several houses together with associated outbuildings, paths, field boundaries, cultivation soils and refuse middens. Much of the original design of the buildings is clearly discernible; in many cases the walls survive to a height of over 1 m. Inside, clues to the daily life of the settlement lie in the artefact-rich organic deposits covering the floors. Bone is exceptionally well preserved, in contrast to many other sites of this period.

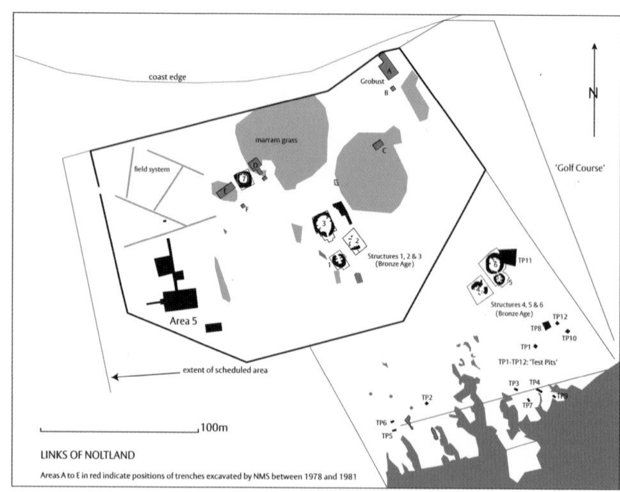

2 Location of known archaeological interventions, 1978–2009

Preliminary analyses indicate that settlement developed over a lengthy period of time, with origins from at least around 2900 cal BC.

The national and international significance of Links of Noltland is beyond question. Neolithic settlement is in any case rare and in its state of preservation, Links of Noltland is comparable to Skara Brae, the importance of which is internationally recognised by its incorporation in a World Heritage Site. As with Skara Brae, the remains here allow for 'a level of interpretation unmatched on other excavated settlement sites of this period in Europe' (Historic Scotland 1998). Bronze Age settlement in Orkney is rarer still and in this context offers us the unparalleled opportunity to investigate continuity and change in an early farming community over a long period of time.

Natural Background

The site lies in an area of coastal machair, extending to some 42ha (104 acres) in area, located behind Grobust Bay on the north coast of Westray. The dune system, which formerly stood behind the beach, has now largely deflated. Substantial deposits of loose, shell-rich sand cover a thin layer of boulder clay over Old Red Sandstone flags. Outcrops of aeolianite (cemented sand) are present along the shore. Much of the area is now bare of vegetation and resembles an undulating 'moonscape' of drifting sand. In some places the sand has been scoured completely away, occasionally revealing traces of older ground surfaces or exposing underlying boulder clay and bedrock. The grassland in the wider area is now under threat from erosion and from over-grazing by rabbits, though recent management efforts here have met with some success.

Prehistoric Links of Noltland

Soil erosion and blowing sand also affected the ancient farmers at Links of Noltland. The evidence indicates that early cultivation soils were prone to inundation by sand and required intensive management through the application of imported domestic midden and, later, animal dung in order to stabilise them (see McKenna and Simpson, this report). The extent of this management and the nature of the prevailing conditions is currently under investigation, but the apparent lack of settlement and cultivation within the main links area after the late second millennium BC points to an abandonment of the area as a result of instability. The area is thought to have been used as a burial ground in the Viking/Norse period, in which case it is unlikely to have been cultivated at that time either.

A Dynamic Landscape

A baseline study of the beaches of Orkney was carried out in the 1970s (Mather, Smith and Ritchie 1974, 116–9). At this time, the majority of the area was covered by vegetation and marram-covered dunes were present. Several large erosion blow-outs were in evidence, however, and it was noted that 'the machair system is undergoing a phase of fairly severe though localised scouring by wind action' (op cit 13.1.4).

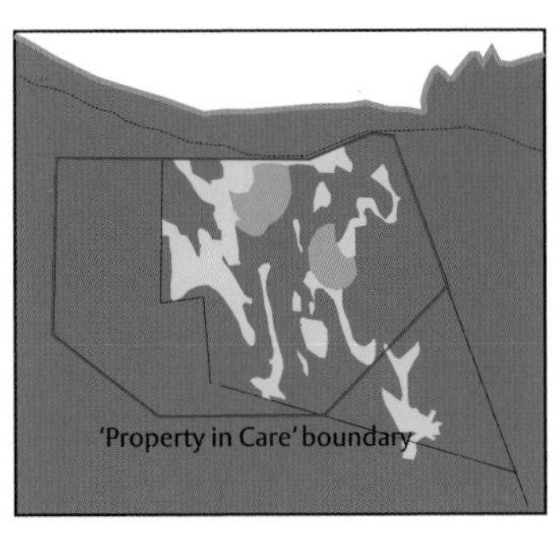

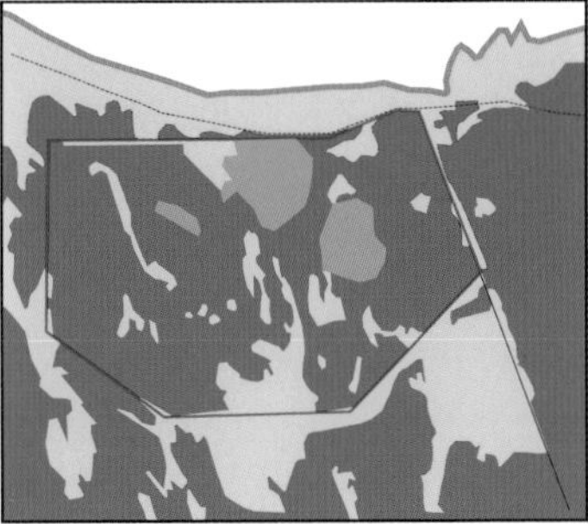

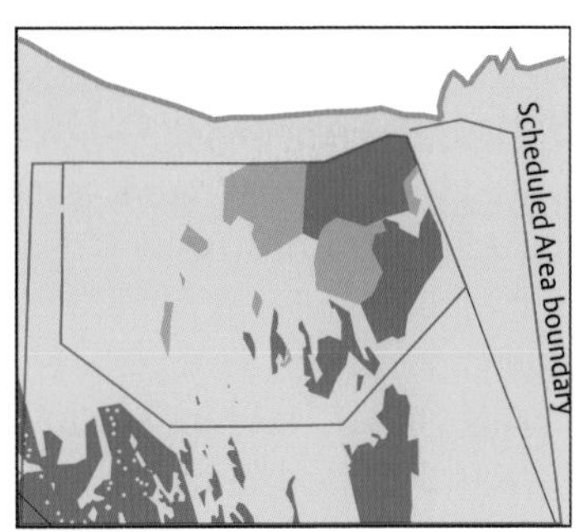

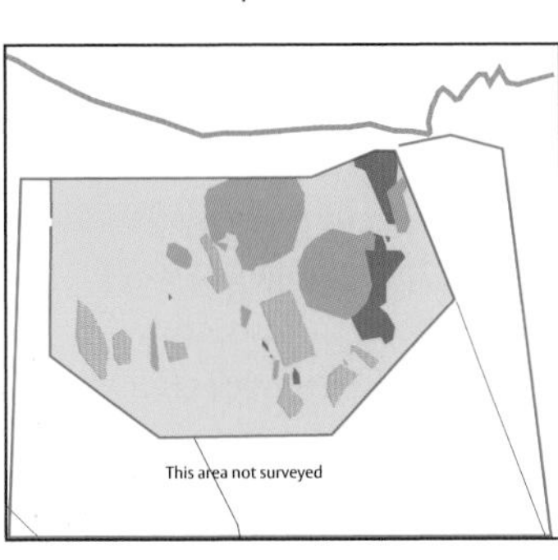

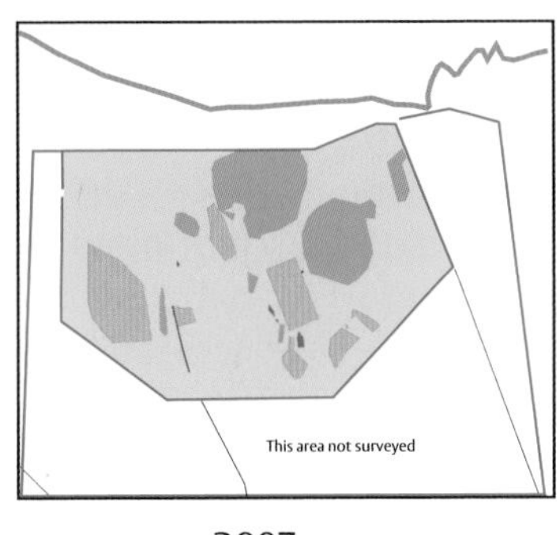

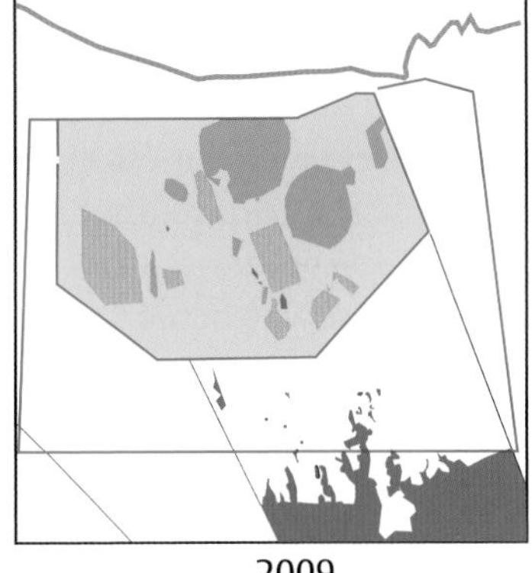

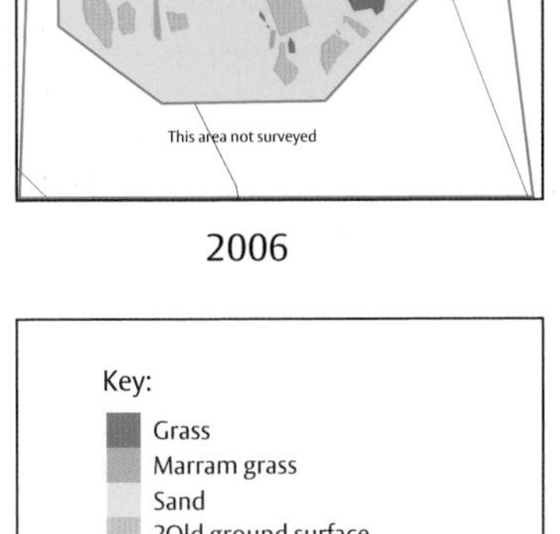

3 Comparison of vegetation surveys, 1981–2009

It was suggested then that this erosion probably occurred cyclically, followed by periods of regeneration.

Secondary agents of erosion were identified as cattle grazing, high rabbit population and quarrying, although these were seen as contributory rather than instigatory in nature. It was suggested that little could be done to decelerate the erosion on the grounds that it probably resulted from the dynamic nature of the land forms and the high intensities of the processes arising from the exposed nature of the site. It was noted that scars caused by erosion during winter were generally healed during the summer and that, with ample supplies of sand present offshore, replenishment of the sand supply was unlikely to present an issue. There appears to be no suggestion that the erosion was likely to escalate substantially beyond the levels seen at that time.

Escalating Erosion

The progress of erosion has been recorded in a series of surveys undertaken by archaeologists from the late 1970s onwards. Topographic surveys were carried out by David Fraser in 1980 and 1981, during the course of Dr Clarke's excavations 1978–81, with a subsequent survey commissioned by Historic Scotland in 1994 (Dunwell 1995). Between 1998 and 2009, a near-annual series of surveys have been undertaken by the authors.

A comparison of the results of these surveys indicates that there has been a near-total loss of vegetation from the area and, that this has largely occurred in the last quarter century. In 1980/81 some 85–90 per cent of the area was vegetated, today less than 25 per cent is covered. It is also apparent that the rate of erosion has accelerated considerably more in recent years.

While these observations cover a relatively short period and were compiled as part of an archaeological rather than a geomorphological study, the findings suggest that the changes taking place at Links of Noltland do not follow the pattern predicted by Mather *et al* (1974). There has been no evidence of cyclical regeneration of blow-out scars and erosion has moved considerably inland and now affects the improved ground bordering the machair plain.

In addition to a progressive loss of vegetation throughout this period, the findings indicate that the ground level has dropped significantly. In places a net drop of 6m has been calculated by reference to the surviving talards. Traces of a gravel surface created during the 1978–81 excavations now stands some 1.5m above the level of the surrounding sand.

The plight of the kelp kilns provides another insight. Used for burning seaweed to produce kelp, these stone-lined pits date mainly to the late 19th century and were originally set into the ground surface. Several dozen were distributed throughout the links area and many were recorded by archaeological surveys. Most of these features have disappeared over the past ten years, and the few still remaining exhibit damage resulting from the deflation of the ground surface into which they were built. Some are now reduced to unstructured heaps of stone, while others are still recognisable, but either preserved on isolated sand platforms or in the process of collapse.

Eyewitness accounts and reference to photographic evidence from the 1978–81 excavations also agree that the landscape has deflated in so extreme a manner in the interim as to render it difficult to reconcile with the present environment (D V Clarke, C Wickham-Jones pers comm).

Archaeology Exposed

The frequency at which new exposures are occurring has increased substantially over the past ten years. From the three main foci of interest (comprising one structure, field walls and midden spreads) investigated by Clarke in 1978–81 can be added a further 13 structures known to be of prehistoric date, together with numerous associated features and soils. It is of note that between 1998 and 2006 the emerging remains were of Bronze Age date, while the more recent exposures appear to be of Neolithic date. This suggests that old land surfaces are being laminated away in reverse chronological order and, furthermore, that they have now been stripped back to the earliest period of settlement. It may be that the changes documented above result from locally severe erosion forming part of a cyclical process, but it is of particular concern that many of the archaeological remains now exposed had not previously been uncovered since their abandonment in prehistory. While two of the Bronze Age settlements were found to have been partially exposed at some point in the past, the Neolithic remains currently under investigation had not. These buildings were buried beneath extensive middens after they went out of use and were subsequently covered by sand. The re-emergence now of these remains would indicate that the ground surface has been scoured back today to an extent never previously reached in the past. This factor alone argues that the level of erosion currently affecting the area is exceptional and unprecedented. Though they have been extremely well preserved up to now, the remains which are now exposed are at great risk from continued erosion and will not survive beyond the short term without intervention.

Causes of Erosion

The factors influencing the increase in the scale of erosion may include increased storminess and changes in weather patterns, wind direction and tidal dynamics, possibly associated with climate change. It is also suggested that a loss of offshore sand deposits may be implicated. A substantial sand bar said to lie offshore is locally thought to have diminished or disappeared in relatively recent times. This feature is said to have been substantial enough in the 19th century to support sheep grazing (L Brown pers comm) and while it has not been visible above the water within living memory, Mather *et al* (1974) found there to be plentiful deposits of offshore sand at the time of their survey. The possibility remains, however, that these

4: Aerial photograph of Links of Noltland taken during 2005
Aerial Photography: Licensed to Historic Scotland for PGA through Next Perspectives ™

deposits have since disappeared, possibly as the result in changes in submarine sediment transport. This would result in a cessation of the sand supply on to the land and, as the existing loose sand is blown further inland, would see the machair plain becoming ever more depleted. Such a scenario may explain the rapid loss of the dune system and erosion of the ground surface to the present levels.

5: Erosion in action: strong winds and heavy rain expose a field boundary during 2009

Subsidiary factors identified by Mather *et al* (1974) as influencing erosion – the high rabbit population, cattle grazing and sand quarrying – no longer play a significant role. The loss of vegetation has relocated the rabbit problem to greener areas further inland. The area is now too barren to support grazing and quarrying has ceased.

Archaeological Background

Between the 17th and 19th centuries a number of Viking/ Norse period burials were discovered in the area between Links of Noltland, Rackwick Bay and Pierowall Village (Illus 2). While few contemporary records exist and the remains have since been scattered and lost, the evidence suggests that this was the largest pagan Norse cemetery yet found in Britain (Graham-Campbell and Batey 1998, 129–31; Thorsteinsson 1968, 150–73). Some of the burials are reported to have been located on the north-west shore of the island (*First Statistical Account of Scotland* 1795) and may have been located at Links of Noltland. This is supported by local tradition which avers that Viking burials have been found in the 'Links of Grobust' (M Drever pers comm, reported in King and Barrett 2002). Some of the burials are said to have been uncovered as the result of sand blow, indicating that the area was already prone to erosion at that time.

In the 19th century, the antiquarian George Petrie found fragments of grooved ware pottery and skaill knives in eroding deposits and deduced the existence of settlement comparable in date to Skara Brae (Petrie nd, notebook no 9, 26–9).

Excavations 1979–1981

The extent and importance of the site was recognised only much later on, as the result of investigations directed by Dr David Clarke, National Museums of Scotland (Clarke, Hope and Wickham-Jones 1978; Clarke and Sharples, 1985). The impetus for this work was the erosion of archaeological remains among the sand dunes. At this time the dune system was scarred by blow-outs but remained relatively intact.

The findings revealed structural remains of Neolithic date which, together with contemporary agricultural soils, field walls and features such as butchery surfaces had been preserved beneath deep blown sand deposits. Elsewhere in the area, a large expanse of anthropogenic soils labelled the 'West Midden' was uncovered. An unusual discovery was the carcases of over 15 red deer, found piled together to one side of a cultivated field (Sharples 2000).

6: The partially excavated 'Grobust' building, as revealed during monitoring work in 2007. The planks in the foreground protect a whale rib left *in situ*

The main focus of the excavation was a stone structure, situated adjacent to Grobust Bay, to the north-east corner of the Links of Noltland area. The 'Grobust' building, as it became known, comprised two rooms joined by a passage and was constructed inside a midden-lined pit which had been cut into a sand dune (Illus 6). A large number of artefacts were recovered from these fills, including worked bone, grooved ware pottery, stone and flint tools and beads, together with plant and animal remains.

In date, scale and state of preservation, the remains at Links of Noltland were considered comparable to those at Skara Brae. The majority of these remains had been only partially excavated, however, when the programme concluded in 1981.

Most of the deposits and structures encountered by this work were dated to the Late Neolithic through a combination of finds analysis and radiocarbon dating (see Radiocarbon Dating, below). This places the settlement as contemporary with Barnhouse (Richards 2005), Skara Brae (Ashmore 2000) and Phase 3 at Pool (Hunter 2007). The only hint of later activity was a few sherds of Beaker pottery found in association with a hearth (Ashmore 2000; Sheridan 1999).

This work demonstrated that the preservation, likely extent, variety of the remains and potential of the site was widely recognised. The partial and unfinished nature of the excavation, which remains unpublished, has left the full significance of Links of Noltland yet to be realised.

Conservation Programme

In 1985, the Grobust building and a surrounding area, covering some 2.5ha, were taken into state care. This area, together with a surrounding margin, together totalling some 3.5ha, are designated as a Scheduled Ancient Monument (HS Index 90337). Thereafter, the management of the site concentrated on conservation of the remains *in situ* and in efforts to stabilise the surrounding landscape.

In 1986, an inspection of the site revealed that erosion had increased since the close of the excavations in 1981. It was observed that some of the excavation trenches had been stripped bare of their backfill, to the extent that archaeological deposits had been re-exposed and were vulnerable to erosion. In response to these circumstances, Historic Scotland sponsored a programme of consolidation work within the PIC area (Owen 1986). The excavation trenches were backfilled and the Grobust building were totally filled with sand bags and covered over. At the same time, some mechanical landscaping of the ground surface in the vicinity of the excavation trenches was undertaken to level out hummocks and fill in blow-out hollows. These levelled areas were then reseeded.

A subsequent inspection in 1992 reported that these measures had been largely effective in securing those areas which had been at risk in 1986, but, it was observed, the focus of erosion had shifted and several new exposures of archaeological remains had since been created (Sharples 1992).

Throughout the 1990s more archaeological remains were reported over an ever-widening area (BOAT 1998; Dunwell 1995; Lynn and Bell 1990; Moore and Wilson 1998). In 2001, an extensive site assessment was commissioned to coincide with Historic Scotland's review of its own management strategy for this site as part of its Property in Care Condition Survey Programme. The findings of this work provided a comprehensive statement on the archaeological potential, together with an analysis of the erosion and an exploration of management options (Moore, Wilson and Barrett 2002).

To Excavate or Protect?

In conclusion, the results of the management review found that to preserve the archaeology at Links of Noltland *in situ* would require intensive management of the wider landscape. The scale of the problem was now so great that any consolidation work would have to be carried out over a huge (and growing) area. Furthermore, the associated costs were likely to be substantial, while the results may be of only short-term benefit.

While resources could be targeted towards the preservation of some or all of the stone structures, it is unlikely that the contemporary fields, boundaries and other landscape features, which make Links of Noltland unique among sites of this period, could be protected.

In considering the outcomes of various management strategies, evidence accumulated over many years of monitoring shows that, once exposed to the elements, archaeological remains at Links of Noltland are extremely vulnerable to the combined forces of attrition, desiccation and contamination. The quality of retrievable information reduces the longer the site is exposed. Materials such as bone and pottery survive particularly badly on the surface. Sites degrade quickly and even stone structures can be entirely erased in a short period of time.

7: Structure 4, looking east

The case of one of the Bronze Age structures illustrates the fate of exposed archaeological remains in this environment. First recorded in 1998, Structure 4 (see below) was assessed in 2001 using topographical survey and trial trenching. It was visible as a low but prominent mound defined by substantial stone walling. The inner and outer wall faces of the oval structure were clearly distinguishable, as were internal divisions and a central hearth setting, both also made from stone. The trial trenching indicated that floor deposits survived on the inside of the building and outside, a contemporary ground surface surrounded the building. These soils were stratified and contained a rich assortment of artefacts and environmental materials.

Subsequently excavated in 2007, this structure had all but disappeared. Most of the walling and internal features had gone, leaving only occasional earth-fast stones, and the associated deposits were severely truncated. These were poorly stratified and yielded few artefacts. Had it been investigated earlier, it is highly likely that Structure 4 would have proved to be as well preserved as Structures 5 and 6 (see below).

2 ARCHAEOLOGICAL INVESTIGATION

Assessment 2000–2006

Between 2000 and 2006, Historic Scotland commissioned three seasons of assessment at Links of Noltland. The aim of this work was to gather data on the quality, quantity and potential of the remains to assist in defining priorities and in framing a tailored response. This comprised topographic survey, trial trenching and small-scale excavation and was undertaken under the direction of the current authors (Moore and Wilson 2000; 2002; 2006). This work was complemented by a soils and environmental sampling programme of the wider hinterland.

The results were both exciting and significant: two hitherto unrecorded Bronze Age settlements were discovered, together with traces of associated features, middens and cultivation soils. The settlements each comprised three buildings; all were exposed and actively eroding. These new findings greatly expanded our appreciation of the site, demonstrating that it was both more extensive and the settlement of greater longevity than had previously been thought. It was immediately apparent that these factors, together with the quality of preservation of the remains, marked out this site as being of exceptional importance. With the risk posed by continuing severe erosion, further intervention was, now more than ever, urgently required.

8: Erosion in action: strong winds and heavy rain expose an old ground surface during 2009

Assessment and Excavation 2007

A major rescue campaign was mounted in 2007. Over two long seasons, the exposed Bronze Age settlements were excavated and a further programme of topographical, geophysical and augur survey and trial trenching was undertaken (Moore and Wilson 2007a; 2007b). In addition, the Grobust building was reopened, assessed and subsequently reburied.

Six Bronze Age buildings and associated features were investigated. Four of the buildings were found to survive in sufficiently good condition that the full ground plan could be discerned, together with some internal and external features. Some of the buildings showed signs of modification during their lifetime; all appeared to have been robbed of stone after their abandonment. They are discussed in more detail below.

Geophysical survey was carried out by Sue Ovenden, Geophysics Unit, Orkney College. A gradiometer survey of the entire PIC area was complemented by a ground penetrating radar survey (GPR) of the Grobust building and its surroundings. The aim was to identify potential features lying buried below the ground surface as well as providing additional information about known features of archaeological interest. Although no new features were identified, the findings indicated that several of the areas of interest were likely to be more substantial than had been previously assumed.

An augur survey was undertaken by Dr Tessa Poller, University of Glasgow. The survey probed underlying deposits to a depth of 2m along three transects located to the northern part of the PIC area. The aim was to see if it was possible to relocate the 'West Midden' which had been identified during the 1979–81 excavation. This extensive spread of anthropogenic soil was said to cover a 1100m^2 area and to contain Neolithic artefacts; it lay to the west of the Grobust structure (Clarke and Sharples 1985). In the absence of any known nearby settlement, it was hypothesised that these deposits may have been stockpiled for later reuse as a building material or, alternatively, as a substrate for cultivation. The extent of erosion in this area in the intervening period had been so severe that it was uncertain whether these remains would survive.

9: Geophysical survey undertaken during 2007

Fortunately, the augur survey found ample evidence of stratified deposits across this area. Preliminary analysis, however, indicated that the 'West Midden' was not a homogenous deposit, as had previously been thought. Both the augur survey and the follow-up trenching identified two distinct soil horizons, separated by wind-blown sand and found that the composition of these deposits varies greatly from place to place, and at least in part probably represents cultivation soils.

The results of the topographic, augur and geophysical surveys were correlated and a programme of trial trenching was then undertaken to examine subsurface deposits in more detail. Following this, small-scale excavation was undertaken in three locations (labelled Areas 4, 5 and 6) where new foci of interest had been identified (Illus 2). The aims were to determine the nature, condition and, where possible, the extent of the remains. The results conclusively identified three stone-built structures of probable Neolithic date. These are discussed in more detail below (Neolithic Links of Noltland).

10: Neolithic wall (Structure 8) exposed in test pit during 2007

At the end of the 2007 campaign, it was concluded that a major settlement of probable Neolithic origin lay within the south-western area of the PIC; this was now visible as a topographic feature and the identification was supported by the evidence of the geophysical survey and trial trenching. The 'West Midden', reassessed in the light of new evidence, comprised multiple elements, including settlement remains, extensive traces of an old ground surface and localised midden dumping.

Excavation 2008–2009

The 2008 excavation programme concentrated on the south-western area of the PIC. Here, a Neolithic settlement (Area 5) occupies an elevated position and is greatly threatened by erosion. The aim of this targeted assessment was to recover information to define the nature and scale of the remains more closely, with a view to informing a management and research strategy. The work uncovered part of a settlement of extended duration (Structure 8), together with a field bank and cultivation soils. Midden deposits, comprising highly organic soils rich in artefacts, encircled the settlement and covered the building. Many of the artefacts were chronologically diagnostic and suggest a Late Neolithic date.

The 2009 season saw a continuation and expansion of work on Structure 8, together with the investigation of closely associated structures and features. In addition, an assessment was carried out of newly exposed remains located outside the PIC. Major new discoveries were made, among which a carved stone figurine, now recognised as the earliest representation of the human form found in Scotland, and a Neolithic structure with cattle skulls deliberately placed within its foundations are most notable. Other new discoveries included a cemetery of Bronze Age date and three new structures, one of probable Neolithic date and two of probable Bronze Age date.

11: General view of Area 5 at close of 2008 season, walling emerging in foreground

12: View across Area 5 to the north-east

3 KEY FINDINGS OF THE FIELDWORK

Neolithic Links of Noltland

Prior to the recent programme of fieldwork, the only substantial Neolithic structural remains known to survive at Links of Noltland was the Grobust building, part-excavated by Dr David Clarke, National Museums of Scotland. Recent campaigns have ranged more widely over the landscape and have had significant success in locating further structures; by the end of the 2009 field season, the number of probable or verified Neolithic structures had increased to six, not including the several phases represented at Structure 8. Of these, only one has been verified by radiocarbon dating (Structure 8); the others are provisionally dated by reference to their form and the typologies of associated artefacts. The following section provides a brief summary of the findings.

Grobust

The Grobust building was excavated between 1978 and 1981 and the published accounts indicate that it was elongated and cellular in plan and comprised two interconnecting rooms (Clarke and Sharples 1985). It was built into a pit which had been dug into a sand dune and lined with midden. The walls survived to over 1m in height and contained features such as integral cupboards and shelves. The entrance stood on the seaward side. After it went out of use, the building was filled with domestic refuse.

While excavation of the outer room did not progress beyond the uppermost fill, deposits within the inner room were investigated more extensively, to a depth of c 1m, but floor levels were not reached. The evidence suggest that the outer room had been modified on at least one occasion, when a dividing wall was inserted. The material filling both rooms, and most particularly in the outer room, contained a high concentration of artefacts, including a large number of fine worked bone items, which may imply a degree of deliberate infill.

13: Detail of interior of the Grobust building, inner room

The Grobust structure was reopened in 2007 to investigate its condition. The findings indicate that while the structure is unsound and fragile, it has not deteriorated appreciably since it was backfilled in 1986. Unexcavated deposits within the building were found to remain intact and well preserved. The structure was refilled with the help of the local Historic Scotland squad.

Structure 8

Undoubtedly the most unexpected discovery of the recent work was that of Structure 8, a large structural complex on an elevated ridge in the south-western corner of the PIC.

The area had not previously yielded archaeological material, although it contained structural remains associated with 19th-century kelp burning. A substantial loss of sand during winter 2006–7 revealed a stony spread, amongst which the suggestion of masonry was noted, together with desiccated midden spreads containing shell, bone and flint. It subsequently appeared on the geophysical survey as a large, irregular anomaly. Trial trenching here recovered large fragments of decorated grooved ware and flint and indicated the likely presence of buried remains of Neolithic date.

14: Plan of Structure 8

These remains are considered to be the most threatened in the PIC area: they stand on a ridge facing out to the Atlantic, have entirely lost their protective sand covering and are actively eroding. The wind and rain regularly wash out artefacts; the more fragile of which, such as pottery, rapidly degrade once they are exposed to the weather and are seldom found on the surface despite being abundant in lower strata.

15: Structure 8 under excavation

Excavations in 2008 and 2009 focused on part of this structural complex revealing it to comprise a very substantial stone building (Structure 8), and several later phases of activity. The excavated portion of the interior is roughly cruciform in plan, measuring some 5m by 5m at the widest point. The building is defined by a stout wall, up to 4m thick and standing up to 0.8m high. This comprises at least three separate and approximately concentric skins of walling, each of which is revetted into a clay core. The exterior wall face, seen in a trial trench, was of very high quality (Illus 10). It was constructed from large quarried blocks set over a wider basal plinth, the latter placed on a platform of yellow clay. A probable entrance passage leads towards the east of the complex where the presence of more masonry suggests a second room or cell. It remains to be seen whether these spaces represent a series of contiguous buildings or rather multiple rooms within a single building, as was the case at Grobust. Traces of a possible outer enclosure wall, up to 2m thick, were identified on the west side of the complex. This is set some 4m away from Structure 8, with a courtyard area occupying the space in between. A stone setting in this yard possibly served as a hearth.

16: Structure 8, detail of deposits

18: Animal bone spreads within the Late Neolithic midden covering Area 5

After its abandonment, the interior of the building filled with rubble deposits as the walls slowly collapsed. It was from amongst these deposits that a stone figurine was recovered. It was subsequently covered with dumps of domestic refuse to a depth of 0.4m and more.

Interpreted collectively as midden, these soils are highly organic and have produced a large and very well preserved assemblage of mammal, bird and fish bone, including some articulated remains. There have also been numerous finds of grooved ware pottery, some with distinctive motifs, and many hundreds of worked flints. Tools and objects in stone and bone are also numerous and there is evidence for on-site bead manufacture. Other finds of note include worked shell, red ochre and haematite. The artefacts are in good condition, if fragile, and do not appear to have been disturbed following their original deposition. Preliminary sample processing indicates the survival of carbonised plant material, small fish and mammal bone, flint flakes and large amounts of marine and snail shell. The artefactual evidence suggests that these deposits are of Late Neolithic origin. Radiocarbon dates obtained from articulated animal bone recovered from these deposits support this (GU-27899: 2630–2470 cal BC and GU-27900: 2870–2570 cal BC).

During a later phase of activity, a paved surface was laid down over part of the infilled building. This is thought to be the last remnants of a structure. It has yet to be fully uncovered, however, and the overall plan remains unclear.

Later again, a further stone feature was constructed. Linear in form with a small, square, stone cell at its western end, it appears to have been sited so as to reuse the former paved surface. The 2m-long linear element resembled a flue, with the cell being reminiscent of a kiln (Illus 19). Dumps of clay found in the base of the structure may derive from a collapsed superstructure. That this feature had been used for heating was indicated by heat-damaged masonry within the 'kiln' and copious deposits of ashy soils outside (Illus 20). It is not clear, at present, what the exact function of this feature was; the presence of animal bone may indicate its use as a cooking place or smokehouse. It is hoped that future specialist analysis of the recovered materials may provide an answer. Part of an articulated cow leg, recovered from within the flue, may represent a 'closing deposit'. This has been radiocarbon dated (GU-27902: 2860–2490 cal BC) and is considered to represent a *terminus ante quem* for the use of this feature. A second radiocarbon date (GU-27903: 2890–2660 cal BC) was obtained from an articulated sheep vertebrae found within the rubble and clay filling into the kiln.

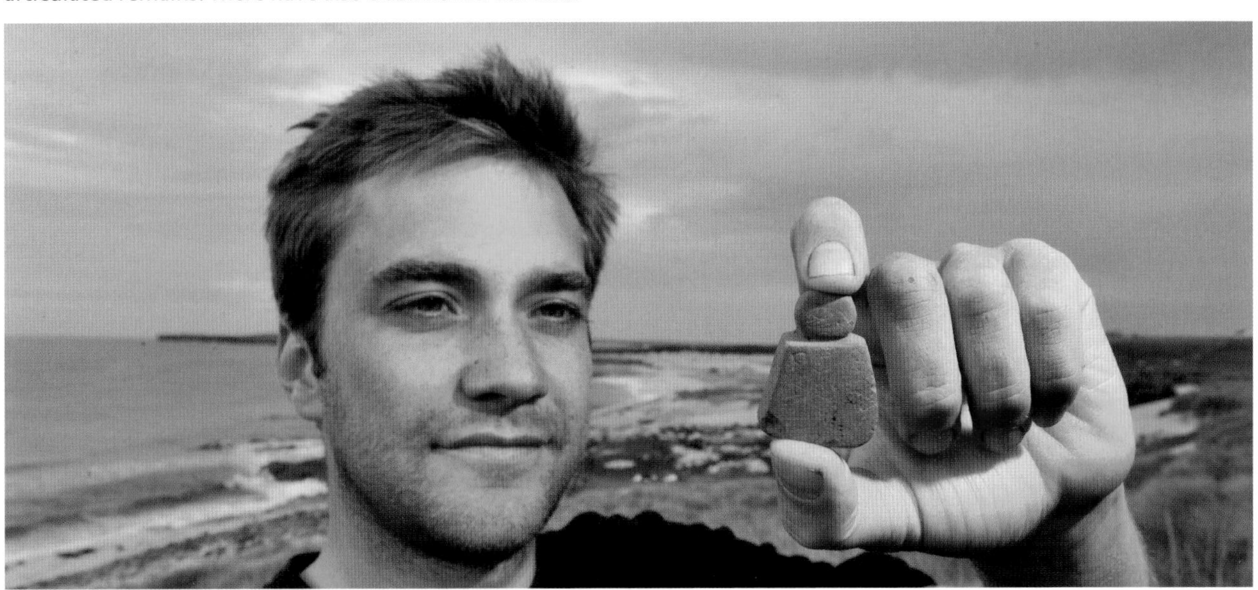

17: The figurine with Jakob Kainz

20: Detail of fine layers within ashy dumps associated with the kiln feature

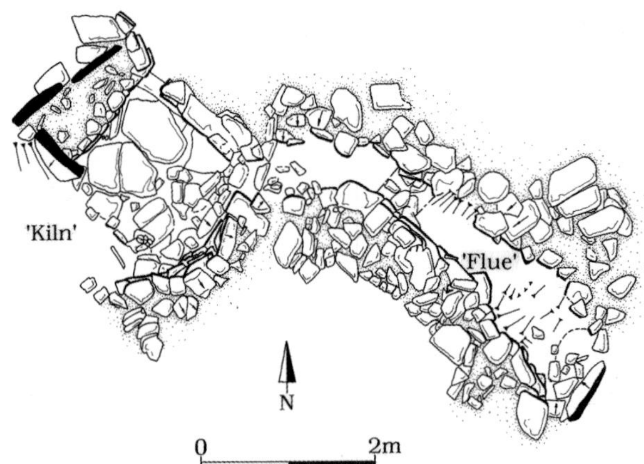

19: The kiln feature with 'flue'

21: Basal deposit within flue leading to kiln feature, in background

23: Structure 7 under excavation, looking west. The casing wall is visible in foreground, partly covered by midden

Structure 7

Investigations to relocate the 'West Midden' led to the discovery of a previously unsuspected substantial stone building (Structure 7). Limited excavation was undertaken, showing that it was rectilinear in shape, measuring some 7m by 7m externally. The enclosing wall comprised several skins or casements and was over 2m thick (Illus 22). On the interior, traces of a structure set within a stone-lined recess on the north wall suggested a dresser here. The interior of the building was filled with midden deposits containing quantities of flint, pottery, bone and shell. Further excavation is planned.

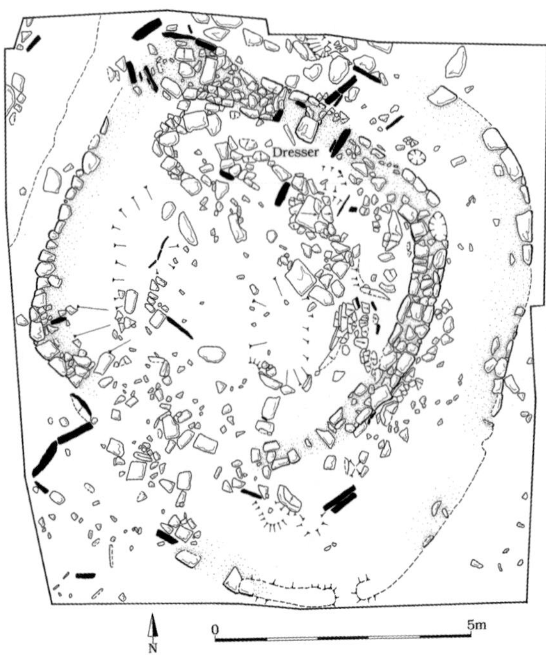

22: Plan of Structure 7

Area 6 Structure

Preliminary investigation in the area of exposed midden deposits lying adjacent to the excavated Bronze Age structures and within the vicinity of the 'West Midden' also uncovered traces of a curvilinear building. This structure underlies and has been partially truncated by one of the Bronze Age houses (Structure 3). A paved surface, associated with the building, was covered with artefact-rich midden deposits. On their northern extent, these remains have been abruptly cropped, either as a result of sand quarrying or by an erosion blow-out. This area has not yet been fully investigated, but the possibility that these remains may represent a Late Neolithic–Bronze Age transition marks it as a high priority for future enquiry.

Structure 9

Structure 9 was discovered in 2009 during an exploratory exercise designed to provide information about the field system to the north of Structure 8. A linear concentration of cattle skulls and some masonry were found associated with a subrectangular structure which, though buried by only centimetres of loose sand, had not been identified by geophysical or topographical survey. The building has an angular or cruciform interior and is enclosed by a thick wall in which at least two facings are apparent (Illus 24). It measures some 7m by 6m. The most unique feature of this building was found within the wall core: here, the skulls of adult cattle were placed carefully side by side to form a continuous ring, in some instances with horns interlocked. The skulls were arranged upside-down with horns facing into the interior (Illus 25). Time limitations permitted an examination of only the easternmost portion of this building, by which point some 12 cattle skulls had been uncovered. There are indications, however, that more skulls exist and that they may extend around the entire circuit of the wall. The complete excavation of this building will be undertaken in 2010.

Other Structural Remains

Part of a further possible building was discovered between Structures 8 and 9. Here, upright slabs and coursed masonry forming a right angle are thought to represent the corner of a building. The wall incorporated a cup-marked slab. The stonework was buried beneath rich midden deposits which contained a large number of artefacts, especially of flint flakes. Too little of this building has yet been uncovered to hypothesise on its overall plan or size. It is anticipated that further excavation will be carried out in 2010.

25: Cattle skulls within the core of the wall of Structure 9, east side of building.

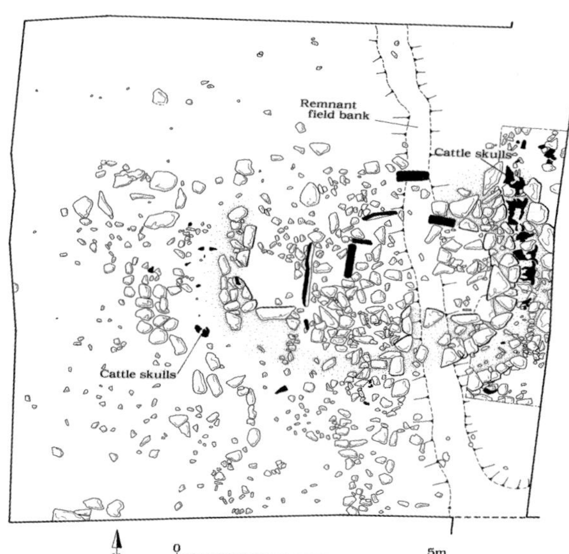

24: Plan of Structure 9

Soils and Field Systems

26: View of Structure 9 looking north-east, field bank visible running over the top of the building

A specialist evaluation of the site by Professor Ian Simpson, University of Stirling, concluded that the remains at Links of Noltland present a rare opportunity to investigate landscape dynamics from the Neolithic to Bronze Age periods: 'The uniqueness of the site lies in the range and extent of anthropic sediments and anthrosols associated at the same locality, allowing the first opportunity to consider relationships between midden material and cultivated areas to be established' (Simpson and Wilson 2008).

27: View of sondage through cultivated soils dug in 2007. Structure 1 (Bronze Age) is visible in background and is associated with the remnant ground surface upon which the top ranging rod lies

Initial augur survey and test trenching have identified and begun to map cultivation horizons and midden spreads and intensive sampling has been undertaken during all excavation work. A research studentship, jointly sponsored by the University of Stirling and Historic Scotland, will continue and expand this work in 2010. Future work will seek to broaden our understanding of the formation processes, and the relationships between, the middens, the cultivated soils and the floors within the houses at Links of Noltland.

Bronze Age Links of Noltland

The presence of Bronze Age settlement had not been suspected before the current programme of work. The excavation results indicate that several of the Bronze Age structures had been exposed in the past and it may seem surprising, therefore, that they went unrecorded. There may be a number of explanations for this. For example, it may be that the midden deposits associated with these settlements were not as extensive or as readily identifiable as those associated with the Neolithic remains. Certainly, they contained fewer artefacts and very few chronologically diagnostic items. The remains may have been uncovered and recovered on numerous occasions and perhaps were not exposed during monitoring visits. A further possibility is that, given the extreme paucity of Bronze Age settlement remains in Orkney, they were not expected and, being less conspicuous, either went unnoticed or were not ascribed to this period.

The discovery of eight complete or partial buildings of Bronze Age date during the present campaign was, therefore, both unexpected and extremely exciting. Although these remains are affected by erosion, they are largely intact and survive as upstanding structures. They cluster in two complexes, some 80m apart, with one outlier, and are thought to represent separate farmsteads. One group (Structures 1–3) is located within the PIC; the other (Structures 4–6) lies within the adjacent Scheduled Monument Area (see Illus 2).

Each group contained a set of paired oval buildings of unequal size, with opposing entrances. In each case the larger (northern) building appears to have had a domestic function. An open central area with a hearth was surrounded by a paved surface and, beyond this, by a series of more enclosed recesses set against the inner wall face. The smaller buildings appear more specialised: one had a clay-lined floor, the other was dominated by a stone-lined tank. In both groups, the third building was badly eroded and difficult to discern. Deposits associated with these buildings yielded stone and bone artefacts, together with some fragments of steatite vessels, the latter representing imports, probably from Shetland. The structures are dated by reference to their form and the typologies of associated artefacts. In 2009, random trenching close to the settlement in the Scheduled Monument Area led to the discovery of human remains. These have been radiocarbon dated (see below).

The following section provides a brief summary of the findings.

Structure 1

Structure 1, a well-constructed stone building, formed a pair with Structure 3 and was smaller than its neighbour (Illus 28).

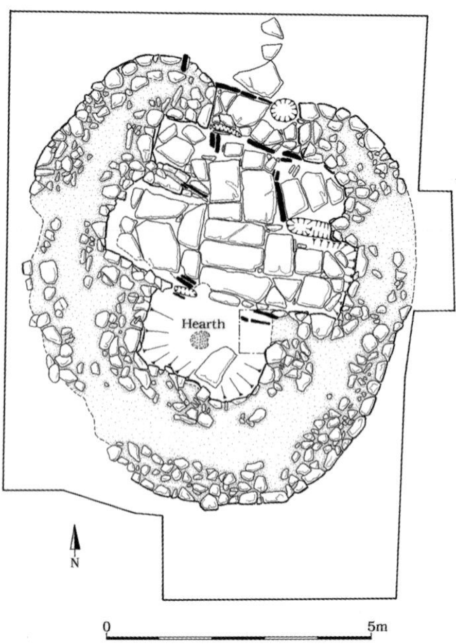

28: Plan of Structure 1

It measured 8m N–S by 8m E–W, externally. The wall had a soil/midden core with revetted drystone facings and stood up to five courses high (0.35m). The entrance faced north, directly in line with and opposing the entrance of Structure 3. The exterior walls were straight with rounded corners and were up to 2.1m thick. The interior was divided into five rectangular cells by a series of upright slabs. The floor was neatly paved throughout, with the exception of the southern cell, which had a clay floor. A distinctive feature was the use of clay luting at the junction between the floor and the walls. This had been repaired or replaced at least twice. It is hypothesised that this building served a specialist function, perhaps as a store. Certainly the internal arrangements would have greatly restricted movement, while the clay luting may have provided insulation. Very few finds were recovered.

29: View of Structure 1 looking south-east. The entrance is visible on the left of the picture

Structure 2

Structure 2 survived as a concentration of stone, including upright slabs set into pits. The arrangement of the surviving upright slabs suggests that they had formed part of a curvilinear wall with two associated stone piers. Two further sets of upright slabs are thought to be the remains of associated internal features such as stone-lined boxes or tanks. The remains of a rectangular hearth setting were found to the north side. The lack of identifiable walling and paucity of rubble are regarded as indications that this building had been largely robbed out in antiquity. No floor deposits could be clearly identified. Although few in number, the artefacts recovered from this area included items such as bone points and pottery similar to those recovered from Structures 1 and 3.

Structure 3

Structure 3 was a large oval building with walls up to 2.5m thick (Illus 31). The interior measured some 11m by 9m. The central floor area lay at a slightly lower level than the surrounding exterior ground surface. It was surfaced with compacted clay in which traces of a hearth were evident. A raised platform of compacted earth extended around the inner wall face. This was divided by radial stone partitions into a series of recesses. An extensive area of paving covered the floor in front of the platform and in the area of the entrance. Four notched slabs set upright within this floor may have served as tethers for animals. Two elongated slots found in the area between the paved surface and the raised platform may have once supported a screen or internal division, separating the inner and outer zones.

30: Plan of Structure 2

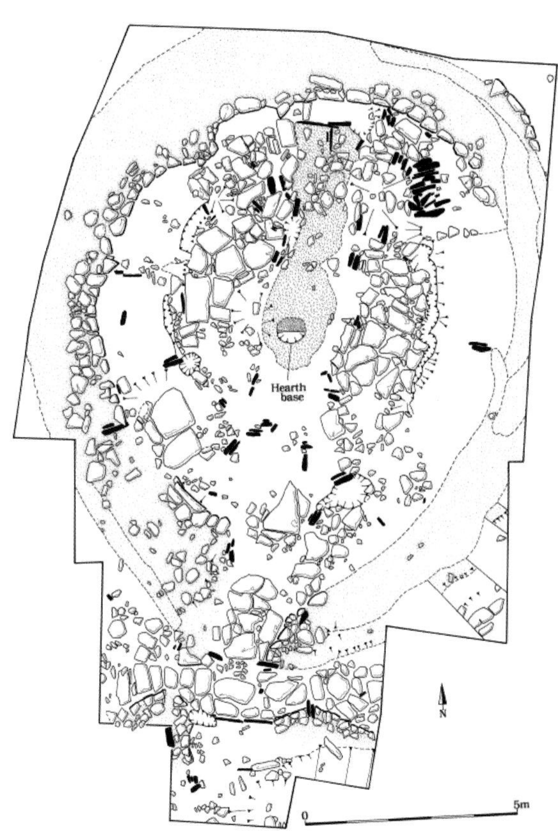

31: Plan of Structure 3

The weathered condition of some of the slabs is of interest: some showed clear signs of abrasion resulting from blowing sand: one had been worn to a point. The evidence of the monitoring programme indicates that these remains cannot have been exposed for more than 12 months in the ten years prior to excavation. It must therefore be presumed that they were exposed in the past, and for some considerable time. Perhaps the building remained open to the elements following its abandonment or perhaps it was subsequently exposed at some period or periods in the past.

A pit located beside a radial partition on the west side of the interior contained a whale vertebra (Illus 32). A series of depressions had been gouged into this bone and it may have supported a small post for interior furniture. The south-facing entrance opened into a 'porch' feature and looked directly on to the entrance of Structure 1. More notched upright slabs in the paved area (Illus 33) may have been used to tether animals. Evidence of repairs to the original structure were seen on the north-east of the interior, where a series of upright slabs had been buttressed against a slumping section of the original wall to stabilise it.

This building yielded the largest number of artefacts, with notable concentrations located at the entrance and at the northern, innermost end of the interior. These include a few small sherds of coarse, straight-sided pottery, a large number of worked bone tools (mostly 'points' and awls), some stone tools, and some struck flint. There was a notable concentration of steatite vessel sherds, some of which are decorated, at the northern end of the interior.

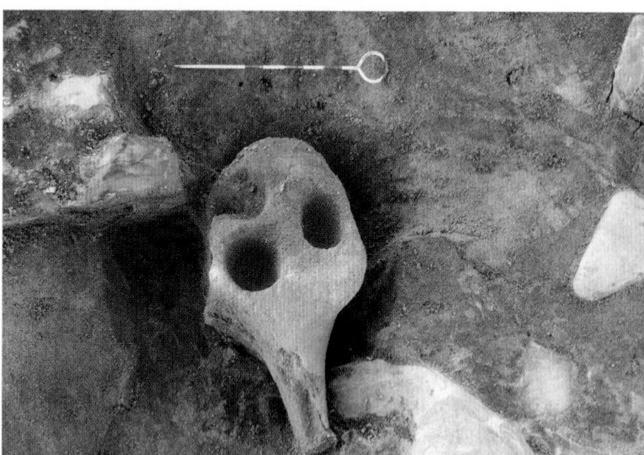

32: Cetacean bone post-socket in Structure 3 interior

33: Notched tether stone set upright in paved area in interior of Structure 3

34: Structure 3, looking north

Structure 4

Structure 4 was first recorded in 1998 and was the most exposed of the structures seen at that time (Illus 35). It continued to deteriorate rapidly over the next nine years and by the time of its excavation in 2007 only scant traces of walling survived (see Illus 7). It was a curvilinear, probably oval, structure and the surviving evidence suggest that the interior was radially divided. Stone-built piers formed a series of recesses set into the inner wall face. Traces of internal furniture, in the form of upright slabs, were noted, as was the last remnant of a paved surface. A square hearth was set into the floor on the north side of the interior. The scant deposits associated with this building were poorly stratified and contained few inclusions or artefacts.

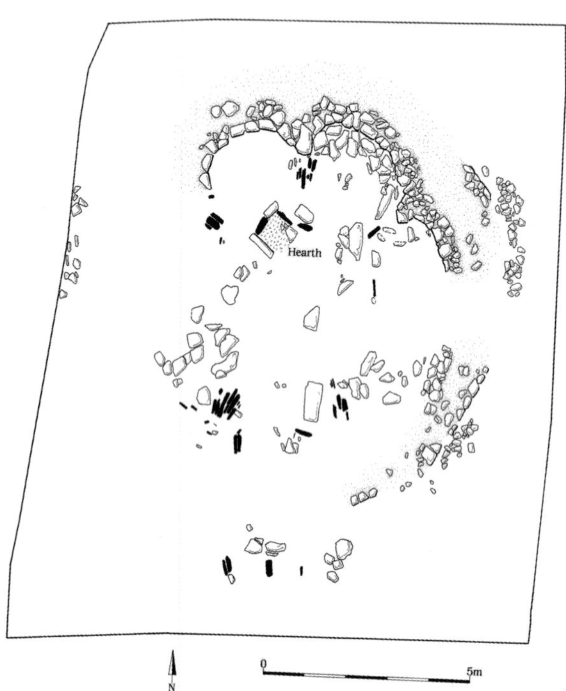

35: Plan of Structure 4

Structure 5

Structure 5 was located to the south of Structure 6 and appears to have formed an annexe to its larger neighbour (Illus 36). It measured 6.4m N–S by 7m transversely. From the outside it appeared approximately circular in plan. The wall was constructed of randomly coursed stone with a core of midden. It varied in thickness, up to a maximum of 1.5m, and stood almost 0.5m in height. The entrance, with threshold slab *in situ*, was on the north side and faced directly onto the entrance of Structure 6, from which it was separated by a paved passage. The interior was divided into a series of five recesses set around an open central area. The floor was neatly paved with slabs bonded by clay. A stone-lined tank was present, set into the floor and surrounded by stone partitions, and formed the focal feature (Illus 37). It bore no signs of clay luting. A stone-lined drain was set into the wall in the area of the tank. Although few finds were recovered, of note is a large handled stone cleaver, similar to those found in Structure 6.

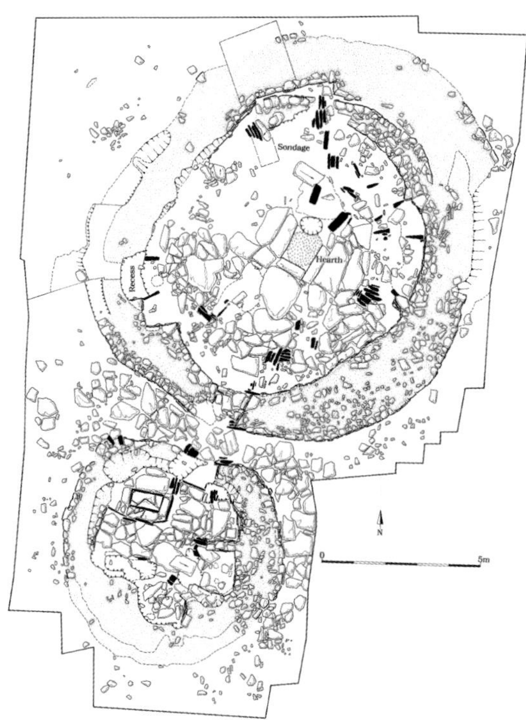

36: Plan of Structures 5 (bottom) and Structure 6 (top)

37: Detail of tank sunken into floor of Structure 5

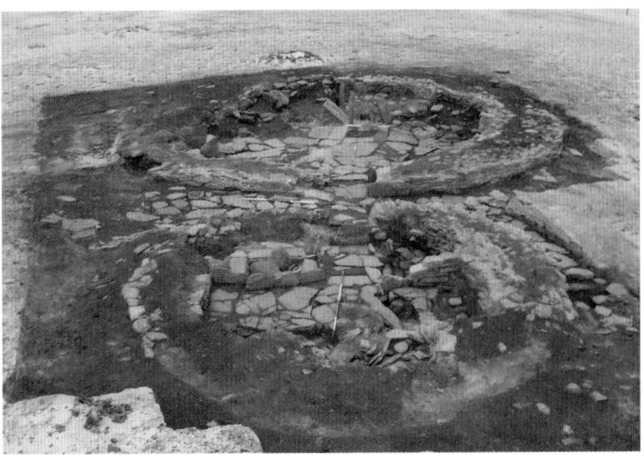

38: Structures 5 and 6 looking north, Structure 5 in foreground

Structure 6

Structure 6 comprised a well-preserved, large, subcircular building measuring some 12.8m N–S by 11.6m transversely (Illus 36; Illus 39). The entrance, flanked by large upright stones, lay on the south side, facing directly on to that of Structure 5. The double-faced stone wall was randomly coursed with a core of packed soil and midden. It stood up to 0.45m high and varied in thickness between 1.26m at the entrance and 3m on the north side. Parts of the wall circuit were substantially thickened during the lifetime of the building. The interior was divided radially by six piers or radial partitions and a small recess was present on the west side. The floor was almost entirely paved with large, neatly laid slabs and a square hearth was set into the central floor area. Steatite vessel sherds, handled club fragments and two caches of worked bone points were notable amongst the small assemblage recovered from this building.

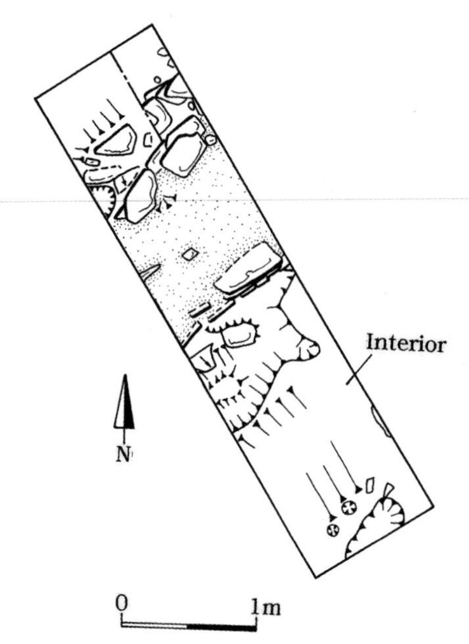

42: Structural remains identified in Test Pit 4

39: Structure 6

Human Burials

In 2009, an investigation of surface scatters of disarticulated bone and midden spreads to the south-east of the Scheduled Area recovered evidence of human burial (Illus 2). Both adult and child inhumations were represented by the loose bone and some cremated bone was also noted. Trenching in the wider area revealed one complete and one partial burial. The burials were set over glacial till with a thin cover of wind-blown sand. The surrounding area was strewn with coral and marine shell. Coral, although native to the surrounding waters, has not been commonly found in any quantity at Links of Noltland and in this context may have been placed as an offering or marker. The burials have been assessed (see Gooney, this report). It is considered possible that further remains may lie nearby: this will be investigated in 2010.

The partial burial comprised both articulated and disarticulated remains; provisional assessment has indicated that they may represent a male of older age. No trace of a cut or of grave furniture was seen. These remains have been radiocarbon dated (GU-27901: 1630–1460 cal BC).

40: Inhumation 9054

The complete burial has been identified as a female of between 35 and 45 years of age. The body was crouched on the right side, with one hand close to the head. No trace of a grave cut was visible. The upper torso and head were covered by a rough stone setting comprising a flat slab, supported on upright stones. Several of these uprights rested directly on the body indicating that the structure was erected after the body had been placed in the grave. The remains have been radiocarbon dated (GU-27908: 1690–1510 cal BC).

Other Remains

Two further sets of structural remains have been found within the Scheduled Area to the south-east of the PIC, and are thought most likely to be of Bronze Age date. Neither has been investigated fully yet, but the findings of preliminary assessment can be reported briefly.

Part of a substantial curvilinear building extends beneath the eastern wall of Structure 6 and appears to represent a direct precursor (Illus 2, Test Pit 11; Illus 41). The wall head was partially uncovered in 2009, but little was seen of the interior. The wall stands to 1.4m high and has a coursed outer face, a midden-packed core and a stone revetment on the interior. It appears to be on a similar scale to Structure 6. The interior was filled with shelly midden deposits which post-date its abandonment. Further investigations are planned here in 2010.

41: Structural remains identified in Test Pit 11

A less well-defined structure was identified during survey to the immediate south of the Scheduled Area (Illus 2, TP4; Illus 42). It lies on the boundary of the eroding area and has just begun to be affected: archaeological remains have only been exposed since late 2008. Test trenching in 2009 investigated only the exposed portion of this structure and indicate a curvilinear building of probable Bronze Age date. The wall is of double-faced construction, with a packed soil/midden core and measures 1.5m wide by 0.3m high. Anthropic deposits are present, both inside and surrounding the building. However, the remains have been seriously undermined by rabbit burrowing. Further monitoring and investigation work is anticipated in 2010.

4 DISCUSSION

The ongoing programme of work at Links of Noltland has substantially enhanced our understanding of this site and is already beginning to change perceptions about life in prehistoric Orkney. The discovery of numerous structural remains of Neolithic and Bronze Age date show this to have been settled more densely and occupied over a considerably longer period than had hitherto been suspected.

43: SF2289: Orkney Venus figurine

Alongside the headline discoveries, such as the figurine and cattle skull building (Structure 9), a mass of data concerning the environment, subsistence and material culture is being gathered and analysed. Our preliminary thoughts are that this is a typical Orcadian farming settlement made remarkable by the sheer scale of survival and the quality of its preservation.

Neolithic Links of Noltland

The present evidence suggests that Noltland was settled by around 3000 cal BC, although this date may be pushed back as excavation progresses. There is currently too little data available to determine if the buildings (Structures 7–9) were contemporary, if their use overlapped, or if they represent a sequence of replacements. Radiocarbon dating of infill material suggests that deposits filling Structure 8 may be slightly earlier than those associated with the Grobust house. The similarity in artefact types found in association with Structure 8 and Grobust (for example, see Sheridan, this report) would tend to suggest that the midden deposits covering these building was of roughly contemporary date. However, Structure 9 appears to be stratigraphically earlier than Structure 8 and, if proved to be the case, could account for the differential survival of these buildings, with Structure 9 perhaps razed before or during the occupation of Structure 8. Structure 7 appears similar in form to buildings found at Skara Brae (Childe 1931; 1950), Rinyo (Childe 1939; Childe and Grant) and Barnhouse (Richards 2005) and might therefore be provisionally dated to the first half of the third millennium BC, thus fitting into the known dating range for the Grobust structure (Ashmore 2000).

These buildings display a range of forms: Grobust and Structure 8 are multicellular, while Structures 7 and 9 are not. Furthermore, Grobust and Structure 7 stand alone, while Structures 8 and 9 are closely associated and surrounded with other probable buildings. Structures 8 and 9 appear to have cruciform interiors. There is evidence of secondary activity at Structure 8, while Grobust was substantially modified during its lifetime.

44: Work in progress on Structure 8

At present, it is hypothesised that all belong generally within the Late Neolithic period and that some or all may have overlapped chronologically, collectively forming a dispersed village rather than the single isolated settlement as was previously thought. This pattern, with multiple homesteads situated amongst farmed land has been more usually associated with Europe and Ireland than Scotland (Grogan 2004).

New findings in the area of the 'West Midden', as identified during the 1979–81 excavations, have prompted a reassessment of these deposits (see above), demonstrating their heterogeneity and the presence of a hitherto unsuspected settlement (Structure 7). In discussing the significance of the heaped red deer carcases, Sharples suggested that the singularity of this find was further emphasised by its location away from settlement (Sharples 2000, 111–12). The discovery of Structure 7 does not alter the significance of the deer find, but beggars the question of its relationship to the nearby settlement.

45: Cache of pot boilers in Structure 8 interior

The survival of cultivation soils, field boundaries and 'middens' in association with the buildings makes it possible to investigate the relationships between the settlements and their landscapes and to discern and compare patterns of activity at multiple locations over an extended area. Furthermore, the preservation of palaeoenvironmental remains offers the opportunity to gather valuable new data relating to the local environment, economy and cultural life of the settlements. The relationships between the settlements and their surrounding landscapes, land management practices and contemporary environmental conditions will be investigated as part of doctoral research by Laura McKenna, School of Biological and Environmental Sciences, University of Stirling, commencing in 2010.

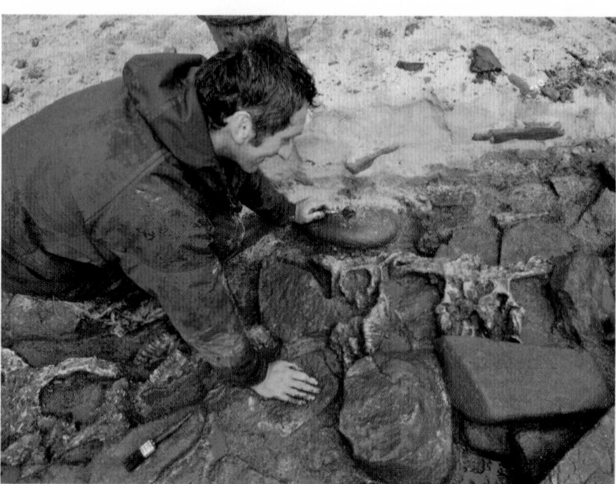

46: Structure 9: cattle skulls in wall

The preservation of bone and plant material, for example, will inform investigations into animal and crop husbandry and the use of wild resources. Preliminary assessment of the plant material has identified cultivated barley and the use of peat, driftwood and heathy turf for fuel and has suggested that crowberries may have been collected as a foodstuff. The diversity of the sample under analysis was limited and represents mainly upper midden deposits. It is anticipated that more deeply buried deposits and contexts such as floors and wall cores may produce a wider range of material.

A study of the animal bone, to be undertaken as a doctoral research by Sheena Fraser, University of Edinburgh, will examine key issues such as the origins of the domesticated animals, evidence for dairying and the place of animals in the cultural, material and spiritual life of the settlement. This study is expected to commence in 2010. A preliminary assessment emphasises the large size and high quality of the animal bone assemblage and its potential for bioarchaeological investigation, such as isotopic and DNA analyses.

47: Work in progress in Area 5 during 2009

The study of the material culture at Links of Noltland is greatly aided by the quality of preservation and abundance of artefacts which have been recovered. Several assemblages have now been assessed by specialists (see below). The results indicate a similarity with material from other Late Neolithic sites in Orkney and with the Grobust assemblage (Sheridan, Saville, McLaren, Rice, all this report). This supports the suggestion that Links of Noltland be regarded as a typical farming settlement of this period. Many of the bone and stone artefacts are interpreted as tools associated with farming and craft working. There is evidence for the manufacture of flint and stone tools, pottery and bone objects. The presence of decorated stones and pottery, together with evidence of items of personal adornment, such as bone beads and pins (Illus 48), pigments such as ochre, and more unusual items, such as haematite, provide additional insights into life at this time.

48: SF1750: antler pin

In placing Links of Noltland within its Orcadian context some features, such as the structural forms and artefact assemblages, find close comparisons at Skara Brae, Barnhouse and Rinyo. Moreover, in common with Tofts Ness, Pool and Rinyo, the Links of Noltland settlement represents an apparently unexceptional agricultural community situated far from the ceremonial centre of mainland Orkney. Other aspects are less readily paralleled, however. Neither the settlement pattern nor the preservation of the contemporary landscape can be directly matched in Orkney or in mainland Scotland. The remains at Links of Noltland are better preserved than most other settlements and certainly more extensive and for these reasons it holds the potential to disclose a more complete insight into life in Neolithic Orkney.

Bronze Age Links of Noltland

The discovery of extensive settlement remains at Links of Noltland significantly enhances our knowledge of the Bronze Age in Orkney and substantially augments the number of settlements, previously known, for example Spurdagrove (Ovrevik 1985), Tofts Ness (Dockrill 2007) and Skaill, Deerness (Buteux 1997). Furthermore, the Links of Noltland examples appear to represent a form not previously encountered: a dispersed village in which individual households are composed of groups of buildings, apparently of differing function. Prior to these discoveries, no village of this period had been known in Orkney (Downes and Richards 2000, 165).

49: Work in progress on Structure 2

In the past, the paucity of Bronze Age settlement has been linked to increasing isolation and recession (Ritchie 1995), the adoption of a semi-nomadic lifestyle (Hedges 1975) and the interpretation of burnt mounds as houses (however, cf Moore and Wilson 1997). In their very ubiquity, however, burnt mounds provide us with clear evidence that settlement continued throughout this period, even though archaeological evidence of structures may be scant. The presence of at least six structures of this period at Links of Noltland may be the product of exceptional survival, but is unlikely to be unrepresentative. It strengthens the case for stable settlement in the Bronze Age while providing a clearer picture of what these settlements looked like.

The Links of Noltland examples display a distinctive and complex use of space inside buildings and the pairing of structures, a feature also found at Skaill, Deerness (Buteux 1997) and Sumburgh, Shetland (Downes and Lamb 2000). Further links with Shetland are indicated by the use of steatite vessels (Forster, this report) and stone tool types (McLaren, this report). The recovery of steatite vessel sherds from the Bronze Age houses at Links of Noltland is particularly significant and adds weight to the argument that this material was in wider domestic use in Orkney than has hitherto been suspected.

50: Structure 1 under excavation

The existence of two similar but separate settlement complexes offers opportunities for comparison and the elucidation of patterns of activity. Key topics for future investigation will include an analysis of the economy at each site, determination of how the individual buildings were used, their chronologies and their relationships.

At Links of Noltland, Neolithic and Bronze Age settlement occurs in the same landscape, and the evidence is strongly suggests continuity rather than disjuncture. The land continued to be farmed, the same animals were kept and crops grown, wild resources continued to be exploited, craft working undertaken and permanent stone houses were constructed. The houses differed in form, but the pattern of individual households dispersed within the landscape remained constant. Some differences are apparent, the use of steatite and types of bone and stone implements in use, for example, but nonetheless the picture is one of development over time.

51: The paved passage between Structure 5 (left) and Structure 6 (right)

It is significant, however, that with two possible exceptions, the Bronze Age and Neolithic settlements do not overlap. It is possible that cultural considerations were responsible for the shift in location. The exceptions, two instances where structures have been found to underlie Bronze Age buildings (Structures 3 and 6), may provide us with clearer insights into the transition period.

It is also notable that none of the Bronze Age buildings appear to have been backfilled after their abandonment; many appear also to have been robbed of stone in antiquity. In general, the midden deposits associated with these buildings are less substantial: preliminary analysis also indicates that they contain fewer and different types of inclusions and are less humic in nature. The reasons for this are not yet understood and will be addressed by future analysis, including an examination of possible extenuating environmental factors and changes in the agricultural regimes.

52: The hearth in Structure 6

The difficulty in locating Bronze Age structures elsewhere in Orkney may be due to the fact that, as at Links of Noltland, they tend not to be located in the same places as either earlier or later settlements and that they are not represented within multiperiod mounds which are more visible and have claimed much of the archaeological attention. It is perhaps fortunate that at Links of Noltland a much wider tract of landscape has been exposed for investigation, albeit as the result of erosion, than has generally been scrutinised in the past.

It may now be timely to reassess evidence for contact with Shetland during this period and to compare other aspects of life on the two island groups. The perception of a Bronze Age recession in Orkney in part stems from the apparent diminution of contacts with mainland Scotland and beyond. But this ignores the increasing importance of Links of Noltland with its northern neighbour and the fact that Shetland, with its more varied geology, had access to valuable resources such as steatite and copper which were not available in Orkney.

5 CONCLUSIONS

It is perhaps ironic that the factors which threaten to destroy these remains at the same time present opportunities for much-needed new research, the like of which exists nowhere else in Scotland and rarely elsewhere in Europe. The accelerated erosion of the sand cover from large areas of land is revealing an entire archaeological landscape. This is highly unusual in the Orcadian context, where sites tend to survive in isolation and where much excavation work has been concerned with individual structures or large settlement mounds while the wider site hinterland is either not examined or not available for investigation.

53: A visit to Pierowall school with the figurine

The importance of the remains at Links of Noltland cannot be overstated; they represent rare examples of Neolithic and Bronze Age settlement in a contemporary landscape; they are in extremely fine condition and, although now threatened by erosion, are amenable to rapid and high-quality excavation and can, thereby, be 'rescued' for the future.

Recent research agendas reiterate the need for more and better data collection, for exploration of under-represented sites and periods and of transition periods, for the investigation of economic and environmental circumstances and consideration of sites within their landscape settings and their wider settlement hinterlands (for example, Barclay 1997; Downes *et al* 2005; Sheridan and Brophy 2008). It is evident that, despite the challenges posed by erosion, Links of Noltland offers an unparalleled opportunity to meet these requirements.

Fieldwork 2010

A four-month-long programme of work is planned over summer 2010. This will primarily comprise excavation with some survey and assessment. The highest priority for investigation will be the Neolithic remains comprising Structures 8 and 9, the adjacent field system and surrounding structural remains. This part of the site is elevated, has the highest density of exposed remains and is most threatened by erosion. It is hoped that work in this area will be concluded during the forthcoming season.

54: The open day during the 2009 season

Further investigation of the Bronze Age remains in the Scheduled Area will also be carried out. Here, priority will be given to the eroding structures and to a fuller assessment of the burial area. In the event that vulnerable human burials are identified, these will be excavated.

A rapid assessment of Structure 7 will be carried out to monitor its current condition. Finally, survey of the PIC and Scheduled Areas will locate and record all new archaeological exposure and track the progress of known sites.

55: Planning in progress, Structure 8

The fieldwork will be undertaken by a team of qualified archaeologists and environmentalists, with some provision for some student training. The public outreach programme will include daily site tours, an on-site exhibition of recovered materials, information panels and leaflets, one or more Open Days and liaison with local schools and other interested groups. It will be complemented by the exhibition at the Westray Heritage Centre of the 'Westray Wife' figurine, found in 2009.

6 METHODOLOGY

Excavation

Fieldwork investigations mainly employed open area excavation, with trial trenching used for assessment purposes. All excavation was conducted by hand. The trenches were first cleared of loose sand and then a pre-excavation drawing was made of the uppermost archaeological deposits. Thereafter, excavation proceeded in plan, with deposits removed stratigraphically. Baulks and running sections were used to provide horizontal control. A mixture of single context and multicontext plans, sections and profiles were drawn at key points during the excavation. A context record was compiled with a written and illustrated description of each context encountered during excavation. A comprehensive visual record, using digital, slide and black and white film, was used to record individual contexts and features and to document the progress of the work. The site record was digitised and large-scale survey and location plans were compiled. Data Structure Reports, describing the aims, methodology and findings of every fieldwork season were produced and summary reports were submitted to *Discovery and Excavation in Scotland.*

Two site codes have been issued and are used in this document: SLN refers to the Scheduled Area only (outwith the PIC area); LON refers to the scheduled PIC Area.

Materials Recovery

In recognition of the importance and quality of the remains at Links of Noltland, and their potential to fill significant gaps in our knowledge, this project has incorporated an extensive sampling programme, with methodologies devised with expert input and, in some cases, undertaken by specialists. Both sampling and sample processing methods are periodically reviewed and are upgraded as necessary.

56: Dry sieving of spoil for finds

The aim has been to provide the best possible recovery system within the bounds of a fixed budget. This requires some selectivity: the scale of the remains and the speed at which excavation must progress in the face of erosion mean 100 per cent recovery is not feasible, even if it were affordable.

57: The wet sieving station

It should be noted that the researchers and specialists associated with this project may employ additional field and laboratory methods which have not been documented here.

Sampling Strategy

The sampling regime aims to recover as wide and representative an assemblage of environmental and artefactual remains as possible. These materials include charcoal, macroplant, bird, fish and faunal remains, together with artefacts too small to be collected by hand. The methodologies used are screening (dry-sieving) and wet processing (flotation). In addition, samples have also been collected for microscopic and chemical analyses and for thin section analyses.

58: Phosphate sampling on Structure 2

Screening: The screening programme is designed to maximise the opportunities for artefact/ecofact recovery without unduly slowing the pace of excavation. A percentage of all excavated deposits is screened or dry-sieved through a 1cm mesh, with recovered material labelled per context. In the case of artefact-rich deposits (such as middens), the totality of excavated soils is generally screened. Where contexts were only partially sieved, the volume of the sieved portion is recorded along with the total volume of the deposit: at a minimum, this will permit statistical inferences to be made on the basis of material recovered. Experimentation with smaller mesh sizes has and will continue to be undertaken, but has been found to slow proceedings down considerably while not producing a significant increase in the number or type of artefacts being recovered.

Sampling: Bulk soil samples, a minimum of 30 litres in volume, are routinely collected from every context encountered during excavation. Where insufficient material is available, contexts are sampled in their entirety. In many instances, additional samples are collected from deposits identified during excavation or processing as being of high potential. These include deposits containing macroplant or other environmental materials. Extra samples are also collected from deposits in key stratigraphic locations in order to maximise the opportunities for radiocarbon dating.

Where accumulations, such as floors, have been identified, multiple samples are collected using a grid system, to provide a more detailed level of information on the distribution of materials within these deposits. Such features are 100 per cent sampled. Bulk samples are processed using a water separation or flotation tank. The products of this work (floated fractions and non-floating fractions) are air dried, packed and stored. An assessment of the nature and variety of inclusions within each sample is recorded during processing. This provides advance information for specialists, helps determine if further sample recovery is desirable, and can aid the selection of material suitable for radiocarbon dating.

Artefact Recovery

Artefacts have been recovered in one of four ways:

Small Finds: The majority of artefacts are collected by hand during the course of excavation. Other than unworked bone and shell, all artefacts are given a unique 'Small Find' number and recorded by context, with locations electronically recorded in three dimensions. Artefacts which are manufactured or modified are always treated as special finds, as are more uncommon ecofactual finds, such as coprolites, whale bone, articulated bone, complete skulls, and discrete caches of shell and bone.

Bulk Finds: Bulk deposits of unmodified shell and animal bone which are collected by hand during the course of excavation are recorded by context. The volumes of these materials, especially in the midden deposits, is so large as to make more detailed recording impractical.

Screening: Artefacts recovered during screening are recorded by context.

Wet Processing: Artefacts recovered from soil samples processed via water flotation are recorded by context.

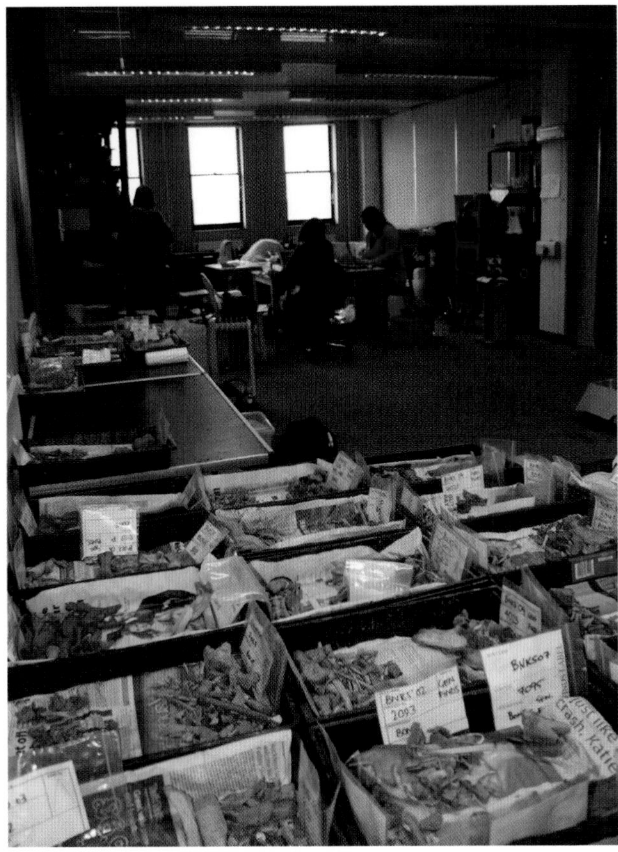

59: Finds processing, winter 2009

Post-excavation Processing

Charlotte Crowston

Post-excavation materials processing has now been undertaken on the majority of artefacts, animal bone and shell recovered from the 2007–9 excavations. This work was undertaken in the EASE Archaeology facility in Edinburgh by a specialist team. Advice and support on matters relating to artefact handling, storage and conservation were provided by Richard Welander, Head of Collections, Historic Scotland, and Alison Sheridan, National Museums of Scotland.

During processing all Small Finds were re-examined and fully catalogued. Depending on the material type, they were washed or dry brushed. Many were also photographed. The hand-collected 'general finds' comprising bone and shell were sorted and examined more closely for signs of working and butchery. The materials were then packed for dispatch either to specialists or to the store.

Processing Methodologies

Animal bone and shell: The larger pieces were washed by hand with a brush; the smaller fragments were washed in a >500 micron sieve. They were then air dried, packed in clean plastic bags and stored in sealed crates.

Pottery and worked bone: These materials were air dried and repacked. A small number of sherds have been removed for lipids analysis (see Sheridan, this report).

Flint: The flint is generally clean and was not washed or rebagged prior to specialist assessment.

Stone: Coarse stone objects were generally washed, air dried, packed in clean plastic bags and stored in sealed crates.

Discussion

In total, over 3000 small finds have been recorded from the 2007–9 seasons. The following material types are represented: pottery, lithics, coarse stone objects, worked bone objects, worked shell objects, human bone, mammal, fish and bird bone, coprolites, steatite objects, shell (marine and terrestrial), and organic materials (charred wood, cereal and plant matter). Small amounts of coral, ochre and haematite have also been recovered. Some categories of material, notably bone working waste and worked shell, were more readily identified during processing than in the field.

The post-excavation process has been a valuable exercise, not only for the creation of more detailed and accurate catalogues of the various assemblages, but also for providing feedback which will be of assistance in interpreting the findings of fieldwork and in improving and updating future recovery methodologies. In particular, certain artefacts, such as bead-making debris and astragali polishers, were mainly identified during this stage of the work. Knowledge of their existence and form will improve our ability to recognise such items on-site during future fieldwork. Many of the processed assemblages have been assessed by relevant specialists and the results are provided within this report.

7 RADIOCARBON DATING

A key aim of the sampling programme was to recover material suitable for radiocarbon dating. The materials preferred for this are single entity carbonised cereal grain and articulated bone. Preliminary assessment of the processed flots by an archaeobotanical specialist (Hastie, this report) suggests that the plant material recovered so far is significantly abraded and, deriving from infill deposits, is likely to be taphonomically unreliable. This could be expected since much of the Neolithic material under discussion comprises midden deposits. It is probable that better quality material survives at a lower level. In the meantime, several samples of articulated bone were selected for dating assay.

A preliminary series of seven radiocarbon dates were obtained in time for inclusion within this interim report. The aim was to secure a small number of secure dates with which to better understand the formation of the deposits currently under excavation. It was further hoped that a comparison of these dates with those from the excavations carried out by Dr Clarke would enable those findings to be put into context with the current work.

All dates derive from single bones taken from an articulated group or, in one case, one bone from a closely associated bone concentration ascribed to a single animal. It was hoped that these selection criteria would make it less likely that the entities dated were residual or intrusive and that they would give a fair indication of the date of the deposits within which they were found.

The dates are as follows:

Two dates, GU-27899 and GU-27900, derive from animal bone recovered from the extensive Area 5 midden. Two others, GU-27902 and GU-27903, are from infill within the kiln/flue feature which directly underlay that midden. Taken together, the four dates indicate that the kiln/flue feature fell into disuse and midden formation began by early in the third millennium BC.

One date, GU-27904, is problematic: it is from a concentration of sheep bone recovered from Structure 8 infill. This deposit is stratigraphically earlier than the kiln/flue and the overlying midden, yet the date is very late. It is not possible, at present, to explain the discrepancy – it is probable that this bone is intrusive and does not relate to the deposit from which it was recovered. It is hoped that further excavation during 2010 will resolve this issue.

Two dates are from articulated human burials found in the Scheduled Area in 2009. The burials did not include any grave goods and did not have stratigraphic relationships, either with each other or with any other deposits. The dates indicate that the bodies were interred during the mid-second millennium BC. This accords well with what is known of the date of Structures 4, 5 and 6 which lie only some 50m to the north, suggesting that these burials are contemporary with the Bronze Age settlement of Links of Noltland.

A total of 14 dates exist for the previous excavations, carried out under the direction of Dr David Clarke. These were commissioned during the 1980s through Historic Scotland's predecessor, the Scottish Development Department, and have been published elsewhere (Ashmore 1998; Sharples 2000; Sheridan 1999).

Code	**Context**	**Material**	**Date BP**	**Date at 2 sigma**
GU-27899	7302	Cow phalange	4030+/–30	2630–2470 cal BC
GU-27900	7302	Sheep vertebrae	4105+/–30	2870–2570 cal BC
GU-27901	9053	Human femur	3280+/–30	1630–1460 cal BC
GU-27902	9016	Cow calcaneus	4070+/–30	2860–2490 cal BC
GU-27903	9009	Sheep vertebra	4185+/–30	2890–2660 cal BC
GU-27904	9011	Sheep metapodial	3635+/–30	2130–1900 cal BC
GU-27908	9054	Human femur	3315+/–30	1690–1510 cal BC

Code	Material	Date BP (adjusted)	Date at 2 Sigma	Trench
GU-1691	*Bos*, Ovicaprid	4315+/–80	3350–2600 cal BC	E
GU-1429	*Bos*	4215+/–110	3100–2450 cal BC	D
GU-1428	*Bos*	4140+/–110	3050–2350 cal BC	D
GU-1431	*Bos*	3950+/–110	2900–2100 cal BC	D
GU-1432	*Cervus elaphus*	3722+/–110	2500–1750 cal BC	C
GU-1433	Ovicaprid, *Bos, Sus, Cervus elaphus*	3840+/–110	2650–1950 cal BC	A
GU-1430	*Bos*	3860+/–110	2650–1950 cal BC	D
GU-1690	*Cervus elaphus*	3760+/–85	2500–1950 cal BC	C
GU-1692	*Cervus elaphus*	3850+/–65	2490–2130 cal BC	A
GU-1693	*Bos, Cervus elaphus*	3990+/–85	2900–2200 cal BC	C
GU-1694	Ovicaprid	4040+/–80	2900–2300 cal BC	D
GU-1695	*Cervus elaphus*	3750+/–100	2500–1850 cal BC	A
GU-1696	*Bos*	4270+/–75	3100–2600 cal BC	D
GU-1697	*Bos*	4360+/–125	3400–2600 cal BC	D

These dates must be used with caution, for several reasons. Firstly, these older excavations remain unpublished and so the precise context and stratigraphic relationships for many of the dates is not yet known, although general locations have been published (for example, Sharples 2000). Six of the dates have codes which are earlier than 'GU-1500' and, therefore, the quoted error must now be adjusted to take account of known problems with measurements of this age (see Ashmore 1998).

A further reason for caution relates to the material which was dated. Information held by Historic Scotland shows that three of the dates were obtained from mixed animal bone. In the case of GU-1433, for example, the measurement relates to a mix of four species (ovicaprid, *Bos, Sus, Cervus elaphus*). These three dates should be discarded since they are undoubtedly unreliable (Ashmore 1999). With regard to the remaining 11 dates, it is not known whether they derive from articulated bone or even if more than one bone, from the same species, was used per measurement, as might have been necessary to achieve the relatively large weights of material required for dating at that time.

With these provisos, it is nonetheless felt that these dates provide a useful general comparison. They indicate, for instance, that some of the deposits encountered by Dr Clarke are contemporary with midden formation over Structure 8 (Area 5). The suite of seven dates from Trench D, in particular, seems to be closely comparable; those from Trench A (the Grobust building) and Trench C appear to indicate significantly later activity here – the second half of the third millennium as opposed to the first half. The Trench A dates, however, derive from the uppermost fills of the outer room, which is known to have been modified, thus it is not clear how they relate to the building itself. It is possible that the Grobust building is much earlier than the dates would suggest.

8 THE ANIMAL BONE

Sheena Fraser

Introduction

A selection of animal bones from 28 midden, anthrosols and infill contexts excavated from Links of Noltland 2007–9 excavations were the subject of a preliminary examination. The aim of this examination was to assess:

(i) range of animals represented
(ii) comparability with other Neolithic Orkney settlements
(iii) condition and potential measurements of the bones
(iv) future research possibilities

Midden and Anthrosol Deposits

The preliminary examination focused on late Neolithic midden and anthrosol deposits. Additionally, three Bronze Age contexts were noted, as well as one context from a lens, from an infill and from a floor deposit.

Schiffer considered the role of formation processes when interpreting archaeological material and stated that accumulations of animal bone material were not reflections of past activity but of discard behaviour, a cultural process (Schiffer 1976). More recently, Needham and Spence (1997) defined a midden as an occupational deposit with deliberate and sequential accumulation.

Midden material is often referred to as waste or refuse, implying that it has no further value, but in Neolithic Orkney this deposited material may have been useful for building or enhancing cultivation, so it is probable that midden material will be recovered from areas beyond the primary deposition zone.

Bone preservation within a midden and anthrosol is dependent on many factors such as protection from weathering, bacterial and fungal activity, acidity of the soil, gnawing by scavengers, including herbivores (Brothwell 1976), trampling by humans and animals, bioturbation (Bocek 1986), root damage and redistribution (for a summary of factors affecting animal bone after deposition, see Lyman 1994; O'Conner 2000; Reitz and Wing 1999).

An unknown percentage of the bones originally deposited has been preserved, and, of these, only a percentage of the surviving bones has been excavated. It is estimated that approximately 20,000 to 25,000 bones were recovered from the 2007–9 excavation, similar to the number of bones recovered by Dr Clarke in his 1979–81 excavation of an adjacent site (Armour-Chelu unpublished).

Animals Present/Absent

The following animals were present:

(i) cattle *Bos taurus*
(ii) sheep *Ovis aries* (no goat horns or metapods identified to date)
(iii) pig *Sus scrofa*
(iv) red deer *Cervus elaphus*
(v) dog *Canis familiaris*
(vi) otter *Lutra lutra*
(vii) vole *Microtus arvalis*
(viii) whale (vertebrae and cranium)
(ix) bird (unidentified)
(x) fish (unidentified)
(xi) rabbit *Oryctolagus cuniculus* (not present during Neolithic)

In addition, a shed tooth from a meat-eating shark was recovered (at least 18 species of shark are sighted in coastal waters off Scotland, of which at least eight eat larger fish/mammals (www.sharktrust.org).

Sheep and cattle bones were numerically dominant in the 2007–9 collection and found in the majority of contexts examined. Pig and red deer bones were recovered in much lower numbers but present in just under half of the contexts. Dog, otter and whale bones were rare, with dog present in five contexts, otter in three contexts and whale in seven contexts. One otter bone was found.

This distribution of animal bones suggests that the community at Links of Noltland had dependable domestic meat and fat sources and wild animals did not form part of the basic subsistence regime.

Rabbits were recovered from seven contexts, often represented by sets of articulated bone. These contexts were predominantly associated with the upper spits of middens. Otters may have been natural colonisers of the midden or deposited by the community. In the case of rabbits, however, they are unambiguously later intrusions to the midden. Rabbits are thought to have been introduced into Britain in the 12th/13th century (Hull 2007) and were in Orkney by the 17th century (Buckley and Harvie-Brown 1891; Fenton 1978; Martin *et al* 1994).

Burrowing activities by rabbits could alter the stratigraphy of archaeological deposits by segregating soil contents by size and causing artificial concentrations of small materials near the surface. A depth of up to 300–

400mm may be displaced (Bocek 1986; Fowler *et al* 2004). Rabbit bones were also recovered from most layers of the Neolithic site of Knap of Howar, Papa Westray.

The following animals were not identified during the preliminary examination:

(i) goat – domesticated prior to arrival of Neolithic people to Orkney, but not found in any Neolithic settlement or cairn sites to date. Feral goats thrive in some mainland and island sites in Scotland today (Bullock and Rackman 1982; McCormick and Buckland 2003) suggesting that areas of Scotland can support these animals. Goats and sheep have been recovered from Neolithic sites in Ireland (Cooney 2000).

(ii) horse – foal teeth and talus recovered from Quanterness cairn (Clutton-Brock 1979); horse bones noted by Petrie (1868) and Balfour Stewart (1914) at Skara Brae are now known to be intrusive (McCormick and Buckland 2003).

(iii) seal – a few bones at other Neolithic Orkney sites but never abundant, for example Knap of Howar (Noddle 1983), Tofts Ness (Nicholson and Davies 2007). The animals may have been butchered for oil/hide on shore. Meat without bones could have been carried back to the settlement for consumption, but stable isotope analysis (for example, Richards 2004; Richards and Hedges 1999; Schulting 2004), suggests a low marine profile in the Neolithic diet.

(iv) other wild animals – for example, pine martin from Pierowall, Westray (McCormick in Sharples 1984), fox from Quanterness cairn (Clutton-Brock 1975), possible wolf from Stones of Stenness (Clutton-Brock 1976).

Fragmentation

The bone material is in excellent condition. Although heavily fragmented, it was frequently possible to take measurements. Bones from all parts cattle and sheep skeletons were recovered, indicating that the midden was a repository for various settlement wastes, not, for example, just primary butchery or tool-working waste. Most parts of deer were also present, so it appears that they were not imported into the settlement as joints. Pig was represented predominantly by feet, skull and loose teeth, although a few forequarter bones were observed. This may indicate that after initial butchery the carcase was processed and disposed of elsewhere. Almost all bones were disarticulated, although a few cattle and sheep lower limb bones and some sheep vertebrae were recovered in strict connection with each other. Although ribs from cattle, medium mammals and deer were present, mostly broken, these bones may have been under-represented in the collection. Complete bones (apart from neo-natal) are as follows:

	Cattle	Sheep	Red deer	Pig
1st phalange	P	p	P	
2nd phalange	P	p		P
3rd phalange	P	p	p	
Astragalus	P	p	p	P
Calcaneus	P	p		
other tarsals	P	p		
Carpals	P			
Metatarsal		p		p
Metacarpal	P	p		
cervical vertebra		p		P
thoracic vertebra	P	p		
mandible		p		

60: Table of complete bones

Comparison of Faunal Assemblage with other Sites

The preliminary examination focused on comparisons with animal bone reports from other Orkney Neolithic settlement sites since these were more directly comparable than monumental or cairn sites. These settlement sites, however, have slightly different occupation periods and animal bones were recovered from a variety of deposits.

Other settlement sites such as Rings of Rinyo, Rousay (Childe and Grant 1939; 1947) and Barnhouse, Orkney mainland (Richards 2005) were not reviewed because bone preservation was too poor to produce animal bone reports. At Rings of Rinyo a few sheep, cattle, whale and antler fragments were recovered and at Barnhouse sheep, cattle and pig fragments were noted (King 2005). Only a few animal bones were identified from the Neolithic phase of Howe, Orkney mainland, and these were from sheep, cattle, pig and deer (Smith 1994).

Additionally, during the Neolithic period at Northton in Harris, Hebrides, sheep, cattle, deer, seal and the tusk of a boar (possibly wild), were recovered, with sheep bones dominating the collection (Finlay 2006).

Distribution of Animals

The dominance of sheep and cattle bones recorded during the preliminary examination of the 2007–9 Links of Noltland bones was also recorded at Skara Brae (Watson 1931), Tofts Ness (Nicholson and Davies 2007), Pool (Bond 2007a), Knap of Howar (Noddle 1983) and the earlier Links of Noltland excavation (Armour-Chelu unpublished). This distribution in Orkney is noteworthy. Cattle and pig dominate animal bones from most other British and European Neolithic settlement sites, with sheep only becoming important during the late Bronze Age (Armour-Chelu unpublished; Clark 1952). It is speculated that the increase in sheep numbers in most of Britain related to the reduction of woodland

Site	Context types	Period	Authors
Pool, Sandy	Red ash with heavy overburden	Neolithic, phases 1-3 Sequence of grooved ware in middens and houses only partially dated, with 68.2% confidence between 3040 and 2780 cal BC.	Ashmore, 2005, Bond, 2007a, Hunter, 2007
Tofts Ness , Sandy Skara Brae , Mainland	Most bones recovered by hand. Clay-rich nature of many deposits precluded large-scale bulk-sieving Excavation material, predominately midden material. Material from individual houses cannot be distinguished	Neolithic/Early Bronze Age 3100-2500BC	Dockrill, 2007, Nicholson and Davies, 2007, Ashmore, 2005 Callender, 1931, Clarke, 1976, Clarke and Sharples, 1985, Childe, 1931, Petrie, 1866/68. Renfrew, 1979, Trail, 1866/68, Watson, 1931
		Earliest phase may have been as early as 3400 cal BC but is more likely to be 3100 cal BC.	
Knap of Howar , Papa Westray	Upper 2 layers treated separately because of possible modern burials	3500 to 3400/3100 BC	Ashmore, 2009, Noddle in Ritchie, 1983, Ritchie, 1983
Links of Noltland , Westray	Trench D, phase 1 cultivation and deposition of midden, phase 2 cultivation, phase 3 extensive midden, phase 4 plough soil covered. Trench A upper material from passage connecting N and S cell of house and one of the cells	Settlement not before 3000 BC and continued in use until after 2500/2400 BC. phase 2 2190+/-65- 2265 +/-65 BC phase 4 2000+/-65 BC	Armour- Chelu, unpublished, Ashmore, 2005 Clarke *et al*, 1978, Clark and Sharples, 1985,

61: Site comparisons (animal bone)

caused by agricultural activities and that Orkney, where deciduous trees were already rare or absent, already had an environment that allowed sheep to thrive (Clark 1952; Watson 1931).

Arrival of Animals to Orkney

It is probable that cattle arrived into Orkney during the Neolithic. At that period there was no land connection with the rest of Scotland. Recent DNA research suggests that although there were two independent domestications of cattle, European cattle all originated from the Near-East and not from local centres of domestication (Edwards *et al* 2007; Loftus *et al* 1994; Troy *et al* 2001). This would suggest that the cattle in Orkney were not locally domesticated stock from mainland Britain. These cattle must have arrived by boat (Serjeantson 1990) and there were two types of boat in use from the Mesolithic onwards, log boats and skin-covered frame boats (McGrail 1998), that would have been suitable for transporting animals. Sheep are not native to Britain and were also probably imported by Neolithic farmers by boat.

The data for the configuration of land and sea in the Orkney area after the last glaciation is not fully resolved. It is debated as to whether some of the Orcadian terrestrial fauna could have crossed the Pentland Firth before it was inundated shortly after 10,000 BP (McCormick and Buckland 2003) or whether all terrestrial animals were transported to Orkney (Clutton-Brock 1979; Kitchener and Bonsall 1997). It is accepted that animals such as otters and seals could have crossed water bodies themselves to recolonise Orkney without human assistance.

Even if a natural route to Orkney did not exist, red deer may have been imported earlier than the Neolithic (contra Clutton-Brock 1979) as recent researchers (for example, Richards 2005; Saville 2000; Wickham-Jones 2006) suggest that Orkney was occupied during the Mesolithic. As red deer have adopted an evolutionary strategy of shedding antlers, despite the associated energy and mineral loss (Davis 1987; Goss 1983; MacGregor 1985), this alone might make these animals an attractive addition to a Scottish island in Mesolithic times for tool-making.

Domesticated dogs appeared from approximately 7000 BC onwards (Brewer *et al* 2002) and were found in Mesolithic sites in Denmark (Clark 1952), so it is possible that dog was introduced to Orkney during the Mesolithic or Neolithic. It is unlikely that wolf would have been deliberately introduced into Orkney. The only site in Orkney with possible wolf-like bones is Stones of Stenness (Clutton-Brock 1976) so it is probable that there was not localised domestication of wolves in Orkney.

The pig bones recovered may have been domesticated animals brought to Orkney during the Neolithic period, or, alternatively, introduced wild boar. None of the excavations in Orkney have found material that indicates teeth size or tusk formation associated with wild boar, although a wild boar tusk was found at the Neolithic site at Northton, Harris (Finlay 2006).

Researchers consider that the distinctive Orkney vole was introduced, and radiocarbon dating indicates it was present in the Neolithic period (Armour-Chelu unpublished). What is remarkable about this species is that it is not currently found on mainland British sites. Current research on this animal may give some indication of the source of other animals introduced in the Neolithic into Orkney by identifying the source area of these voles.

Orkney Environment during the Neolithic

Terrestrial animals in Neolithic Orkney would have had to cope with an oceanic climate; open pasture and little shelter from frequent and high-speed winds. Since rain falls most frequently in spring and autumn, this may have caused problems during spring lambing or autumn harvesting of hay (Davidson 1979; Davidson and Jones 1985). There would be few trees to provide additional food, but there were large quantities of seaweed that the Orkney animals had adapted to eating in historic times (Fenton 1978; Martin *et al* 1994) and may have adapted to during the Neolithic (Balasse *et al* 2005).

Cattle and sheep would have required a water source, grazing and overwintering food. A method of protecting the spring grazing from deer would have been required if the animals were to thrive. Links of Noltland excavation 1979–81 uncovered a ditch containing large stones and Clarke and Sharples (1985) speculate that this may have been the base for a seaweed wall.

Red deer cannot be domesticated (as defined by Diamond 2002). At present there are around 300,000 red deer in Scotland (Milner *et al* 2002), but there are no longer any in Orkney (Buckley and Harvie-Brown 1891). Density varies from 2 deer/km^2 in Skye to between five and 10/km2 in Lewis and over 25 deer/km^2 in the Grampian area (Scottish Natural Heritage 1996). The red deer in Scotland have had to adapt to moorland, a less optimal grazing and browsing environment (Chaplin 1983; Clutton Brock and Albon 1989; Clutton Brock *et al* 1982; Ritchie 1920). Westray has an area of approximately 47km^2, so at current stocking levels for Scottish islands there may have been at least 94 to 470 red deer on Westray in Neolithic times, a viable breeding unit.

Burning and Root Marks on Animal Bones

Some burnt bones were recovered from 14 contexts, but the numbers from each context were low, probably of the order of 1 per cent. These bones ranged from slightly charred through to fully calcined (Stiner and Kuhn 1995), with most in the black or locally calcined categories, indicating exposure to temperatures less than 645–940°C (Shipman *et al* 1984). This evidence may indicate that:

(i) Roasting was not the main cooking method.
(ii) Bones deposited in these contexts were not used for fuel.
(iii) There was little *in situ* burning in the deposition areas.

At the earlier excavation of Links of Noltland less than 1 per cent of bones were burnt and were predominantly of a bluish/black colour (Armour-Chelu unpublished). Root marks were observed on approximately one-third of the bones examined. This indicates that plants grew over the midden material at some period of time.

Method of Killing Animals at Links of Noltland

The domestic animals would have been slaughtered at the settlement at Links of Noltland based on requirements and the herd management system in operation. The presence of newborn sheep and cattle in the midden suggests a human involvement at the settlement of at least some domestic animal births.

There is no evidence at Links of Noltland 2007–9 of how pig or sheep were killed, but several cattle skull fragments had breaks that might indicate the cattle were pole-axed. The future excavation of the remaining skulls in a foundation trench at Links of Noltland may produce more conclusive evidence for or against pole-axing.

Most parts of red deer skeletal elements are present at Links of Noltland 2007–9. Shed antlers are present, some hacked in preparation for working, indicating that antlers were collected. Deer bones at the settlement could have come from fallen deer, but it is likely that they were hunted either by drives into a killing zone or by individually targeted weapon hunting. Another possibility is that they were trapped in order to prevent them marauding any crops or prime grazing land. Red deer introduced into Orkney in the mid-19th century produced a herd of 14. Although they survived well, they were killed off because they 'caused too much annoyance about the crofters crops' (Buckley and Harvie-Brown 1891).

There is no evidence from the bones as to how whales were obtained, but the low numbers of bones at all the Orkney settlements could be explained by scavenging of beached whales, although Clark makes a powerful argument that hunting of whale occurred in the Scandinavian Neolithic (Clark 1952).

Articulated Bones

Articulated feet and vertebrae from cattle and sheep were recovered at Links of Noltland 2007–9. Articulated animal bones have also been recovered from other settlement sites in Orkney. At Tofts Ness a partially completed cattle skeleton was found near the surface of a late Neolithic midden (Bond 2007b). At Pool two articulated forelimbs and one hind limb from cattle were recovered, all missing feet; these may have been removed during an earlier butchery process. Sheep metapodials were also excavated in close association with phalanges (Bond 2007a). At Skara Brae the skull and much of the skeleton of a short-horned ox were found in loose midden material above collapsed slabs in Hut 6, Period 4 (Childe 1931). Without radiocarbon dating it may not be possible to state whether this animal was Neolithic. At Links of Noltland two cattle skulls were recovered (Clarke and

Sharples 1985) and at Pool three possible complete skulls were recovered (Bond 2007a).

Additionally, at Links of Noltland excavation 1979–81 the articulated, or partially articulated, skeletons of a at least 15 red deer were excavated in a small area of upper midden and were thought to have been deposited at or just after 2650–1950 cal BC (Armour-Chelu unpublished; Sharples 2000). At Skara Brae the complete skull of a red deer with antlers was recovered from the reoccupation period, layer 3, of Hut 7 and was associated with shells and charred bones (Childe 1931, plate 33 (1)). At Bay of Skaill, close to Skara Brae, another red deer deposit was uncovered, peripheral to main midden and structural activity areas. The deer were only partially articulated, representing the early stages of butchery of several large animals. This deposit was not dated, but the presence of skaill knives suggests it was Neolithic (Sharples 2000). Finally, at Point of Buckquoy, Birsay, five deer, all represented by forelegs and probably articulated, have been tentatively dated from 2560–2200 cal BC through to 1750–1310 cal BC were recovered (Rackman and Young 1989).

Cattle

Cattle of all ages, from newborn through to mature, were noted. The cattle were large for domestic animals, but not as large as wild aurochs. There is no evidence on either horns or leg bones that the cattle were tethered. Butchery marks indicate skinning, removal of horn cores, disarticulation and filleting. Helical breaks on the humerus, femur, tibia and radius and the lack of intact mandibles indicate possible marrow extraction. Some metapodial fragments were the remains of bone-working, other metapodials might have been fractured for marrow. Several cattle skull fragments had breaks that might indicate pole-axing. At Skara Brae Watson suggested that a cattle skull had been pole-axed and Bond considers it probable that an animal was pole-axed at Pool (Bond 2007; Watson 1931). At Links of Noltland 1979–81 Armour-Chelu observed the same damage but determined that this was post-mortem crushing (Armour-Chelu unpublished).

Bone	Mean (mm)	SD (mm)	No in sample	Range (mm)
1st phalange GLpe	59.1	4.2	27	53-68.5
Astragalus GLl	67	3	42	61.7-74.5
Calcaneus GL	135.7	11.7	6	123-155
Tibia Bd	60	6.2	5	53.6-67.5

62: Table of cattle size

Bones from all elements of the body were recovered and were of a large size. This is similar to the results from Skara Brae, Knap of Howar, Links of Noltland 1979–81, Tofts Ness and Pool. Noddle stated that the bone measurements she examined were greater than two Neolithic sites in southern England, Durrington Walls and Windmill Hill, but smaller than Danish wild cattle (Noddle 1983). Tresset agrees that the cattle at Knap of Howar are smaller than aurochs and notes that the large measurements may well be partly due to a more important male component in this series than in other Neolithic assemblages (Tresset 2003). Armour-Chelu describes Links of Noltland late Neolithic cattle as having a larger body size and being more stocky than those from Neolithic sites in the south of England (Armour-Chelu unpublished).

Measurements following Driesch (1976) from Links of Noltland 2007–9 were taken during the preliminary examination and assessment:

Measurement	Mean	Standard deviation	No in sample	Range
GLl	67	3	42	61.7-74.5
GLm	61.7	3	43	56.7-67.7
Bd	41.6	3.1	43	36.2-50.6
Dl	38	2.1	41	33.6-42.2
Dm	33.6	2.5	43	28.7-41.8

62: Table of cattle size

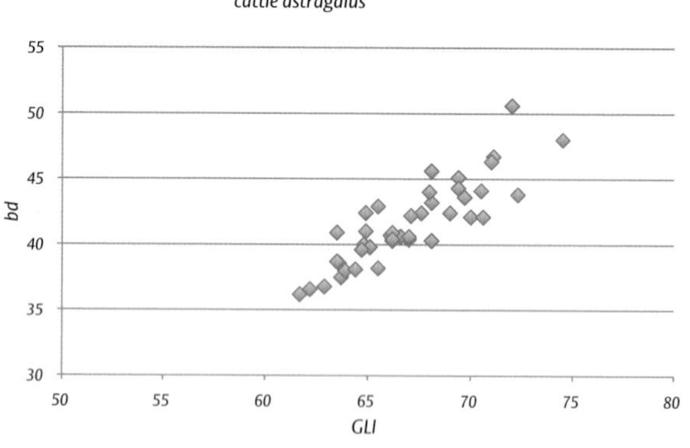

63: Cattle astragalus dimensions (mm)

Bone	Mean	Standard deviation	No in sample	Range
1st phalange GLpe	59.1	4.2	27	53-68.5
2nd phalange GLpe	36.1	3.9	16	30-43.8
Calcaneus GL	135.7	11.7	6	123-155
Tibia Bd	60	6.2	5	53.6-67.5

64: Graph of cattle astragalus dimensions (mm)

The bone measurements have a broad range and a high standard deviation on the mean, perhaps indicating that there may be female and male cattle present and also possibly castrated cattle. The graph of the GLl and Bd of the astragali does not show a linear relationship between the two measurements, again possibly suggesting that different shapes of cattle existed at Links of Noltland. Watson suggested the presence of three groups of cattle for Skara Brae based on his examination of horns (Watson 1931, plates 52 and 53).

The small selection of astragali from non-midden contexts had an average for GLl greater than those from midden contexts, but the difference was not significant using statistical student t-test. No astragali from the Bronze Age contexts were examined.

Services Provided by Cattle

Traction

There is evidence that arable agriculture was practised in Neolithic Orkney. Barley, for example, has been recovered from the Neolithic settlement of Barnhouse (Hinton 2005). Cattle may have provided traction for ploughing, although the light sandy soils may have allowed an ard to be pulled by man since there is no evidence of deep ploughing at Links of Noltland 1979–81 (Clark and Sharples 1985).

When animals are used for traction the loading is increased on their hind legs and this can lead to pathological lesions (Bartosiewicz 2008). A few pathological lesions on cattle were noted in the preliminary examination. These included lipping or exostoses on the glenoid cavity of the scapula, on the articulated surface of the second phalange, and on the proximal articulation of a tibia. These are proliferative lesions that may be associated with ageing or repetitive action on the articulated surfaces (Baker and Brothwell 1980; Chaplin 1971). Although this might be an indication that animals were used for traction, it is not conclusive. It was also noted that some bones had very well-developed muscle insertions, but although this may be associated with traction, other possible causes also exist.

Dairying

The mandibles of the cattle at Links of Noltland were fragmented, but it was noted that a considerable number of unworn dm4 teeth were present, indicating that some cattle died prenatally or at a very young age. This was reinforced by the presence of bones from very young animals. At Knap of Howar 50 per cent of cattle died in the first year of their life.

At Links of Noltland 1979–81 young cattle deaths peaked around birth and at the age of 6 months (Armour-Chelu unpublished). Killing calves at birth could be due to natural causes or a dairying economy lacking enough surplus milk to raise cull calves to a more economic meat weight (McGovern 1985). At Pool, five of twenty mandibles (25 per cent) were from cattle that had died before 6 months (Serjeantson and Bond 2007a). At Tofts Ness fusion data from long bones indicated that 23 per cent of cattle died as neonates or newborn calves, with another 18 per cent dead before 1 year old (Nicholson and Davies 2007). Analysis of mandible data indicates that in the Neolithic period 38 per cent of the animals were dead by 6 months of age (Serjeantson and Bond 2007b). Watson also noted that young cattle were slaughtered regularly at Skara Brae (Watson 1931).

An age-profile for the preliminary data at Links of Noltland 2007–9 has not yet been produced, but fusion evidence using Silver (1969) and Habermehl (quoted in Amorosi 1989) was as follows:

Fusion at 12-18 months

Bone	Less than 12-18m	12-18m	Greater than 12-18m
Humerus distal	p	p	p
Radius proximal	p		p

Fusion at 18m

Bone	Less than 18m	18m	Greater than 18m
1st and 2nd phalange	p	p	p

Fusion at 24-30m

Bone	Less than 24-30m	24-30m	Greater than 24-30m
Tibia distal	p		p
Metacarpal distal	p	p	

Fusion at 36-42m

Bone	Less than 32-42m	32-42m	Greater than 36-42m
Femur proximal	p		

Fusion at 42-48m

Bone	Less than 42-48m	42-48m	Greater than 42-48m
Femur distal	p		p
Radius distal	p		p
Tibia proximal	p		p

65: Table showing other cattle measurements (mm)

As well as deaths of newborn/early life cattle, these tables show that there were bones from cattle that died at less than 12 to 18 months old, cattle that died at approximately 18 months old, cattle that died between 24 and 30 months old and cattle that lived beyond 40 to 42 months.

The output from dairying is five times higher than from meat for the same food intake (Legge 2005) so it may well have been an attractive option if the problems of letting down milk for milking could be overcome. Milk products also have the potential for storage. In Neolithic Orkney dairying would probably only have been possible during the summer months, the period following the birth of calves.

Arguments have been made for and against dairying at Neolithic sites based on the age and sex profile of the animals (see McCormick 1998; Serjeantson and Bond 2007b). It may need further investigation of lipids from pottery as well as more detailed analysis of age profiles and breeding cycles to determine whether dairying took place or not. Lipid analysis at Barnhouse identified cattle fat, which, on balance of probability, may be milk not fat, in Grooved Ware Pottery (Jones *et al* 2005).

Dung

Cattle dung may have been used for fertilisation or fuel at Links of Noltland. There is no evidence on either horns or leg bones that cattle were tethered, so, if dung was collected for fuel, it may have been collected from an area where cattle were penned or from the fields.

Products from Cattle Carcases

It seems possible that cattle carcases from Links of Noltland 2007–9 were used for horn, skins, meat and fat. The preliminary examination identified cut and scrape marks on the feet, suggesting skinning. On the skull, some marks around the horn core indicate that horn may have been removed for further working. Cut marks on bones such as astragali indicated both dismemberment and skinning.

Possible marrow extraction was identified by the helical breaks which were observed in diaphysis of humerus, femur, tibia and radius. Additionally, almost no mandibles were recovered intact, suggesting that they may also have been fragmented for marrow. Most metacarpals and metatarsals were broken, mostly longitudinally, and this may have been for bone-working or the removal of marrow. In caribou, the tibia, metatarsal and femur produce the greatest volume of marrow (Jones and Metcalfe 1988). The pattern of breakage at Links of Noltland therefore seems to be associated with marrow extraction.

Sheep

The sheep were all slender and long-limbed. The measurements were taken following Driesch (1976).

Bone	Mean (mm)	SD (mm)	No in sample	Range (mm)
1st phalange GLpe	36	2.4	30	31-41
Astragalus GLl	27.2	1.5	25	24-30.6
Radius Bp	27.7	2	9	26-31.5
Metacarpal Bp	21.8	1.1	10	

67: Table of sheep measurements, following Driesch (1976)

Mandibles examined for eruption and wear suggested that all ages of sheep were represented on-site, with no distinct killing periods after a period of losses in very young animals.

Site	Under 2 yrs old	Over 2 yrs old
Links of Noltland	47%	53%
St Kilda (modern, feral)	Ewe 60%, ram 73%	Ewe 40%, ram 27%
North Ronaldsay (modern)	48%	52%

68: Comparison of sheep ages with St Kilda and North Ronaldsay (data from Grubb, 1974)

The preliminary examination did not produce evidence of how sheep were killed. Some sheep skulls had been halved or had sections removed to access the brain. Cuts through occipital condyles were also noted, suggesting a method of removing the skull from the rest of the body. These features were also noted in the earlier Links of Noltland excavation (Armour-Chelu unpublished). Cut marks on the bones indicated disarticulation and filleting. It was also noted that the spinal processes of the vertebrae were removed (as illustrated in Noe-Nygaard 1977, Fig 9.1).

The femur and humerus bones had helical breaks, suggesting that some of these bones were used for the extraction of marrow. Unlike the cattle, mandibles do not appear to have been broken for marrow. Other long bones have transverse, stepped, or vertical cracks, suggesting breaks from trampling or movement after deposition. Other bones had been used for tool-making. All body elements of sheep were noted in the preliminary examination from Links of Noltland 1979–81. The sheep bones recovered appeared to be from only one type of sheep. Some bones were measured for the preliminary examination. Noddle suggested that these long slender sheep might have been Scandinavian in origin, and noted that some of the sheep found at Jarlshof in Shetland were of a similar breed (Platt 1956). Measurements follow Driesch (1976).

Site	Mean	Standard deviation	No in sample	Range
Links of Noltland 2007-09	36	2.4	30	31-41
Knap of Howar (from graph in Noddle, 1983)	35.3	2	97	31-39
Ronaldsay sheep (from graph in Noddle, 1983)	31.1	1.5	28	29-34.5

69: Table showing comparisons of sheep 1st phalange GLpe (mm)

Site	Mean	Standard deviation	No in sample	Range
Links of Noltland 2007-09	27.2	1.5	25	24-30.6
Knap of Howar (from graph in Noddle, 1983)	25.9	1.6	63	24-29
Ronaldsay sheep (from graph in Noddle, 1983)	25	0.9	9	23.5-26.5
Shetland sheep (Davis, 1996)	26.6	1.3	27	23.3-29
Tofts Ness Neolithic /EBA				23-28

70: Table showing comparisons of sheep astragalus GLl (mm)

Site	Mean	Standard deviation	No in sample	Range
Links of Noltland 2007-09	27.2	1.5	25	24-30.6
Knap of Howar (from graph in Noddle, 1983)	25.9	1.6	63	24-29
Ronaldsay sheep (from graph in Noddle, 1983)	25	0.9	9	23.5-26.5
Shetland sheep (Davis, 1996)	26.6	1.3	27	23.3-29
Tofts Ness Neolithic /EBA				23-28

71: Table showing comparisons of sheep radius Bp (mm)

Bone	Mean	Standard deviation	No of sample
1st phalange Bd	28.8	3.5	9
Humerus Bd	28	1.8	11
Metacarpal Bp	21.8	1.1	10
Metatarsal Bp	20.2	0.9	7
Calcaneus GL	55	3.7	6
Scapula LG	23	2.4	12

72: Table of other sheep measurements from Links of Noltland 2007–2009 (mm)

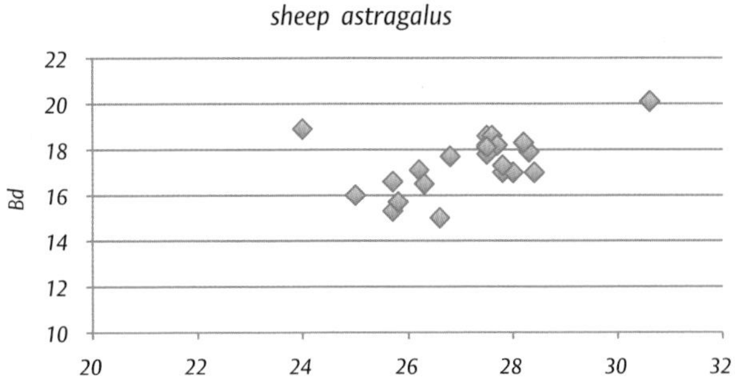

73: Graph of sheep astragalus dimensions (mm)

No pathology was observed on sheep bones apart from some changes to mandibles and a very damaged first phalange with significant additional bone growth and loss of full function.

The first premolars were missing or unerupted in some mandibles. This is a common non-metric variation on prehistoric sites (Andrews and Noddle 1975). It is also claimed that the foramen in sheep femora has a particular distribution on Orkney sites, but this was not recorded during the preliminary examination. A number of slits on articular bone surfaces, also mentioned on other Orkney sites, were noted in the preliminary assessment.

Services Provided by Sheep

To date there have been no artefacts recovered from Links of Noltland that suggest that sheep were kept for wool. This is also the situation at other Neolithic settlements in Orkney. Some newborn lamb bones recovered from the settlement suggest that there may have been some involvement with the birth of lambs. The medium to medium/large dog bones recovered could be compatible with dogs used for herding sheep, although they may only have acted as guards and settlement scavengers.

Products from Sheep Carcases

Sheep provided skins, meat and fat for the settlement. The wear and eruption of mandibles of sheep were examined to try to determine an approximate age profile. However, it should be noted that it is likely some lambs and sheep might die while grazing away from the settlement and that their bodies would not be recovered. This would have the effect of disrupting any age profile. Also, not all lambs are born at precisely the same date each season, so this can cause variation of this method. Finally, nutrition may disrupt the timing of teeth eruption.

This examination suggested that approximately 32 (47 per cent) of the mandibles were from animals under 2 years old and 36 (53 per cent) were from animals over 2 years old. Of the 25 mandible fragments in the 'under 2 years' category that could be aged in more detail, there were 11 at 3 months or below, 9 between 3 and 9 months, 3 at 18 months and 2 at 24 months.

A modern comparison of sheep mortality can be gained by comparison with the unmanaged flock of Soay sheep on St Kilda and the lightly managed Orkney Ronaldsay sheep

(Grubb 1974). In St Kilda 30.5 per cent of ewes and 34.5 per cent of rams die in the first year of life. In North Ronaldsay 31.5 per cent of sheep die within the first year of life. The proportions of under 2 to over 2 are given in Illus 68.

A total of 49 sheep mandibles were sufficiently complete to calculate Grant's wear stages, although it was not always possible to identify tooth in crypt. The results were calculated directly and using the rolling mean of three results, as adopted by Ervynck (2005) for examining tooth wear of pigs and sheep. Both sets of data show no evidence for designated killing periods, after the initial early losses.

In addition to tooth wear and eruption, epiphyseal fusion of sheep bones from Links of Noltland was examined. The results indicate the presence of newborn animals, animals less than 10 months, 10–18 months, 18–24 months, 24–36/42 months and over 42 months.

The age profiles suggest that sheep were kept for meat, not milk. Milking herds tend to have a distinctive death profile, with the early culling of male lambs. A significant proportion survived well into maturity. It is interesting to speculate why, given that milk is an efficient method of obtaining food from sheep, a milking regime was not adopted and whether this was because sheep were allowed to graze in areas distant from the settlement.

At Tofts Ness a different method of dental eruption and wear recording was used, one developed by T Legge and D Serjeantson. Their results also indicate that sheep were not intensively exploited for milk because bones from large numbers of very young male lambs were not recovered. They state that many animals died between the ages of 6 months and 2 years, and this may represent a natural mortality.

Armour-Chelu (unpublished) examining 51 sheep mandibles from Links of Noltland 1979–81 using Grant's wear system, showed two peaks, 43 per cent of the sheep dying in the first year of life, 45 per cent surviving beyond their third year. The sample used in the preliminary examination does not indicate such high losses in the first year of life, but does confirm that many sheep survived beyond their third year of life.

Noddle, using a mixture of teeth indicators and long bone fusion times, determined that at Knap of Howar the sheep bones represented neonatal 32 (17 per cent), weaning 25 (13 per cent), juvenile, (up to 18 months) 36 (19 per cent), immature (18m to 4 years) 51 (27 per cent) and mature 43 (23 per cent).

Pig

Pigs were predominantly represented by skull, loose teeth and feet bones, although a few humerus bones and one vertebra were also recovered. The bones were all from midden contexts.

Pig are different from the other major domestic groups represented at. Firstly, they are omnivores, not herbivores. Secondly, they produce only meat, fat and skin and have no secondary products such as horn, wool and milk. They can play a role, however, in maintaining hygiene in a settlement. The small quantities of bone recovered when compared with cattle and sheep might suggest that this was their role in the Links of Noltland settlement. However, in the 19th century in Orkney pigs were kept on the hills, especially on Hoy, in spring and summer and killed off in autumn for winter use. This was thought to be an ancient custom. They were kept off arable land by turf dykes (Buckley and Harvey Brown 1891).

At Links of Noltland 2007–9 there were too few bones to construct age profiles, but bones were recovered from newborn through to mature animals. At Knap of Howar the 29 pig bones recovered were predominantly older, being in the immature or mature categories.

Site	GLl mean	Standard Deviation	No in sample	Range
Links of Noltland 2007-09	39.2	2.2	5	36-41.1
Knap of Howar (Noddle, 1983)	41.6	1.5	5	40-44
Tofts Ness (Nicholson and Davies, 2007)				38-40.1

74: Table showing comparisons of pig astragalus dimensions (mm)

A statistical student's t-test does not show a significant variation between? the small sample sets from Knap of Howar and Links of Noltland.

Noddle considered that the dimensions of pig at Knap of Howar overlapped with those of wild sow, but deduced that there was little evidence of hunting and that the island (Papa Westray) was probably too small to support a population of wild pig once humans were present. At Links of Noltland 1979–81 pig bones comprised approximately 1 per cent of the total collection and were predominantly represented by juvenile animals. Low numbers of pig bones were also noted at Skara Brae, Tofts Ness and Pool.

The recovery of predominantly head and feet bones at Links of Noltland 2007–9 might suggest that the rest of the pig carcase was deposited elsewhere. Although the surviving pig bones were some of the most dense in the skeleton, the survival of neonatal bones from pig and sheep suggests that bones of lower density did survive in the midden deposits. At Tofts Ness pigs were also represented by relatively few fragments and the skeletal evidence seemed to indicate a slight predominance of heads and lower limbs, although the researchers warned that this may be a function of small sample size and taphonomic loss (Nicholson and Davies 2007).

In the Neolithic site at Durrington Walls the bone recovery pattern of predominantly feet and skulls suggested to the researchers that the pigs were subjected to initial butchery and then roasted (Albarella and Serjeantson 2002).

Dogs

Only a few dog teeth and mandible fragments were noted in the preliminary examination. All were recovered from midden contexts. Based on the size of the teeth and mandible, there appear to be two sizes of dog present – a medium-sized spaniel-type dog, larger than a terrier, and a medium/large dog, approximately the size of a retriever. The teeth were from a puppy and from mature, but not senile, dogs. The mandibles did not appear to be elongated such as those of a greyhound.

Dogs eat meat and in order to receive this food, they must have provided a service to the settlement. There were too few bones to determine whether any butchery marks were present so it cannot be established if they were eaten or not. There is evidence of gnawing and bite marks on some midden bones, with, in some instances, a remarkably clear pattern of indentations, suggesting that dogs played a role in the hygiene of the site (see also Carrott, this report). They may also have had a role as guards.

Clark suggests that Neolithic dogs were medium-sized, powerful, thickset animals, rather like the chows of today (Clark 1952). The teeth and mandible fragments recovered from Links of Noltland were of a similar size. Very few bones were recorded at the other Neolithic sites in Orkney and there were no comments on the type of dog present. The largest collection of dog bones (skulls) was from the cairn at Cuween (Charleson 1902).

Red Deer

Red deer were represented at Links of Noltland by loose teeth, axial, forequarter, hindquarter, hindfoot, foot, antler (categories adapted from Reitz and Wing 1999, 205). Bones associated with the mandible, skull, or forefoot were not recovered. The bones were all recovered from midden or midden/anthrosol contexts. All the limb bones recovered were fused, indicating they were from adult or sub-adult individuals. None of the long bones had helical fractures, perhaps indicating that these bones were not utilised for marrow.

There were cut and hack marks on the bone, indicating manipulation of the carcase. In some cases, spinal processes had been removed from the vertebrae. No pathology was observed apart from a whorl on the articular surface of a proximal radius.

Unshed antler was recovered from which the basal tine had been clearly hacked off, presumably in preparation for tool-working. Other antler fragments were not attached to the skull so it was not possible to determine whether they originated from dead animals or from shed antlers.

At Skara Brae red deer bones examined by Watson were shed antlers, two of which were broken from skulls, and five limb bones (Watson 1931). Petrie noted during an earlier examination of the site that the leg bones of red deer in the midden were unbroken (Petrie 1868).

At Tofts Ness, antler fragments made up 50 per cent of total red deer bones recovered, but bones from the forelimb, hindlimb, hindfoot, foot, mandible and skull were also present. Both adult and juvenile bones were present. There was only one butchery mark, a single chop across the neck of a scapula (Nicholson and Davies 2007). At Pool there were few red deer bones recovered from the Neolithic (Bond 2007a).

At Links of Noltland 1979–81, only 19 bones were not associated with the pile of articulated skeletons. One rib, which had been chopped, suggested this individual might have been eaten (Armour-Chelu unpublished). The point of interest in this excavation, however, was the pile of articulated red deer skeletons. These could have been animals that starved during a hard winter/spring, such as the one Scotland experienced during 2010, or were killed to prevent marauding, or hunted and preserved for some spiritual purpose. Further excavation may help clarify this issue.

The most appropriate modern populations study to provide analogies for red deer in Neolithic Orkney were:

(i) feral Soay sheep in the St Kilda group of islands
(ii) red deer in the Deer Commission for Scotland's site on Rum

The feral Soay sheep have had no wild or feral grazing competitors since 1932 and were subject to low levels of predation (Clutton-Brock 2004; Gwynne and Boyd 1970). Since this date the population has fluctuated greatly, between 610 to 1598 individuals, with greatest mortality in late winter/early spring. Cold springs in particular caused substantial population reduction (Clutton-Brock 2004). In Rum, red deer adult death did not appear to be related to density, but to the harshness of the winter (Clutton-Brock *et al* 1982).

The population of red deer in Westray may have been controlled by food availability and weather (in the probable absence of large predators such as wolf) or by a human hunting regime that harvested, but did not eliminate, the resource.

Whale

A small number of whale bones were recovered. Those that could be identified to element were from vertebrae and cranium. There was no evidence that the bone had been burned. Although a few fragments came from Neolithic midden/anthrosol contexts, the rest came from specific deposits or pits. Some bone had been hollowed out for some structural purpose, perhaps as postholes. No rib fragments were recovered.

At Skara Brae whale bone was used for artefacts such as paint pots; other bones, such as ribs, may have had a structural role (Childe 1931; Petrie 1868). At Knap of Howar whale bone fragments were rare (Noddle 1983). At Links of Noltland 1979–81 nine whale bone fragments were recovered (Armour-Chelu unpublished). A few bones of a middle/large cetacean were found at Pool (Bond 2007a) and at Tofts Ness (Nicholson and Davies 2007).

Future Research

Links of Noltland's substantial Neolithic animal bone deposits creates an opportunity to combine the archaeozoological techniques refined in the later decades of the 20th century, with the bioarchaeology techniques currently under development, such as stable oxygen isotope analysis for assessing seasonality of birth and the use of oxygen and carbon isotope ratios to test for seaweed consumption (for example, Balesse *et al* 2006; Balesse and Tresset 2007) or genetic variation (for example, Geigl and Pruvost 2004). Some of the topics which future research will address are described below.

Origin of Animals – How many introductions took place?

The source of domestic animals in Orkney has not yet been identified and it has not been established whether there was one or multiple introductions. Additionally, although the arrival of red deer has been debated, it has not yet been established if these animals arrived with or without human intervention.

Bioarchaeological investigations can provide insight into these questions. Additionally, careful study of metric and non-metric features may give an indication as to whether the domestic animals arrived as a 'farming package' that remained relatively unchanged over time, or whether the animals adapted to the environment of Orkney and/or changed due to subsequent introductions. The large quantity of animal bones present at Links of Noltland allows for stratigraphic sequencing, important for this type of analysis.

Management Regime for Domestic Animals

Information is already available on age profiles of cattle and sheep (for example Serjeantson and Bond 2007a; 2007b). The animal bones from Links of Noltland can add to this data set and test current interpretations of the secondary data, including proposals for or against dairying in cattle. Bioarchaeological research may move the debate forward (for example, Copley *et al* 2003). Although the mandibles of sheep are complete, those of cattle and pig are not, so methods of analysing individual teeth to obtain ageing data are required (see Haber 2007).

Sex profiles of animals may also give insight into the composition and management of herds. This can be through the examination of particular bones, for example, Watson (1931) examined horn cores at Skara Brae, or biometric analysis of various bones and investigation of clustering to demonstrate the presence of male, female and castrated animals (for example, Davis 2000).

Separate teeth for age profiles of cattle can complement biochemical work, for example a recent DNA test for sex identification in cattle, confirmed biometric results on sex apportionment (Svensson *et al* 2008).

Analysis of animal bones in Orkney settlements has not identified major health problems in the domestic stock. Further examination of health indicators may help establish whether herd living for sheep and cattle was stressful and/or whether malnutrition was a factor during any period.

Current research on the consumption of seaweed may highlight when this food was introduced as a winter fodder for domestic animals. Material from the current Links of Noltland excavation could be made available for this research (for example, Balesse and Ambrose 2005).

The role of pig and dog at the settlements has been little explored to date, due to low recovery rates. With bones from the current excavation, combined with those of other Orkney sites, it may be possible to establish the role that both these animals played in the life of the Neolithic settlements and possibly to pursue mitochondrial DNA work to try to establish the centre of domestication for Orkney pigs (Larsen *et al* 2005; 2007).

There are a considerable number of loose pig teeth present. These could be analysed to determine the health of pigs using the 'LEH method' highlighted by Dobney *et al* (2007).

Role of Wild Animals

Wild animals played a minor role at all Orkney Neolithic sites investigated to date. It has yet to be established whether the red deer bones recovered during the 1979–81 excavation represent animals that were hunted, died during severe winters adjacent to the settlements, or were trapped to prevent them marauding crops. It is also not known how and why red deer were introduced into Orkney. By combining information from the current Links of Noltland investigation with all the other Orkney red deer bone information and using the data from modern research into Scottish red deer populations, it may be possible to build up a profile of red deer in Orkney.

A few whale bones have been recovered from the current excavation, including worked bones. There is potential to identify some of these bones (J Herman pers comm) so an analysis of whale bones from all Orkney sites would be worthwhile in order to increase species information at the sites and to revisit the question on whether they were stranded or captured animals (see also Mulville 2002).

No seal bones were found on the current excavation and those found at other settlements do not seem to form a sufficient body of material to promote further analysis. It is interesting to note that seals were exploited at other European Neolithic sites, for example Er Yoh in southern Brittany (Boyle 2005).

Otter bones from the current excavation are sparse, but there is substantial analysis of this species in the earlier Links of Noltland excavation (Armour-Chelu unpublished).

Products Obtained from Animals

More detailed analysis of the presence/absence of key bone types in different stratigraphic layers may indicate whether import or export of animal joints took place.

It is not known if cattle were used for traction at Links of Noltland. Further examination of pathology, have been identified, following methods outlined by researchers such as Bartosiewicz (2008) and Fabis (2005), may answer this question. The question of dairying, whether of cattle or of sheep, has still to be resolved.

Butchery marks have been noted at all sites and has led to the assumption that domestic animal carcases were exploited for meat, fat, skins and to supply material for tool-working. It is unlikely that analysis of Links of Noltland animal bones will contradict this assumption. Further investigation may focus on how animal products were cooked. It might be of interest, for example, to measure the lengths of ribs and their breakage patterns to determine if they were cooked in pots and whether the preparation of pig carcases varied from that of other domestic stock.

Further detailed work on the fracturing of bones may add to understanding of how much marrow was extracted. This may give insight into the amount of food available over time at the settlement.

Changes in Farming and Hunting over Time

The substantial quantity of bones at Links of Noltland will allow comparisons with different context types within the site rather than having to combine all the data, as, for example, at Pool (Bond 2007a) or Howe (Smith 1994) to create an animal bone report. This may give insight into activities and exploitation regimes over time. In particular, if the opportunity arose to examine the interface between the Neolithic and Bronze Age, this would add to the understanding to the changes in stock-keeping over this period. It is reported that there was a change in climate, and vegetation in Scotland at around this time (for example, Anderson *et al* 1998; Tipping and Tisdall 2004).

Relationship with Animal Bones at Orkney Settlements and Other Orkney Sites

The large collection of bones from Links of Noltland can be compared with the other sites in Orkney. This can add to the understanding of changes in the farming regime over time and whether different islands in Orkney had similar or different stock.

Additionally, the data could form the basis for examination of the smaller collections of animal bones from non-settlement sites to establish if these bone collections vary significantly from those of the settlements.

Evidence of Special Treatment of Animals

At Links of Noltland the discovery of cattle heads carefully positioned below the foundations of a building is a demonstration of the special significance of cattle to the people living at Links of Noltland. The excavation of this material will add greatly to the biometric, taphonomic and butchery detail for the site, but also to the understanding of the spiritual element of the settlement. It will be interesting to try to establish, via examination of factors such as state of weathering, whether the skulls were curated in anticipation of use as foundation deposits. Other cattle heads from Orkney sites, perhaps in less well-defined positions should be revisited in the light of this discovery.

Other unusual deposits, such as the articulated deer from the earlier Links of Noltland investigation, could also be revisited on the basis of information gained from the examination of the cattle.

Comparisons with Other British and European Sites

Although various researchers have carried out comparisons with animal bone collections from other British sites (Armour-Chelu unpublished; Noddle 1983) recent work (for example, Tresset 2003) demonstrates the necessity to look at a wider range of comparative sites. The large collection offers an excellent opportunity to generate enough basic biometric data to generate valuable data for statistical comparisons with other sites (Albarella 2002; Brothwell 1993; Meadows 1999).

Most of these questions have still to be answered fully. Animal bone research is now complex and multidisciplinary. As a starting point for further investigations, it is considered especially important that the current excavated material is examined, labelled and recorded appropriately in order to allow convenient access to other researchers with particular areas of expertise. Additionally the primary data is being recorded using published methods to allow unambiguous comparison with other data sets. This may include, for example, more than one method of recording tooth wear, because sites in Orkney have already used two methods: Grant (Armour-Chelu unpublished) and Legge and Serjeantson (Serjeantson and Bond 2007a). The examination of all bone fragments is important, not just complete or substantially complete bones. The description of fragment size, weight and shape adds information to site analysis as much as the measurements of a complete bone.

Appendix: Assessment Methodology

The following criteria were considered in the preliminary assessment. It should be noted that the preliminary examination was a scoping exercise and not a quantitative review of the material from Links of Noltland 2007–9.

Ageing

Assessing the approximate age of skeletal remains gives an age of death profile, not a live population age profile. So, for example, immature skeletons illustrate as much about fertility as mortality. All other factors being equal, if there is increased fertility, there will be a greater number of immature deaths. This limits the interpretation of data. Most current zoological studies use the age of live animals, particularly those tagged at birth.

Age at death criteria such as tooth eruption or fusion rates of long bones can vary with the health and nutrition of the animal, as well as its breed. This creates a problem with the selection of animal data to use as comparisons with archaeological material. One method has been to assume that unimproved breeds from the 19th and 20th centuries give suitable measurements for comparison (for example, Davis 1996; Silver 1969; Simonds 1854), but they may not be precisely comparable with Neolithic domestic stock. Also descriptions in older records can sometimes be ambiguous. So, for example, it is not always clear in older records if teeth eruption relates to the eruption of teeth through the bone or gum.

Tooth eruption is considered to give the most accurate data for age until the full set of adult teeth has erupted. Once the teeth are fully erupted, it is the level of wear which is considered (Grant 1982; Payne 1987), but this can be influenced by the animal's health and diet.

Fusion of long bones is considered less accurate but is also used to help determine age at death profiles (Noddle 1984; Watson 1978). The same problem of comparison with standards arises as does with tooth wear and eruption. For a summary of the issues relating to ageing of archaeological animal bones see Amorosi (1989), Grant (1982), Reitz and Wing (1999).

Pathology

Pathology was considered in order to determine the health of the animals. Most diseases do not make an impression on the bone, but certain effects, such as osteoarthritis, have been tabulated for use on archaeological material. Additionally, some types of pathology may indicate that animals were used for load bearing or traction (Baker and Brothwell 1980).

Butchery

Butchering is considered to be the human reduction and modification of an animal carcase into consumable parts (Bonnichsen and Sorg 1989; Fisher 1995; Lyman 1987; 1994). Anthropological studies, for example, a recent study of pig carcase preparation (Studer and Pillonel 2007), have shown that some butchering activities do not leave any marks on the bone,. It is also often difficult to assess which marks are made by humans and which have been created by other means. Some marks have been obliterated by erosion after deposition.

The butchery marks noted from the Links of Noltland 2007–9 bone assemblage are those associated with skinning, dismemberment and filleting of meat. Skinning marks are associated with scrape and cut marks on the skull and feet. Dismemberment may be shown by hacking, such as rough cuts through the occipital condyles observed on some sheep skulls. Filleting is when parallel lines can be observed on bones such as ribs, suggesting the removal of meat from the bone.

A specialised form of butchery is breaking open the medial cavities of bones to obtain marrow. If limb bones have helical breaks, it may indicate fresh bone breaks associated with the extraction of marrow. The amount of marrow extracted could give evidence of marginality because in a well-provisioned settlement only optimal bones are broken, but in times of hardship more types of bones are broken (Outram 2001; 2002; 2004).

The consumption of meat alone is not a subsistence strategy because the amount of protein that can be ingested without fat or carbohydrate is limited to 0.4kg per day (Cachel 2000), so fat would have been important to the inhabitants of Links of Noltland. Additionally, fat gives 225 per cent of the energy of carbohydrates and protein (Outram and Mulville 2005) as well as being useful for the treatment of animal skins, waterproofing, fuel, lighting, base for paints, treating bowstrings (Binford 1978; Outram and Mulville 2005; Shipman 1981).

Tool Debitage

Another factor is tool-making. Tools are correctly considered separately as artefacts, but the material used should be listed in animal bone reports because they represent part of the animal bone collection. Additionally, often animal bone material contains debitage from tool-working and it can be useful to examine the distribution of this material to evaluate whether it was placed with general settlement waste or whether there were specific areas of deposition.

Measurements

Measurements were taken to the nearest 0.1mm using the methods proposed by Driesch (1976).

9 THE CARBONISED PLANT REMAINS

Mhairi Hastie

Introduction

One hundred and thirty-six flot fractions (<1mm fraction) were submitted for the assessment of carbonised plant remains. The flot fractions were collected from samples retained during the excavations at Links of Noltland 2007–9.

Methodology

Each flot fraction was scanned using a binocular microscope, magnification x10–x100, and the quantity and quality/preservation of carbonised plant remains was recorded. No plant remains were removed from the flot fractions during the assessment. Results were tabulated in an Microsoft Excel spreadsheet, and recorded quantitatively using a four-point scale:

- + = rare (1–10 cereal grains)
- ++ = occasional (11–50 cereal grains)
- +++ = common (51–100 cereal grains)
- ++++ = abundant (>101 cereal grains)

The plant material identified was split into seven main groups: cereal grains, weed seeds, reed material/small twigs, rhizomes, heather charcoal, wood charcoal, and peat fragments. All identifications were made with reference to the modern collection of CFA Archaeology Ltd and standard seed atlases. The presence of land snails, marine shell, small mammal bone/fishbone and silicate fragments were also noted, but are not discussed below.

The main aim was to quickly characterise the deposits highlighting any samples that were distinctive and any trends in the data. Results are presented in Illus 75, 76 and 77.

75: Carbonised plant remains: composition of flot from 2007 season (>1mm fraction)

Area	Context no	Context description	Flot vol (ml)	Cereal grain	Weed seeds	Rhizomes	Heather charcoal	Wood charcoal	Land snails	Small mammal bones	Marine shell fragments	Peat fragments	Silicate	Preservation of cereal grains	Composition of cereal grain and weed seeds
1	7003	Old ground surface	10	++					+					Varying	Barley (hulled) +
															cf. Oat sp. x 1
1	7004	Sand deposit	<10	+					+					Much abraded	Barley indet +
1	7027	Fill of pit	10	+					++					Much abraded	Preservation of grains very poor - couple appear to be barley suggesting that the others are too.
1	7030	Sand deposit	10	++	+				+			+		Abraded	Barley indet ++
															Oat sp. +
1	7035	Sand deposit	<10	+	+									Much abraded	Very abraded and fragmentary - possible barley
1	7037	Fill of cut for orthostats	<10	++		+			+					Much abraded	Barley indet +
1	7039	Fill of cut for orthostats	<10	+					+					Extremely abraded	Cereal indet x 1
1	7041	Fill of cut for orthostats	<10	+					+					Much abraded	Barley indet x 2
1	7043	Fill of cut for orthostats	<10	+	+				+					Much abraded	Barley indet x 1
															cf. Barley indet x 2
															Empetrum nigrum x 1
1	7045	Fill of cut for orthostats	<10	+					+					Much abraded	Cereal indet x 1

75: Carbonised plant remains: composition of flot from 2007 season (>1mm fraction)

Area	Context no	Context	Flot vol (ml)	Cereal grain	Weed seeds	Rhizomes	Heather	Wood	Land snails	Small mammal	Marine shell	Peat	Silicate	Preservation of	Composition of cereal grain
		description					charcoal	charcoal		bones	fragments	fragments		cereal grains	and weed seeds
1	7047	Fill of cut for orthostats	<10	+								+		Very fragmentary and abraded	Cereal indet +
1	7055	Fill of cut for orthostats	<10						+						
1	7062	Fill of cut for orthostats	<10	+					+					Much abraded	Barley indet x 1
1	7071	Silty sand deposit around orthostats	<10	+										Much abraded	cf. Barley indet x 1
1	7073	Fill of cut for orthostats	<10	+					+					Much abraded	Barley indet x 1 Cereal indet x 3
1	7076 (should this be 7077)	Packing for hearth base stone	<10	+										Much abraded	Barley indet x 1 Cereal indet x 2
1	7079	Sand deposit	<10	+					+					Much abraded	Barley indet x 6 Indeterminate seed x 1
1	7095	Sand deposit	<10	++					+					Varying	Barley (hulled) - including 1 grain of twisted hulled barley
1	7096	Sand deposit	20	+										Much abraded	Barley indet +
1	7097	Sand deposit	<10	+					+					Abraded	Barley indet x 1
2	7082	Sand deposit	10	+	+				++					Slightly abraded	Barley indet x 1 Indeterminate seed x 1

75: Carbonised plant remains: composition of flot from 2007 season (>1mm fraction)

Area	Context no	Context description	Flot vol (ml)	Cereal grain	Weed seeds	Rhizomes	Heather charcoal	Wood charcoal	Land snails	Small mammal bones	Marine shell fragments	Peat fragments	Silicate	Preservation of cereal grains	Composition of cereal grain and weed seeds
2	7083A	Thin layer of mixed sand	<10	+		+			+					Very abraded	cf. Barley x 1
2	7083B	Thin layer of mixed sand	10	+					++					Extremely abraded	Cereal indet x 7
2	7083C	Thin layer of mixed sand	<10	+		+			++					Slightly abraded	Barley indet x 3
2	7084	Windblown sand deposit	30						+++						
2	7085	Sand deposit	10						+						
2	7087	Windblown sand deposit	<10	+					+					Slightly abraded	Barley indet x 2
2	7090	Compact clean sand layer	<10	+					+					Much abraded	Cereal indet x 1
2	7092	Sand deposit	<10						+						
2	7104	Sand containing frequent marine shell and animal bone	10	+					++					Much abraded	Barley indet +
2	7105	Sand deposit	<10	++					+					Varying	Barley indet +
2	7107B	Clayey sand deposit lying on paving	<10						+						
2	7109A	Sand layer lying on paving	10			+			+						
2	7109B	Sand layer lying on paving	10	+					++			+			Barley indet x 1 Cereal indet x 1 Vitrified peat fragments

75: Carbonised plant remains: composition of flot from 2007 season (>1mm fraction)

Area	Context no	Context description	Flot vol (ml)	Cereal grain	Weed seeds	Rhizomes	Heather charcoal	Wood charcoal	Land snails	Small mammal bones	Marine shell fragments	Peat fragments	Silicate	Preservation of cereal grains	Composition of cereal grain and weed seeds
2	7110	Clayey sand deposit lying on paving	20	+					++++					Much abraded	cf. Barley indet x 2 Cereal indet x 2
2	7112	Sand deposit containing some marine shell and animal bone	10	+		+								Slightly abraded - Much abraded	Barley indet +
2	7116	Lense of red clay	<10						+						
2	7117 SF56	Sand containing frequent marine shell and animal bone	10						++						
2	7117	Sand containing frequent marine shell and animal bone	10	+					++					Much abraded	cf. Barley indet x 1
2	7123A	Clayey silt deposit	<10	+	+	+								Much abraded	Barley indet x 4 Cereal indet x 1 Empetrium nigrum x 1
2	7123B	Clayey silt deposit	10	+	+	+		+	++					Much abraded	Barley indet x 2 Cereal indet x 2 Carex sp. x 1
2	7123C	Clayey silt deposit	<10	+					+					Much abraded	
2	7133	Sandy silt deposit	10	+		+			++					Much abraded	Barley +
2	7134	Hearth material	<10						+						

75: Carbonised plant remains: composition of flot from 2007 season (>1mm fraction)

Area	Context no	Context description	Flot vol (ml)	Cereal grain	Weed seeds	Rhizomes	Heather charcoal	Wood charcoal	Land snails	Small mammal bones	Marine shell fragments	Peat fragments	Silicate	Preservation of cereal grains	Composition of cereal grain and weed seeds
2	7138	Burnt clay forming undulated surface in entrance area	<10	+					+					Much abraded	Cereal indet x 3
2	7139	Silty clay deposit (same as 7155)	10	+		+			++					Varying	Barley (hulled) +
2	7140	Clayey sand deposit	<10	+					+					Much abraded	Barley indet +
2	7141	Sand containing frequent marine shell	10	+					++					Much abraded	Barley +
2	7143	Comapct sandy clay deposit	<10	+				+						Much abraded	Barley indet +
2	7144	Comapct silty clay deposit	<10	+					+				+	Varying slightly abraded - much abraded	Hulled barley x 2 Barley indet +
2	7145	Peat ash dump at entrance	<10	+					+					Much abraded	Barley indet x 2 Cereal indet x 8 (prob all barley)
2	7151	Sandy silt deposit	10	+	+				+					Much abraded	Hulled barley x 1 Barley indet x 5 Indeterminate seed
2	7154	Compact silty sand deposit containing shell and animal bone	20	+		+			++					Much abraded	Barley indet x 1 Cereal indet x 1

75: Carbonised plant remains: composition of flot from 2007 season (>1mm fraction)

Area	Context no	Context	Flot vol (ml)	Cereal grain	Weed seeds	Rhizomes	Heather	Wood	Land snails	Small mammal	Marine shell	Peat	Silicate	Preservation of	Composition of cereal grain
		description					charcoal	charcoal		bones	fragments	fragments		cereal grains	and weed seeds
2	7155	Silty clay deposit (same as 7139)	10	++	+				+					Varying	Barley (hulled) ++
															Empetrum nigrum x 1
2	7157	Sand deposit with occasional shell and animal bone - forms matrix around buttressing slabs	10	+					++					Much abraded	At least one barley grain and a few fragments of other cereal grains but not identifiable
2	7159	Sand deposit below buttressing slabs	20	+					++					Much abraded	Barley indet +
2	7160	Sand deposit	10	+	+	+			+					Much abraded	Barley indet +
															Danthonia decumbens x 1
2	7161	Silty sand deposit	10	+					++					Slightly abraded	Barley indet x 1
															Carex sp. x 1
2	7162	Sand deposit	10	+	+				++					Much abraded	Barley indet +
															poss. Gramineae x 1
															Carex / Ranunculus sp. x 1
															cf. Empetrum nigrum x 1
2	7163	Silty sand deposit	10	++	+	+		+	+	fish bone +				Much abraded	Barley indet ++
															Indeterminate seed x 3

75: Carbonised plant remains: composition of flot from 2007 season (>1mm fraction)

Area	Context no	Context description	Flot vol (ml)	Cereal grain	Weed seeds	Rhizomes	Heather charcoal	Wood charcoal	Land snails	Small mammal bones	Marine shell fragments	Peat fragments	Silicate	Preservation of cereal grains	Composition of cereal grain and weed seeds
2	7164	Lense of clay sand deposit within deposit 7160	10	+	+	+			++					Much abaraded	Barley indet x 1
															cf. Barley indet x 1
															Cereal indet x 1
2	7165	Silty sand deposit	10	++	+	+			++					Much abraded	Barley indet ++ (many cereal fragments prob all barley)
2	7167	Clay layer	<10					+							Very small fragments of charcoal
2	7168	Silty sand deposit	<10	+	+	+			+					Much abraded	Barley indet x 1
															Cereal indet x 1
															Danthonia decumbens x 1
3	7032	Spread of stone shatter, shell and bone	10	+					+					Much abradaed	Barley indet x 2
3	7033	No description provided	<10	+										Much abraded	cf. Barley indet x 1
3	7080	Sand deposit filling interior of Structure 1	<10						+						
3	7101	Windblown sand deposit	<10	+					+					Much abraded	Barley indet x 1
3	7111	Windblown sand deposit	<10	+					+					Slightly abraded	Barley indet x 1
3	7115	Windblown sand deposit	<10	Archaeologically sterile											1 x modern uncharred weed seed

75: Carbonised plant remains: composition of flot from 2007 season (>1mm fraction)

Area	Context no	Context	Flot vol (ml)	Cereal grain	Weed seeds	Rhizomes	Heather	Wood	Land snails	Small mammal	Marine shell	Peat	Silicate	Preservation of	Composition of cereal grain
		description					charcoal	charcoal		bones	fragments	fragments		cereal grains	and weed seeds
3	7119	Silty clay containing charcoal, shell and animal bone	<10	+					+					Much abraded	Barley indet x 1
3	7120	Clay deposit	<10						+						
3	7121	Silty clay deposit	<10												
3	7122	Sandy clay deposit	<10	+					+					Much abraded	Barley indet x 2
3	7124	Silty sand deposit	<10						+						
3	7130	Clay deposit	<10	+										Much abraded	cf. Barley indet x 2
3	7132	Clayey silt deposit	<10	+					+					Slightly abraded	Barley indet x 1
3	7136	Sandy clay deposit	<10	+					+					Much abraded	Cereal indet x 1
3	7152B	Sand containing frequent marine shell	<10	+					+					Much abraded	Barley indet x 1
3	7512D	Sand containing frequent marine shell	<10		+	+		+	+						Galeopsis sp. x 1
Test Pit 1	7149	Clayey sand deposit	20	+++	+	+			+	+				Much abraded	Barley indet +++ Empetrum migrum + Carex sp. +
N/a	7301		10			+			+						
N/a	7302		10				+		++						
N/a	7302 (SPIT3)		10			+		+	+	#NAME?	+				

75: Carbonised plant remains: composition of flot from 2007 season (>1mm fraction)

Area	Context no	Context	Flot vol (ml)	Cereal grain	Weed seeds	Rhizomes	Heather	Wood	Land snails	Small mammal	Marine shell	Peat	Silicate	Preservation of	Composition of cereal grain
		description					charcoal	charcoal		bones	fragments	fragments		cereal grains	and weed seeds
N/a	7302 (SPIT4)		20		+	++		+	+	+					Carex sp. +
															Danthonia decumbens +
N/a	7302 (SPIT5)		10		+	++		+	+			+			Danthonia decumbens +
															Carex sp. +
N/a	7302 (SPIT7)		20		+	+			+	++	++				cf. Gramineae sp. x 1
N/a	7302 (SPIT8)		10			+		+	+						Tiny fragts of wood charcoal
N/a	7303		20			+		+							Tiny frags of wood charcoal
N/a	7304		10		++	++			+						Carex sp. ++
															Danthonia decumbens +
															Empetrum nigrum +
N/a	7305		<10		++	+									Dianthonia decumbens +
															Carex sp. ++
															Empetrum nigrum +
N/a	7306		20		++	++			+	+					Carex sp. ++
															cf. Danthonia decumbens +
															Polygonum sp. +

75: Carbonised plant remains: composition of flot from 2007 season (>1mm fraction)

Area	Context no	Context	Flot vol (ml)	Cereal grain	Weed seeds	Rhizomes	Heather	Wood	Land snails	Small mammal	Marine shell	Peat	Silicate	Preservation of	Composition of cereal grain
		description					charcoal	charcoal		bones	fragments	fragments		cereal grains	and weed seeds
N/a	7307		100		++++	+	++		+	+					Large quantity of weed seeds particualrly Danthonia decumbens and Carex sp.
N/a	7312		10			+				+	+				
N/a	7313		<10					+							Charcoal frags extremely small
N/a	7323		100		+	+			++++	#NAME?				Much abraded	Barley indet +
															Rumex sp. +
N/a	7324		50	++	+	++	+		++					Much abraded	Barley indet ++
															Empetrium nigrum +
															Ranunculus sp. +

76: Carbonised plant remains: composition of flot from 2008 and 2009 seasons (>1mm fraction)

Area	Context no	Context	Flot vol (ml)	Cereal grain	Weed seeds	Rhizomes	Heather	Wood	Land snails	Small mammal	Marine shell	Peat	Silicate	Preservation of	Composition of cereal grain
		description					charcoal	charcoal		bones	fragments	fragments		cereal grains	and weed seeds
LON08															
N/a	8000	Clay lens	<10		+				+						Danthonia decumbens +
N/a	8001 (SPIT1)	Silty clay deposit containing frequent animal bone, shell and artefacts	10		+			+	+						Carex sp. +
															cf. Ranunculus sp. x 1
N/a	8001 (SPIT2)	Silty clay deposit containing frequent animal bone, shell and artefacts	10			+		+	+						
N/a	8002	Compact silty clay deposit	20		+	++							++		Danthonia decumebns +
															Carex sp. +
N/a	8003	Compact silty clay deposit	10		++	+		+		+			+	Much abraded	Danthonia decumbens ++
															Carex sp. +
															NB One very small fragment of wood charcoal
N/a	8004	Concentration of limpet shells	20		+	+		+	+		++				Danthonia decumbens +
															Indeterminate seeds +
N/a	8008	Spread of rubble	10		+	+		+					+		Carex sp. +
															Galeopsis sp. +

76: Carbonised plant remains: composition of flot from 2008 and 2009 seasons (>1mm fraction)

Area	Context no	Context	Flot vol (ml)	Cereal grain	Weed seeds	Rhizomes	Heather	Wood	Land snails	Small mammal	Marine shell	Peat	Silicate	Preservation of	Composition of cereal grain
		description					charcoal	charcoal		bones	fragments	fragments		cereal grains	and weed seeds
N/a	8010	Compact silty clay deposit	20		+	++		+	+	+	+				Carex sp. +
N/a	8010 (SPIT1)	Compact silty clay deposit	10												
N/a	8010 (SPIT2)	Compact silty clay deposit	<10		+	+			+						Indeterminate seeds +
N/a	8018	Compact silty clay deposit	<10		+										Rumex sp. x 2
N/a	8022	Silty clay deposit with patches of peat ash	<10		+										Ranunculus sp. x 2
N/a	8029	Compact silty clay deposit	10		+	+		++	+						Danthonia decumbens +
LON09															
N/a	9000 (SPIT1)	Midden deposit	10		+	+		+	+						Danthonia decumbens +
N/a	9000 (SPIT2)	Midden deposit	<10		+		+								Danthonia decumbens +
															Carex sp. +
N/a	9000 (SPIT3)	Midden deposit	10					++							Eleochuris sp. x 1
															Plantago lanceolata x 1
N/a	9003	Midden deposit	<10		+	+			+						Danthonia decumbens x 1
N/a	9004	Fill of kiln flue	10		+			++							Danthonia decumbens +
N/a	9005	Fill of kiln flue	<10			+		+	+						

76: Carbonised plant remains: composition of flot from 2008 and 2009 seasons (>1mm fraction)

Area	Context no	Context description	Flot vol (ml)	Cereal grain	Weed seeds	Rhizomes	Heather charcoal	Wood charcoal	Land snails	Small mammal bones	Marine shell fragments	Peat fragments	Silicate	Preservation of cereal grains	Composition of cereal grain and weed seeds
N/a	9006	Fill of kiln flue	10		++	+									Danthonia decumbens +
															Carex sp. +
N/a	9009	Fill over collapsed kiln bowl	10			+		+	+						

77: Carbonised plant remains: composition of flot from structures in scheduled area (>1mm fraction)

Area	Context no	Context	Flot vol (ml)	Cereal grain	Weed seeds	Rhizomes	Heather	Wood	Land snails	Small mammal	Marine shell	Peat	Silicate	Preservation of	Composition of cereal grain
		description					charcoal	charcoal		bones	fragments	fragments		cereal grains	and weed seeds
LON08															
N/a	8000	Clay lens	<10		+				+						Danthonia decumbens +
N/a	8001 (SPIT1)	Silty clay deposit containing frequent animal bone, shell and artefacts	10		+			+	+						Carex sp. +
															cf. Ranunculus sp. x 1
N/a	8001 (SPIT2)	Silty clay deposit containing frequent animal bone, shell and artefacts	10			+		+	+						
N/a	8002	Compact silty clay deposit	20		+	++							++		Danthonia decumebns +
															Carex sp. +
N/a	8003	Compact silty clay deposit	10		++	+		+		+			+	Much abraded	Danthonia decumbens ++
															Carex sp. +
															NB One very small fragment of wood charcoal

77: Carbonised plant remains: composition of flot from structures in scheduled area (>1mm fraction)

Area	Context no	Context	Flot vol (ml)	Cereal grain	Weed seeds	Rhizomes	Heather	Wood	Land snails	Small mammal	Marine shell	Peat	Silicate	Preservation of	Composition of cereal grain
		description					charcoal	charcoal		bones	fragments	fragments		cereal grains	and weed seeds
N/a	8004	Concentration of limpet shells	20		+	+		+	+		++				Danthonia decumbens + Indeterminate seeds +
N/a	8008	Spread of rubble	10		+	+		+					+		Carex sp. + Galeopsis sp. +
N/a	8010	Compact silty clay deposit	20		+	++		+	+	+	+				Carex sp. +
N/a	8010 (SPIT1)	Compact silty clay deposit	10												
N/a	8010 (SPIT2)	Compact silty clay deposit	<10		+	+			+						Indeterminate seeds +
N/a	8018	Compact silty clay deposit	<10		+										Rumex sp. x 2
N/a	8022	Silty clay deposit with patches of peat ash	<10		+										Ranunculus sp. x 2
N/a	8029	Compact silty clay deposit	10		+	+		++	+						Danthonia decumbens +
LON09															
N/a	9000 (SPIT1)	Midden deposit	10		+	+		+	+						Danthonia decumbens +
N/a	9000 (SPIT2)	Midden deposit	<10		+		+								Danthonia decumbens + Carex sp. +

77: Carbonised plant remains: composition of flot from structures in scheduled area (>1mm fraction)

Area	Context no	Context description	Flot vol (ml)	Cereal grain	Weed seeds	Rhizomes	Heather charcoal	Wood charcoal	Land snails	Small mammal bones	Marine shell fragments	Peat fragments	Silicate	Preservation of cereal grains	Composition of cereal grain and weed seeds
N/a	9000 (SPIT3)	Midden deposit	10					++							Eleochuris sp. x 1
															Plantago lanceolata x 1
N/a	9003	Midden deposit	<10		+	+			+						Danthonia decumbens x 1
N/a	9004	Fill of kiln flue	10		+			++							Danthonia decumbens +
N/a	9005	Fill of kiln flue	<10			+		+	+						
N/a	9006	Fill of kiln flue	10		++	+									Danthonia decumbens +
															Carex sp. +
N/a	9009	Fill over collapsed kiln bowl	10			+		+	+						

Results

One hundred and twenty-six of the flot fractions contained carbonised plant remains, including cereal grain, a range of weed seeds, rhizomes (underground stem fragments), charcoal (both wood and heather) and small peat fragments.

Cereal Grains

The vast majority of the flot fractions contained carbonised cereal grains. No high concentrations of grains were present and only a small amount of grain was recovered from each flot, in most cases each containing less than 10 grains. Preservation was generally poor, the cereal grain being much abraded, and much of it could only be identified to the level of species. Occasional well-preserved grains were recovered, but these were rare.

The bulk of the grains were identified as barley and, where preservation allowed, the hulled variety was recorded. Two possible oat grains were also uncovered; however, neither was sufficiently preserved to allow distinction between the wild or cultivated species. Given the number of oat grains recovered it would seem most likely that the wild species, *Avena fatua*, which occurs as a weed of cereal crops, was represented. No chaff or straw remains were recovered from any of the samples.

Weed Seeds

Well-preserved carbonised weed seeds were recovered from 54 of the flot fractions. In most cases, the weed assemblages were small, with only one or two seeds being recovered from each flot, although occasional larger quantities of seeds were recovered, particularly from one context 7307 (LON07). The diversity of the weed seeds recovered was limited. The seeds comprised particularly a suite of species indicative of acid heath environments, including both dry heathland and damper marshy areas, such as *Empetrum nigrum* (cowberry), *Danthonia decumbens* (heathgrass), *Rumex acetosella* (sheep's sorrel), *Carex spp* (sedge) and *Galeopsis* spp (hemp-nettle). Other species which would be more common along the coast, including *Atriplex* sp. (orache), which is particularly common on sandy coastlines, and *Ranunculus spp* (buttercup), were also present although in only very small quantities.

Rhizomes

Charred rhizome fragments (underground stem fragments) were present throughout the flot fractions, particularly in samples that contained increased quantities of weed seed. A variety of rhizomes were identified including possible *Juncus* sp (rush), *Cyperaceae* (sedge) and the possible bulbous rhizomes of *Arrenatheum elatius* (onion couch).

Charcoal

Small quantities of charred heather twigs were recovered from 5 samples, and very small fragments of wood charcoal were recovered from 23 samples. Much of the wood charcoal consists of very small slivers and is not suitable for identification. Initial identification of larger fragments of wood charcoal suggests that it is coniferous wood.

Peat

Occasional burnt lumps of peat were present in a small quantity of the samples.

Discussion

Plant Preservation and Diversity

The carbonised plant remains consisted principally of charred barley grain, the bulk of them being much abraded indicating that they had undergone lots of movement prior to burial. No chaff or other crop processing by-products such as straw were recovered, hence clean grain predominates. Lack of chaff or other crop-processing debris does not necessarily indicate that crop-processing was not being carried out on-site, but rather that activities such as threshing were being done away from a source of fire, and that chaff remains were being discarded on middens or spread on fields instead of being disposed on to the hearth.

Small quantities of twiggy material, heather charcoal, small wood charcoal fragments and peat were present throughout many different contexts. The large concentration of seeds indicative of acid heath along with heather charcoal and peat fragments indicates that the main source of fuel was peat or heathy turfs. Indeed, this is reflected by the recovery of peat ash within some of the deposits associated with a number of the excavated structures. Woodland for fuel was scarce on Orkney from the Neolithic onwards and evidence from other archaeological sites across the island indicates that peat or turves were the main source of fuel. The recovery of coniferous wood, albeit in very small quantities, does suggest potentially that driftwood was being utilised as a fuel.

Interestingly, there is a distinct lack of weed species more commonly associated with crop fields, although occasional possible onion couch rhizomes are recorded and these are associated with arable or grassland. Seeds such as *Chenopodium album* (fat hen), *Stellaria media* (corn spurrey), *Plantago lanceolata* (ribwort) and Gramineae (grass family), which are common arable weeds and have been recovered from other prehistoric sites on Westray and the mainlands of Orkney and Shetland (for example at Kebister, Dickson 1999; Bayanne, Hastie forthcoming a; and Langskaill, Hastie forthcoming b) are not present in this assemblage. This lack of weeds of arable fields at Links of Noltland may suggest that processing of the grain was being carried out away from the settlement site; it is not currently possible, however, to determine if the grain was being processed in a nearby unexcavated area of the site, or if the grain was being brought to the site from much further afield. It is hoped that this can be better assessed when more material becomes available.

The large quantity of *Empetrum nigrum* (crowberry) seeds recovered from some of the flot fractions may indicate the deliberate collection of the berries as a food source. The berries, which would have been available from the autumn, would have been relatively easy to gather and can be stored without much preparation. Ethnohistorical evidence records that the crowberry was a vital addition to the diet of the Inuit and Sami and the leaves and stem of the crowberry are used by the Den'aina (Alaska native) people as a medicine for diarrhoea and stomach problems (National Park Service 2006).

Distribution

Carbonised plant remains, including cereal grain, weed seeds and charcoal fragments, were recovered as a general low-level spread across the excavated areas. There is very little evidence for spatial patterning of plant remains, with a uniform spread of grain present throughout most features.

Of some note is the lack of cereals from structures that date to the Neolithic period. The lack of grain from these Neolithic deposits does not specifically indicate that cultivation was not being carried out during this period. Analysis from soil samples taken from the site suggests that areas close to the Neolithic settlement were being deliberately enhanced with the addition of midden material and animal dung specifically for cultivation (McKenna and Simpson, this report) and if this is indeed the case, then the lack of grain from this area may simply suggests that crop-processing or corn-drying activities were not being carried out in this part of the site. No cereal grains were recovered from samples taken from the kiln-like feature excavated during 2009.

The plant assemblages recovered from the areas excavated in 2007 were very similar both in composition and quantity of plant remains. The structures and deposits uncovered in these areas are believed to be of Bronze Age date and the plant assemblages with hulled barley and a mix of heathland plants fits into a well established pattern from the Northern Isles.

No large concentrations of cereal grains were noted, and none of the charred deposits are likely to represent *in situ* burning. The grain were recovered principally from deposits that contained a mixture of plant remains, burnt fuel, marine shell, animal bone and pottery fragments, indicating that the vast majority of the debris is likely to be the remnants of midden material that has been spread across the site and into many different contexts. This general spread of low-level burnt grain has been identified on similar prehistoric sites, both in the Northern Isles and on the mainland. The grain being burnt during small-scale drying activities where the grain was dried, on an *ad hoc* basis when required, over the domestic hearth to help remove the hulls enclosing the grain and to make the grain easier to grind. , Over time, grain burnt accidentally during these activities would become mixed with other sediments to create a low and relatively homogenous background level of charred grain.

10 THE HUMAN REMAINS

Dawn Gooney

Introduction

A brief assessment was carried out on stray human bone recovered from three locations at Links of Noltland. A fuller examination was undertaken of material from the Scheduled Area to the south-east of the PIC area, which included one complete and one partial burial (Illus 2, Test Pit 4).

Scattered Remains outside the Scheduled Area

In 2000, a concentration of fragmentary human bone was found to the south of the Links of Noltland area, outside but close to the Scheduled Area. The remains included a femur, tibia and humerus fragments, skull and mandible fragments and some vertebrae. They represent at least three individuals. The remains may represent ex situ burials; they were found amongst deposits banked up against a fence and may have been redeposited to this location in the recent past. A table with description has been provided for the site archive.

Scattered Remains in the PIC Area

A small amount of human bone was recovered during the excavation of the Neolithic remains within the PIC area. This includes adult, adolescent and child bones. The majority of the bone is likely to have been deposited in the Neolithic period and was found amongst midden deposits and within wall core material. A table with description has been provided for the site archive.

Burials and Remains from the Scheduled Area

Human remains were recovered from the Scheduled Area in 2007 and 2009. The 2007 remains were recovered from surface scatters. In 2009, three contexts excavated during test trenching produced human bone: 9048, 9053 and 9054. Context 9048 represents a surface spread of bone, including some animal bone; context 9053 was a collection of *in situ* and *ex situ* human bone; and context 9054 was a complete inhumation. A small number of bones found during the 2007 season of investigation in this area were also examined as part of this assessment.

Methods

The remains were washed by members of EASE post-excavation team in plain water and allowed to air dry. Examination of the remains was carried out in accordance with and using methods and resources approved by Institute of Field Archaeologists/British Association for Biological Anthropology and Osteoarchaeology (IFA/BABAO) guidelines (Brickley and McKinley 2004). The main sources used for these assessments were Bass (2005) and Buikstra and Ubelaker (1994). Due to the incomplete and very fragmentary nature of the assemblage, a confident assessment of age and sex could only be determined for the complete inhumation.

Condition of the Bones

Much of the remains are fragmentary and some are bleached white by exposure to the elements while lying disturbed on the ground surface. The presence of rabbit bones in part of the collection and the very sandy environment at Links of Noltland explains much of the disturbance to burials in the area.

When undisturbed, however, as in the case of the complete inhumation (9054), the bone is in good condition, with complete long bones and skull, though the sandy soils have eroded much of the bone surfaces possibly removing evidence of disease or infection.

Bone from the Scheduled Area, South-east of the PIC Area

2007 Bone Scatters

A small amount of human bone was collected during investigations in 2007. This includes a collection of cremated long bone fragments collected from the ground surface, an adult left talus, a fragment of lumbar vertebra and an adult left side triquetral carpal bone from Context 1.

2009: Context 9048

This context included two fragments of long bones probably from a child, pelvis fragments and a number of adult teeth. Further adult teeth were recovered through screening of the excavated deposits. The teeth included one maxillary third molar, one maxillary incisor, two mandibular third molars, two mandibular first incisors, one mandibular canine and a number of molar fragments. All of the teeth showed some degree of attrition, but, due to the disturbed nature of this collection, they cannot confidently be ascribed to the same individual.

2009: Context 9053

This context represents the disturbed burial of one individual, and consisted of two collections of bones described as *ex situ* and *in situ*, which the excavators noted were in close association and partly articulated.

The *in situ* collection included left carpals, left radius and ulna fragments, left scapula fragments, left and right rib fragments and fragments of lumbar and thoracic vertebrae. The *ex situ* collection included foot and hand bones, rib and vertebrae fragments, fragments of left femur and right ulna. Matching fragments of the left tibia and right humerus were mixed between the *in situ* and *ex situ* collections.

There was a large quantity of weathered and bleached bone in this collection and parts of some of the long bones were also white and bleached from exposure to the elements in recent times. The robust appearance of the long bones and the seemingly narrow appearance of the greater sciatic notch on a pelvis fragment suggest that this individual may have been male. A number of the lumbar vertebral body fragments show signs of osteophytic growth which can be indicative of degeneration of the spine and may suggest older age. Given the extremely fragmentary nature of the remains, however, this assessment of sex and age is not definite.

2009: Context 9054

This context represents a single inhumation adult burial. All skeletal elements were represented apart from the cervical vertebrae, of which only atlas fragments were present. There was some fragmentation of the facial area of the skull, the left pelvis, the sacrum and the scapulae. Some bones of the right side, in particular the leg bones, showed black discoloration due to the body's position, lying on the right side, in the grave.

Age

Dental attrition of the molars suggested an age between 25 and 35 years. However, examination of the pelvis (Todd Phase 8), the sternal ends of the ribs and skull suture closure reveal an age of 40 to 50 years. The appearance of the bones together with these results suggests an age in the middle age range of 35 to 45 years.

Sex

A visual assessment of the most sexually dimorphic elements of the skull and pelvis indicate that this individual was female. This is supported by the dimensions of the long bones apart from the femur, the measurements of which yielded results in the indeterminate range.

Stature

A height of 160.1cm +/–3.55 was calculated from combined measurements of the femur and tibia. Stature has been recorded as between 154cm and 161cm for females during the Bronze Age (Roberts and Cox 2003, 86).

Dental Pathology

Increased dental disease has been noted between the Neolithic and Bronze Age periods, with an increase in calculus, abscess and ante-mortem tooth loss, thought to be connected with the increased cereal consumption from accelerated agricultural activity. Ante-mortem tooth loss was recorded in the cremated remains from Cairn 2 at Rapness (Barber *et al* 1996, 113). In the case of 9054, calculus was noted on the buccal sides of a number of the teeth and the teeth are high in the alveolar bone with exposed gums which can be indicative of periodontal disease. In the mandible, the right first incisor was lost during life and a large abscess can be seen at the site of the right canine (Illus 78). Although the canine is present in the collection, it would have been very loose in the gums during life with little or no alveolar bone remaining to hold it in place. All maxillary incisors and canines were lost during life (Illus 79) and the alveolar bone is healed with little evidence of remaining infection.

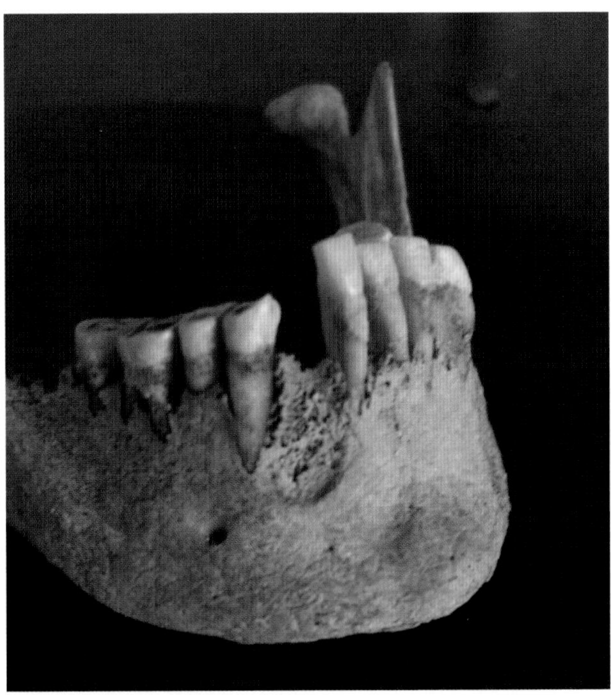

78: Human burial 9054: dental abscess

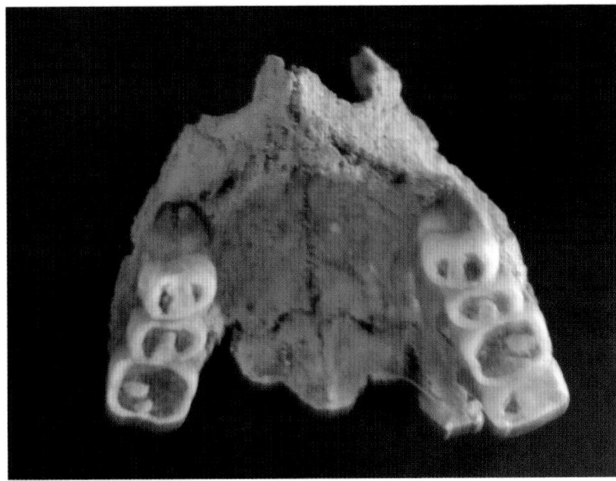

79: Human burial 9054: ante-mortem tooth loss

Other Pathology

The left scapula shows signs of slight infection and widening of the anterior edge of the glenoid cavity (Illus 80). Corresponding to this on the anterior side of the left humerus is a smoothed area of new articulation, possibly the result of a dislocation of the humeral head which would have caused the upper arm to turn with the back of the elbow facing outwards.

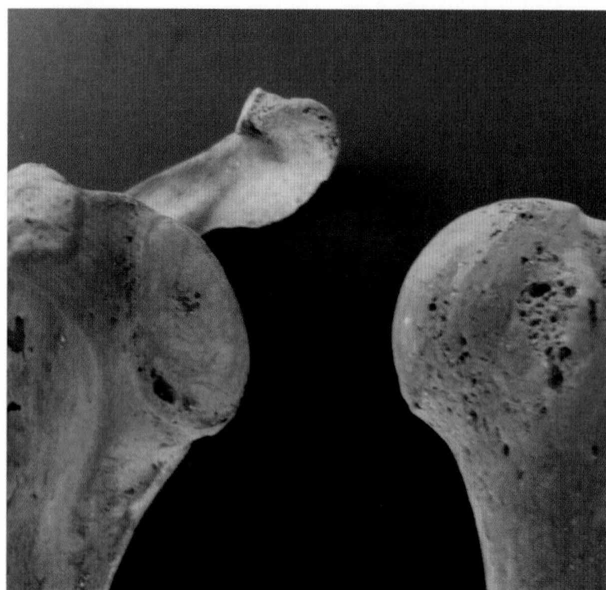

80: Human burial 9054: left shoulder, possible dislocation

Spondylolysis of the fifth lumbar vertebra was also noted (Illus 81). The separated parts of the vertebra also show slight signs of eburnation from rubbing against each other during physical activity. This is a condition whereby the body and spinal process of the vertebra have become separated and can be the result of congenital weakness or of repeated stress at the location from bending and lifting (Roberts and Cox 2003, 80).

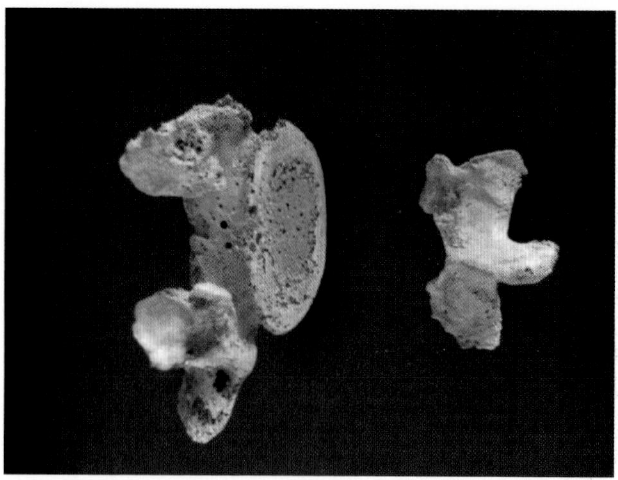

81: Human burial 9054: spondylolysis of Lumbar 5

The eroded surfaces of many of the bones and the sandy soils in which this individual was buried have removed any evidence there may have been on the surfaces of the bone of any other surface traumas or infections.

Conclusions

Given the sandy environment and the disturbed nature of the human burials found in the wider hinterland, the occurrence of scattered human remains in archaeological deposits of varying dates is unsurprising. Many are likely to represent material which has been scattered from its original location and ended up in a deflation surface containing inclusions of all dates.

The remains from the Scheduled Area represent at least two discrete individual adult inhumation burials and at least one other, most probably a child. The small amount of cremated bone recovered from the ground surface here in 2007 suggests that more than one form of burial custom may have been practised in the vicinity.

11 [EXTRACT FROM] ANTHROPIC SEDIMENTS AND ANTHROSOLS AT LINKS OF NOLTLAND: THE POTENTIAL FOR INTEGRATED PALAEO-LANDSCAPE INTERPRETATIONS

Ian A Simpson and Graeme Wilson (May 2008)

Introduction

Surveys and excavations at Links of Noltland have now identified several Neolithic and Bronze Age structures together with stratigraphic sequences that include anthropic sediments (midden deposits) associated with the structures and more extensive deposits of contrasting fossil anthrosols (soils associated with agricultural activity (World Reference Base 2006) beyond the areas of structure and which may form field systems (Moore and Wilson 2007). A day field visit to the site in May 2008 confirmed the presence of anthropic sediments and anthrosols, and the stratigraphic relationships of these with sites and sand deposits, identified by the previous surveys (Moore and Wilson 2007a; 2007b; 2007c).

Relict and fossil properties of soils and sediments associated with archaeological sites and the early cultural landscape in Orkney, as well as in the wider north Atlantic region, are now well-established as records of cultural and environmental change. The application of novel methodologies including thin section micromorphology with associated image analyses and 'on-slide' chemical analyses, biomarker analyses, model-based land productivity assessments and optically stimulated luminescence (OSL) measurement have given new insights into the forms, functions and dynamics of early north Atlantic landscapes.

On Orkney, Neolithic anthropic sediments have been analysed at Skara Brae (Simpson *et al* 2006) and Neolithic and Bronze Age anthrosols have been analysed at Tofts Ness (Guttmann *et al* 2006; Simpson *et al* 1998; 2007). Analyses of midden deposits within the Skara Brae settlement using thin section micromorphology, supported by particle size distribution and total phosphorus, suggested that both earlier and later phases of the site showed accumulation of household wastes dominated by fuel residues and that these wastes may have been used to help stabilise wind-blown sand deposits during the later settlement phases. In addition, the use of clay material tempered with household waste is associated with wall construction. Animal manures were only evident in anthropic deposits on the edge of the main settlement site where composting may have taken place, and there is no evidence for their use in site construction (Simpson *et al* 2006). Integration of thin section micromorphology and lipid biomarkers was used to analyse the fossil anthrosols at Tofts Ness, Orkney, and indicated that they were cultivated soils that were formed through the application of grassy turf material together with domestic waste midden that was dominated by human manures (Guttmann *et al* 2006; Simpson *et al* 1998; 2007). Chronologies for these soils were initially derived from radiocarbon measurement of bulk acid insoluble soil material integrated with stratigraphic relationships to the excavated archaeological site at Tofts Ness. Subsequent assessment of OSL measurements gave broadly consistent chronologies against radiocarbon measurements. For the site and soils (Sommerville *et al* 2001); our more recent experience of OSL measurement on anthrosols in Greenland has give error values of ±40 years. Analyses of soils and sediments associated with the Viking Age to medieval transition in Orkney has also been undertaken where thin section micromorphology, biomarker and stable carbon isotope analyses have allowed integrated analyses of fish midden, farm mound and deep topsoil deposits. This has enabled unique insight into the relationships between farming and fishing during this transition period (Simpson 1997; Simpson and Barrett 1996; Simpson *et al* 1999; 2005).

From our field observations of the anthropic sediments and anthrosols at Links of Noltland site and our experience of working on the analyses of these soils and sediments as cultural and environmental records in Orkney and the wider north Atlantic region, Links of Noltland emerges as a unique location where key questions of Neolithic to Bronze Age landscape dynamics can be addressed. The uniqueness of the site is in the range and extent of anthropic sediments and anthrosols associated at the same locality, allowing the first opportunity to consider relationships between midden material and cultivated areas to be established. Furthermore, the occurrence of Neolithic and Bronze Age settlement and associated sediments and soils in the same vicinity provides an outstanding opportunity to consider the dynamics of landscape change across the Neolithic to Bronze Age transition. The deflation and erosion on the site and the failure to stabilise the site through management intervention adds to the urgency to ensure that the locality is at least 'preserved by record' through excavation intervention.

The key sets of questions we would wish to consider are as follows:

- *What materials make up the midden deposits within and immediately adjacent the archaeological structures (animal and human manures; fuel residues, turf materials)?*
  – Does the distribution of these materials indicate partitioned use in site construction and land management organisation?
  – What is the relative balance of social and environmental explanations of any such partitioned distribution? – How comparable are Links of Noltland midden materials and distributions to that of Skara Brae?
- *What materials make up the more extensive anthrosols beyond the settlement sites?*
  – Are there differences in material composition in soils associated with Neolithic and Bronze Age settlement sites?
  – What function did these soils have – arable production, intensive hay production?
  – What evidence is there for field boundaries associated with these soils – as indicated by the geophysics survey (Moore and Wilson 2007)?
  – What yields (expressed in tonnes/ha) of barley and 'improved' grass might have been expected from these soils, and what difference did manuring strategies make to yield levels?

This latter question can be addressed by modelling techniques developed at Stirling that integrate climate, soils and management parameters (see, for example, Simpson *et al* 2002; Adderley and Simpson 2005). While model-based agricultural yield analysis has been applied to the emergence of cultural landscapes with Norse settlement in Faeroe and Iceland, this will be its first application in Neolithic and Bronze Age Orkney. Model-based analysis can be extended to include assessment of Neolithic and Bronze Age vegetation productivities and utilisation rates in rangeland areas by integrating palynological, climatic and zooarchaeological data (Simpson *et al* 1998b; Thomson and Simpson 2007). In doing so new insights into grazing pressures and landscape responses can be derived.

What comparative and detailed chronological phasing, enabled by the sequences of wind-blown sands between cultural deposits at Links of Noltland, can be achieved for the sites, midden deposits and anthrosols through OSL measurement?

In addressing these questions and in integrating their outcomes, we anticipate new understandings of the organisation, function and productivities of the Neolithic and Bronze Age landscape around Links of Noltland. These analyses have a wider resonance with implications for landscape interpretations within the areas surrounding the Heart of Neolithic Orkney World Heritage Sites (Downes *et al* 2005), for the international Neolithic archaeology research community, and for the economic relationships that can be achieved between archaeology and local economy.

12 THIN SECTION MICROMORPHOLOGY OF ANTHROSOLS (AREA 1)

Laura E McKenna and Ian A Simpson

Introduction

Soil properties reflect the environment in which they have been formed and so the identification and interpretation of buried anthrosols (soils modified by human activity) has the potential to offer new or more refined understandings of cultural activities associated with soil formation and archaeological landscapes. Increasingly, thin section micromorphology of buried anthrosols has been applied to the analysis of archaeological landscapes and provides a detailed, microscope-based, consideration of pedogenesis, aiding an understanding of the origins and variability of soil composition, post-depositional processes involved with specific horizons, and the physical relationship between organic, mineral and anthropogenic components (Davidson and Simpson 2001).

Calcareous wind-blown sands have buried early archaeological landscapes throughout Orkney (see for example Simpson *et al* 1998; 2006) contributing to their preservation and at Links of Noltland, Westray, the survival of Neolithic and Bronze Age anthrosols may be attributed to this process. Though the significance of the site has been compared to the Neolithic village of Skara Brae (Lamb 1983), it is now under threat of erosion and a programme of rescue excavation has been undertaken by EASE. As part of these excavations, a column sample using six 8x5x5cm kubiena tins was recovered from a 4m^2 sondage (Illus 82) located beyond the archaeological structures. Three of these tins, (numbered 1–3) were centred upon context 7096, extending to the interfaces with the soil layers above and below. Three (lettered A–C) were centred upon context 7079, extending to include the interfaces with the soils above and below. Our objectives were to establish through thin section micromorphology analysis, the formation processes of contexts 7096 and 7079.

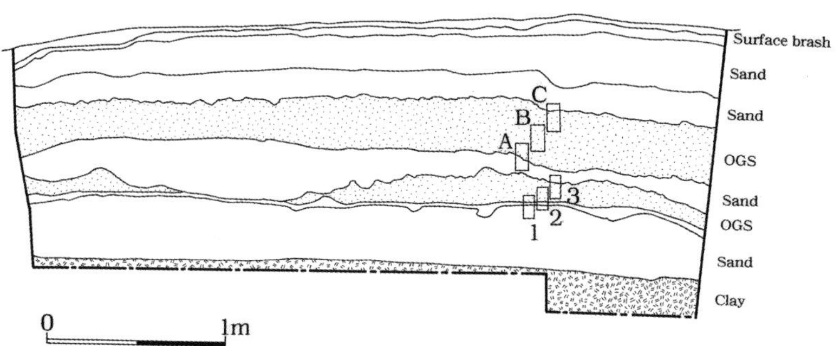

82: Locations of soil thin section samples in 2007 sondage

Methodology

Thin sections were prepared at the Thin Section Micromorphology Laboratory, University of Stirling. All water was removed from the samples by acetone exchange. The samples were then impregnated using polyester 'crystic resin type 17449' and the catalyst Q17447 (methyl ketone peroxide, 50 per cent solution in phthalate). The mixture was thinned with acetone and a standard composition of 180ml resin, 1.8ml catalyst and 25ml acetone used for each kubiena tin. An accelerator was used and the samples were impregnated under vacuum to ensure complete outgassing of the soil. The impregnated soils were cured, culminating with a period in a 40°C oven. Resin-impregnated soils were sliced, bonded to a glass slide and precision lapped to 30µm thickness, and cover slipped to complete the manufacture of the thin section.

The manufactured thin sections were described using an Olympus BX-50 petrological microscope and by following the procedures of the *International Handbook for Thin Section Description* (Bullock *et al* 1985) and the most recent of procedures of Stoops (2003). This allows systematic description of soil microstructure, basic mineral components (MacKenzie and Adams 1994), basic organic components, groundmass and pedofeatures. A range of magnifications (x10–x400) and light sources, plane-polarised (PPL), crossed polars (XPL) and oblique incident (OIL), were used to obtain detailed descriptions and these were recorded semi-quantitatively in a standard table. Interpretation of the observed features rests on the accumulated evidence of a number of workers, notably Courty *et al* (1989) and FitzPatrick (1993).

Results and Discussion

Context 7079, Early Phase (Illus 83)

Slide LON 07 3

This slide intersects three different contexts, identified in the field as a dark-brown sandy soil (7079), possibly of anthropogenic origin, with very small pottery fragments, loose pale yellow shell sand formed through wind-blow (7095) and a mid-orange-brown silty sand (7096) which may represent a cultivated horizon as possible ard marks were identified associated with this context in the field. In thin section the overall c/f related distribution varies very little throughout the slide and distinctions between contexts are very subtle in thin section. The local tendency for a more open porphyric relationship in unit B together with a decrease in black organic particles (1–5 per cent in micro-stratigraphic unit B – 7095 – compared with 5–15 per cent in units A – 7079 – and C – 7076) relates to the shell sand seen in the field, whilst an increase in quartz grains in unit C indicates contrast in coarse mineral materials within the 7096 cultivation context. Anthropogenic features are distributed fairly evenly in small amounts throughout the slide. Distinguishable charcoal fragments (<1 per cent) and turf ash (<1 per cent) are present in unit A and black organic particles make up 5–15 per cent of units A and C. Both burnt and unburnt bone account for <1 per cent of the whole sample. A general lack of visible variation between contexts in this slide evidence homogenisation, possibly related to post-depositional reworking of the wind-blown sand layer. Textural pedofeatures occurring at the lower portion of unit A and the upper portion of unit C, together with iron accumulation (Illus 84), possibly indicate cultivation activity in both of these contexts.

Slide LON 07 2

This slide is centred on context 7096 identified in the field as a possible cultivated soil horizon due to possible ard marks and a differentiation in colour from surrounding soil horizons. In thin section there is a subtle distinction between two microstratigraphic units, A and B; the absence of plant remains and phytoliths in unit A compared to unit B suggests that sand-blow from context 7095 covered vegetation growing in anthropogenic context 7096 and indicates a degree of landscape stability. The anthropogenic nature of this context is indicated by the substantial presence of fine organic material mixed with black organic and red/yellow amorphous material and isotropic punctuations containing diatoms (Illus 85). The distribution of shell (14–40 per cent), sandstone (5–15 per cent) and quartz (5–15 per cent) fragments indicates reduced windblown sand accumulation, homogenised, possibly through cultivation activity, with organic fine material (14–40 per cent) gives an open porphyric c/f related distribution with local enaulic areas. These characteristics together with clusters of phytoliths (5–15 per cent), excremental pedofeatures (2–5 per cent) and plant remains (5–15 per cent) provide further evidence of a more stable environment where sand-blow was not continuous and vegetation began to thrive more easily. The higher proportion of quartz (5–15 per cent) relative to the other samples may suggest evidence of a turf manuring system throughout context 7096 as minerals were brought in, attached to grassy turves, from surrounding areas.

Slide LON 07 1

This slide intersects contexts 7096, a possible cultivated soil horizon with an associated denser microstratigraphy midway through the section, and 7098, a loose pale yellow shell sand. Microstratigraphic unit A (context 7096) displays the most micromorphological evidence for cultivation from current sample set. The mid-brown to orange organo-mineral material with frequencies of 14–40 per cent of the unit contributes to its open phorphyric c/f related distribution. Marine shell fragments occur less (14–40 per cent) than in later phases represented by slides A–C (see below), as do sandstones (5–15 per cent). Individual grains are coated in silts indicating fine organo-mineral movement through the profile to form textural pedofeatures and may be associated with soil disturbance through cultivation activity. The fine organic component in the context mostly consists of trace amounts (<1 per cent) of amorphous yellow, red and black material, while the fine mineral component is highly speckled indicating a silty fabric. The lack of domestic waste features (<1 per cent unburnt bone fragment exclusively) alongside evidence of quartz and feldspar from the fabric would indicate a turf manuring system rather than large amounts of domestic midden. Unit B contrasts markedly with unit A and is consistent with the field description of context 7098. In thin section an enaulic to monic c/f related distribution is exhibited by dominant weathered marine shell (<50 per cent), frequent sandstones (14–40 per cent) and traces of fine organic material which have filtered down from unit A to create the very few textual pedofeatures. This context is likely to be natural.

Context 7096 Later Phase (Illus 86)

Slide LON 07 C

This slide intersects contexts 7004 and 7079 which have been interpreted in the field as wind-blown sand and anthropogenic cultivated soil respectively. The anthropogenic nature of context 7079 is suggested by the very small fragments of pottery observed in the field. In thin section the microstratigraphy confirms the presence of loose shell sand in the upper portion of the slide (unit A – context 7004), with a transition into more anthropogenic soil to the lower portion (unit B – context 7079). The shell sand (unit A) is characterised by dominant marine shell (>50 per cent) and sandstones (5–15 per cent), both of which exhibit signs of weathering and ageing. There is an anthropogenic aspect to this unit indicated by the presence of trace amounts of unburnt bone and a fragment of pottery (Illus 87). Traces of black fine organic material punctuate the very few (1–5 per cent) features of dark-brown (PPL) organo-mineral fabric. The distinction between contexts 7004 and 7079 can be made in thin section based on amounts of fine organo-mineral material; although subtle, there is an increase in this feature in unit B compared to unit A. Unit B is dominated by marine shell (>50 per cent) and sandstones (14–40 per cent), but exhibits slightly more numerous anthropogenic features including unburnt bone (<1 per cent), black fine organic material (<1 per cent) and amorphous brown fine material (<1 per cent). Sandstone in unit B displays signs of iron depletion which could not have taken place in such a calcareous environment; this would suggest that turf material was added to the context from soils that were beginning to exhibit characteristics of podsolisation (Simpson *et al* 1998). The dominantly quartz birefringence fabric supports this interpretation as it does not match the coarse mineral material and must have been brought into the context from another area, probably attached to imported soils. Textural pedofeatures indicate the possibility of cultivation where fine material has filtered down into lower horizons.

Slide LON 07 B

This slide is centred on context 7079. In thin section, unburnt bone fragments (1–5 per cent; Illus 87), charcoal (1–5 per cent), burnt ashes containing minerals and phytoliths (Illlus 89 and 90), animal dung identified by the presence of two calcium spherulites (Illus 91 and 92), and very fine black amorphous material (5–15 per cent) appearing as larger discrete features and smaller fragmented organic debris indicate the deposition of burnt grassy turves and domestic midden material. The dominant coarse mineral component is more densely packed than in sample 'C' and is represented by marine shell (>50 per cent) and sandstone (14–40 per cent), characteristic of continued wind-blown sand deposition throughout the context. Textural coatings and clay infillings with a significant organic component are further evidence of midden material application, perhaps to act as soil stabiliser and allow cultivation. Traces of excremental pedofeatures and channels/vugs attest to a possible standstill period to the lower portion of the slide, this is reinforced by the presence of iron accumulation which is indicative of periodic wetting and drying.

Slide LON 07 A

This slide intersects the lower portion of context 7079, the anthropogenic soil described in slide B above, and the upper portion of context 7095, the loose pale yellow shell sand, described in 3 above. In thin section these two contexts are distinguishable by a subtle decrease in fine organo-mineral material from an enaulic c/f related distribution in unit A (corresponding to context 7079) to gerfuric in unit B (context 7095). Fine black organic material described as organic debris in slide B is present in unit A (5–15 per cent of the unit), though it is of note that a greater proportion appears here as fine debris rather than the larger discrete features identified in slide 'B', indicating that this material has been broken up to a greater degree further down the soil profile. Anthropogenic features are evident throughout the slide; bone (unburnt 1–5 per cent and burnt <1 per cent), charcoal (<1 per cent) and brown amorphous material (1–5 per cent) are intimately mixed with the coarse mineral component, again suggesting midden material was used to stabilise wind-blown sands. The textual coatings and clay infill exhibited in unit A are characteristic of a cultivated horizon, though the small degree of bioturbation suggested by channels in the microstructure may have disturbed the fine material. In unit B black fine organic material is present in lesser amounts (1–5 per cent) than in unit A and the individual coarse marine component consists of marine shell (14–40 per cent) and sandstones (5–15 per cent) along with very few quartz and compound quartz grains (1–5 per cent and <1 per cent). This is characteristic of the calcareous sand in this stratigraphy.

Conclusions

All samples share a similar coarse mineral component, either dominated or largely composed of well-sorted marine shell and sandstone fragments, interpreted as various intensities of calcareous wind-blown sand consistent with the coastal location of the site. The earliest soil formation context (7096) investigated in thin sections 1–3 displays evidence of rapid formation through wind-blown sand accumulation and anthropogenic contributions. These contributions start with the use of imported turf and develop to incorporate domestic wastes that included charcoal, bone fragments and pottery. The most likely explanation for these soil amendments was to stabilise a dynamic and shifted land surface for cultivation. Evidence of enhanced vegetation cover and reduced wind-blown sand movement is found in the upper part of context. A similar deposition process has been identified at Tofts Ness where sharp boundaries between fossil soil cultural horizons and the underlying natural horizons have been interpreted as the result of the initial deposition of considerable volumes of material (Simpson *et al* 1998). As at Tofts Ness, wind-blown sand episodes at Links of Noltland were rapid and sand-blow (context 7095) rapidly covered context 7096. These deposits were subsequently slightly homogenised with context 7079 as intensive anthropogenic deposition began again and the two contexts were initially worked together. Textual pedofeatures in these two contexts suggest the soils were worked through cultivation activity. The later cultural soil formation process visible in thin sections A–C indicates a mixture of domestic waste material and introduced turf alongside animal manure (evidenced by the presence of calcium spherulites), again used to stabilise the wind-blown sand which buried earlier phases of cultivation represented in context 7096. Previous models of prehistoric manuring strategies in the Northern Isles have suggested use of domestic wastes and turves from the Neolithic through to the middle Iron Age, after which the systematic use of domestic animal manures becomes more prevalent (Guttman *et al* 2006). Our findings from Links of Noltland partially support this hypothesis while suggesting that systematic use of animal manures may have been earlier than previously thought.

CONTEXT	THIN SECTION REFERENCE	MICRO-STRATIG-RAPHIC UNIT	COARSE MINERAL MATERIAL							FINE MINERAL MATERIAL	
			(>63µm)							(<63µm)	
			Quartz	Feldspar	Muscovite	Compound quartz grains	Marine Shell	Sandstones	Phytoliths	FINE MINERAL MATIERIAL (PPL)	GROUNDMASS b FABRIC (XPL)
7096/ 7095/ 7079	LON 07 3	A	•	t	t	t	••••	••		Brown (PPL)	Stipple speckled
										Light brown(OIL)	micro-crystallitic
										Organo-mineral	
										•••	
		B	•	t		t	••••	•••		Brown (PPL)	Stipple speckled
										Light brown(OIL)	micro-crystallitic
										Organo-mineral	
										••	
		C	••	t		t	••••	•••		Brown (PPL)	Stipple speckled
										Light brown(OIL)	micro-crystallitic
										Organo-mineral	
										•••	
7096/ 7095	LON07 2	A	••			t	•••	••		Brown (PPL)	Stipple speckled
										Light brown(OIL)	micro-crystallitic
										Organo-mineral	
										•••	
		B	••			t	•••	••	••	Brown (PPL)	Stipple speckled
										Light brown(OIL)	micro-crystallitic
										Organo-mineral	
										•••	
7098/ 7096	LON07 1	A	•	t		t	•••	••		Brown (PPL)	Stipple speckled
										Light brown(OIL)	micro-crystallitic
										Organo-mineral	
										•••	
		B	•	t		t	••••	•••		Brown (PPL)	Stipple speckled
										Light brown (OIL)	micro-crystallitic
										Organo-mineral	
										t - •	

CP =Close Porphyric   •• = few (5 -15%)   ¤¤ = Occasional (2 – 5%)
OP= Open Porphyric   M = Monic   t = trace (<1%)
Frequency class for textual pedofeatures (Bullock *et al.*, 1985) Frequency class refers to the appropriate area of section (Bullock *et al.*, 1985)

83: Results of thin section analysis: slides 1–3

CONTEXT	THIN SECTION REFERENCE	MICRO-STRATIG-RAPHIC UNIT	COARSE ORGANIC COMPONENT			FINE ORGANIC COMPONENT			
			(>63μm)			(<63μm)			
			Plant tissues (slight/moderate decomposition)	Plant tissues (slight/moderate decomposition)	Charcoal	Organic fine material (black)	Amorphous (reddish brown)	Amorphous (yellow)	Rubified Material (OIL)
7096/ 7095/ 7079	LON 07 3	A		t	t	••	•	t	t
		B		t		•	t		t
		C		t		••	t		
7096/ 7095	LON07 2	A				••	•	••	
		B		••		••	•	••	
7098/ 7096	LON07 1	A		t		t	t	t	
		B							

CP =Close Porphyric •• = few (5 -15%) ¤¤ = Occasional (2 – 5%)
OP= Open Porphyric M = Monic t = trace (<1%)
Frequency class for textual pedofeatures (Bullock *et al.*, 1985) Frequency class refers to the appropriate area of section (Bullock *et al.*, 1985)

83: Results of thin section analysis: slides 1–3

CONTEXT	THIN SECTION REFERENCE	MICRO-STRATIG-RAPHIC UNIT	OTHER INCLUSIONS				STRUCTURE	
			Pottery	Bone (burnt)	Bone (unburned)	MICROSTRUCTURE	COARSE MINERAL ARRANGEMEMENT	COARSE/ FINE RELATED DISTRIBUTION
7096/ 7095/ 7079	LON 07 3	A	•	t	t	Moderately developed Blocky Sub-Angular with vughs	Random Well sorted	OP -P
		B			t	Moderately developed Blocky Sub-Angular	Random Well sorted	OP -P
		C			t	Moderately developed Blocky Sub-Angular	Random Well sorted	OP -P
7096/ 7095	LON07 2	A				Moderately developed Blocky Sub-Angular with intergrain microaggregates, channels, vesicles and vughs	Random Well sorted	OP locally E
		B				Moderately developed Blocky Sub-Angular with intergrain microaggregates, channels, vesicles and vughs	Random Well sorted	OP locally E
7098/ 7096	LON07 1	A			t	Moderately developed Blocky Sub-Angular With intergrain microaggregates and vughs	Random Well sorted	OP
		B				Intergrain	Random Well sorted	M- E

CP =Close Porphyric •• = few (5 -15%) ¤¤ = Occasional (2 – 5%)
OP= Open Porphyric M = Monic t = trace (<1%)
Frequency class for textual pedofeatures (Bullock *et al.*, 1985) Frequency class refers to the appropriate area of section (Bullock *et al.*, 1985)

83: Results of thin section analysis: slides 1–3

CONTEXT	THIN SECTION REFERENCE	MICRO-STRATIG-RAPHIC UNIT	PEDOFEATURES			
			Textural (non laminated dusty clay coatings, isotropic/ microcrystallitic)	Silty Clay Coatings	Iron Accumulation	Excremental
7096/ 7095/ 7079	LON 07 3	A	¤	¤	¤	t
		B	¤		t	
		C	¤	¤	t	
7096/ 7095	LON07 2	A		¤	¤	
		B		¤¤	¤	¤¤
7098/ 7096	LON07 1	A	¤¤	¤¤	¤	¤
		B	¤			

CP =Close Porphyric •• = few (5 -15%) ¤¤ = Occasional (2 – 5%)
OP= Open Porphyric M = Monic t = trace (<1%)
Frequency class for textual pedofeatures (Bullock *et al*., 1985) Frequency class refers to the appropriate area of section (Bullock *et al*., 1985)

83: Results of thin section analysis: slides 1–3

CONTEXT	THIN SECTION REFERENCE	MICRO-STRATI-GRAPHIC UNIT	COARSE MINERAL MATERIAL (>63µm)							
			Quartz	Feldspar	Muscovite	Compound Quartz Grains	Rubified Mineral	Marine Shell	Sandstones	Phytoliths
7079/ 7004	LON 07 C	A	t	t		t		••••	••	
		B	t	t			t	••••	•••	
7079	LON07 B	SINGLE	•	t	t	t	t	••••	••	
7095/ 7079	LON07 A	A	•	t	t	t		•••	••	t
		B	•			t		•••	••	

Frequency class refers to the appropriate area of section (Bullock *et al.*, 1985
t = trace (<1%)
• = very few (1 -5%)
•• = few (5 -15%)
••• = frequent (14-40%)
•••• = dominant (>50%)
Frequency class for textual pedofeatures (Bullock *et al.*, 1985)
t = trace (<1%)
¤ = Rare (1-2%)
¤¤ = Occasional (2 – 5%)
¤¤¤ = Many (5 – 10%)

83: Results of thin section analysis: slides 1–3

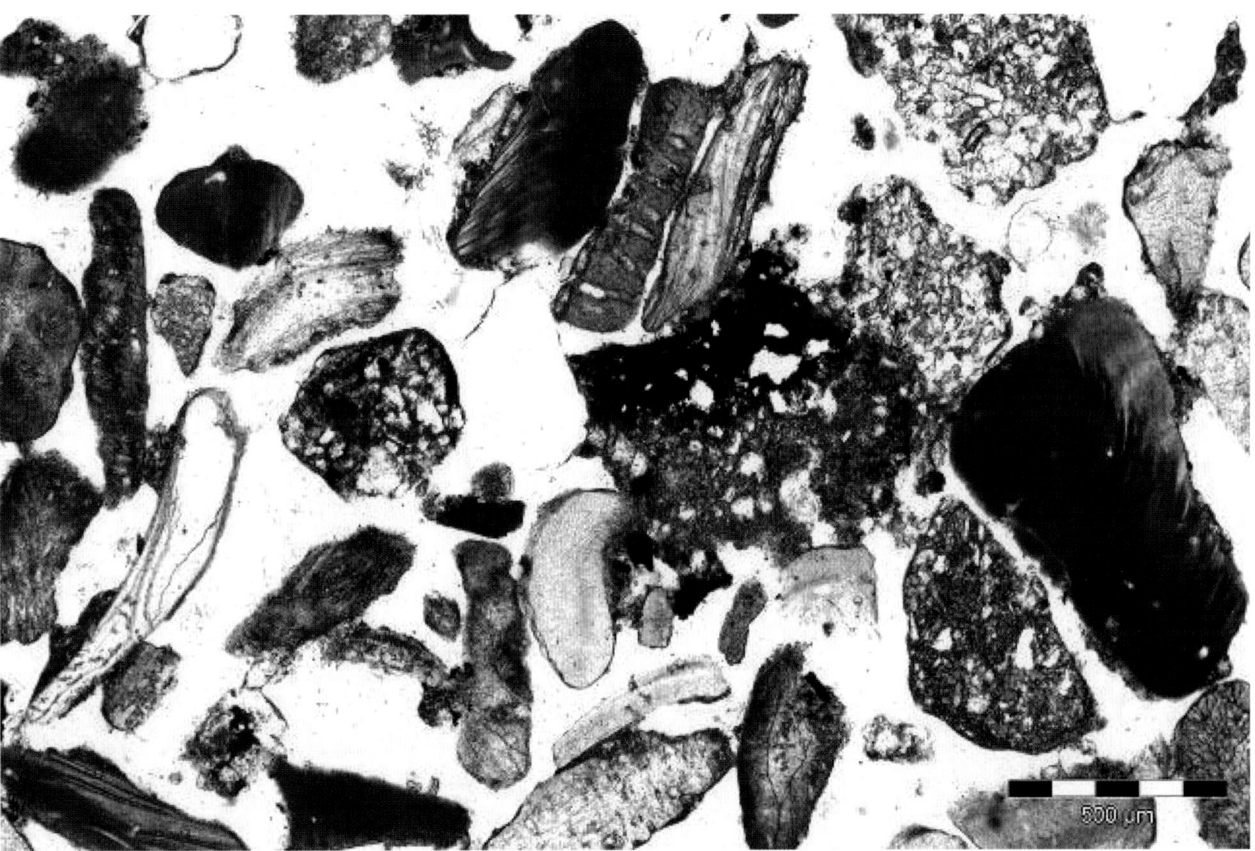

84: Iron accumulation in clay pedofeatures; these cannot develop in alkaline environments so must have been imported with turf inclusions (LON07, 3, PPL).

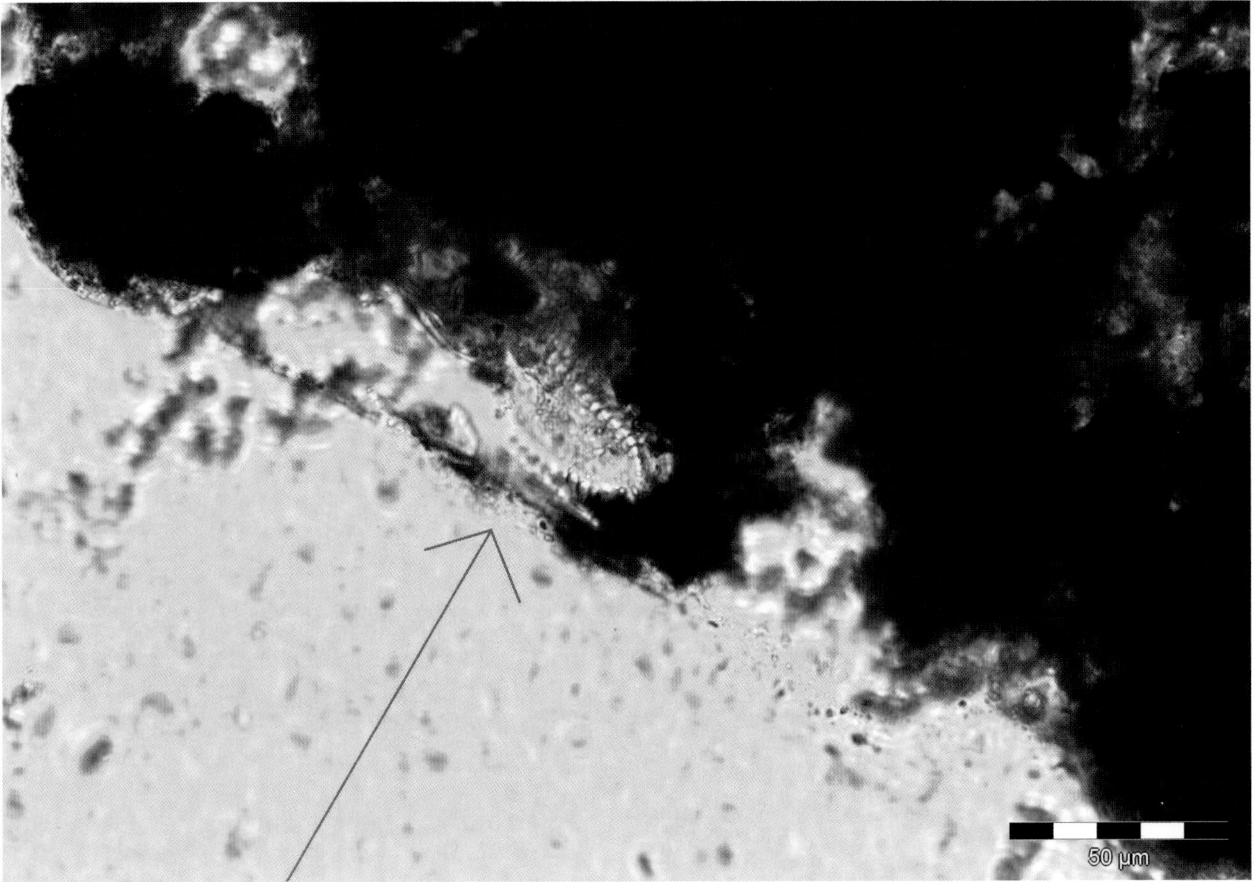

85: Diatom, imported into the context as part of turf/peat (LON07, 2, PPL)

CONTEXT	THIN SECTION REFERENCE	MICRO-STRATI-GRAPHIC UNIT	FINE MINERAL MATERIAL (<63µm)		COARSE ORGANIC COMPONENT (>63µm)			
			NATURE OF FINE MINERAL MATIERIAL (PPL)	GROUNDMASS b FABRIC (XPL)	Plant tissues (slight/moderate decomposition)	Plant tissues (strong/very strong decomposition)	Charcoal	Organic fine material (black)
7079/ 7004	LON 07 C	A	Dark Brown (PPL)	Stipple speckled				t
			Light Brown (OIL)	micro-crystallitic				
			Organo-mineral					
			•					
		B	Dark Brown (PPL)	Stipple speckled				t
			Light Brown (OIL)	micro-crystallitic				
			Organo-mineral					
			••					
7079	LON07 B	SINGLE	Dark Brown (PPL)	Stipple speckled		t	•	••
			Light Brown (OIL)	micro-crystallitic				
			Organo-mineral					
			•••					
7095/ 7079	LON07 A	A	Dark Brown (PPL)	Stipple speckled		t	t	••
			Light Brown(OIL)	micro-crystallitic				
			Organo-mineral					
			••					
		B	Dark Brown (PPL)	Stipple speckled			t	•
			Light Brown(OIL)	micro-crystallitic				
			Organo-mineral					
			•					

Frequency class refers to the appropriate area of section (Bullock *et al.*, 1985
t = trace (<1%)
• = very few (1 -5%)
•• = few (5 -15%)
••• = frequent (14-40%)
•••• = dominant (>50%)
Frequency class for textual pedofeatures (Bullock *et al.*, 1985)
t = trace (<1%)
¤ = Rare (1-2%)
¤¤ = Occasional (2 – 5%)
¤¤¤ = Many (5 – 10%)

86: Results of thin section analysis: slides A–C

CONTEXT	THIN SECTION REFERENCE	MICRO-STRATI-GRAPHIC UNIT	FINE ORGANIC COMPONENT (<63μm)			OTHER INCLUSIONS			STRUCTURE			
			Amorphous (reddish brown)	Amorphous (yellow)	Rubified Material (OIL)	Pottery	Bone (burnt)	Bone (unburnt)	MICROSTRUCTURE	COARSE MINERAL ARRANGEMEMENT	COARSE/FINE RELATED DISTRIBUTION	
	LON 07 C	A				•		t	Bridged grain micro-aggregates and vughs	Random Well sorted	G	¤
		B	t					t	Bridged grain micro-aggregates and vughs	Random Well sorted	E	¤¤
	LON07 B	SINGLE	•	t		t		•	Intergrain structure with channels and micro-aggregates	Random Well sorted	E	¤¤
	LON07 A	A	•			t	t	•	Intergrain structure with channels and micro-aggregates	Random Well sorted	E	¤
		B	t				t		Intergrain with packing voids	Random Well sorted	G	t

Frequency class refers to the appropriate area of section (Bullock *et al.*, 1985
t = trace (<1%)
• = very few (1 -5%)
•• = few (5 -15%)
••• = frequent (14-40%)
•••• = dominant (>50%)
Frequency class for textual pedofeatures (Bullock *et al.*, 1985)
t = trace (<1%)
¤ = Rare (1-2%)
¤¤ = Occasional (2 – 5%)
¤¤¤ = Many (5 – 10%)

86: Results of thin section analysis: slides A–C

CONTEXT	THIN SECTION REFERENCE	MICRO-STRATI-GRAPHIC UNIT	PEDOFEATURES					
			Textural (non laminated dusty clay coatings, isotropic/ microcrystallitic)	Textual (non-laminated dusty clay coatings: anisotropic)	Silty Clay Coatings	Iron Accumulation	Ferruginous (nodules)	Excremental
	LON 07 C	A						
		B						
	LON07 B	SINGLE				¤		t
	LON07 A	A				¤		t
		B			t	t		t

Frequency class refers to the appropriate area of section (Bullock *et al.*, 1985
t = trace (<1%)
• = very few (1 -5%)
•• = few (5 -15%)
••• = frequent (14-40%)
•••• = dominant (>50%)
Frequency class for textual pedofeatures (Bullock *et al.*, 1985)
t = trace (<1%)
¤ = Rare (1-2%)
¤¤ = Occasional (2 – 5%)
¤¤¤ = Many (5 – 10%)

86: Results of thin section analysis: slides A–C

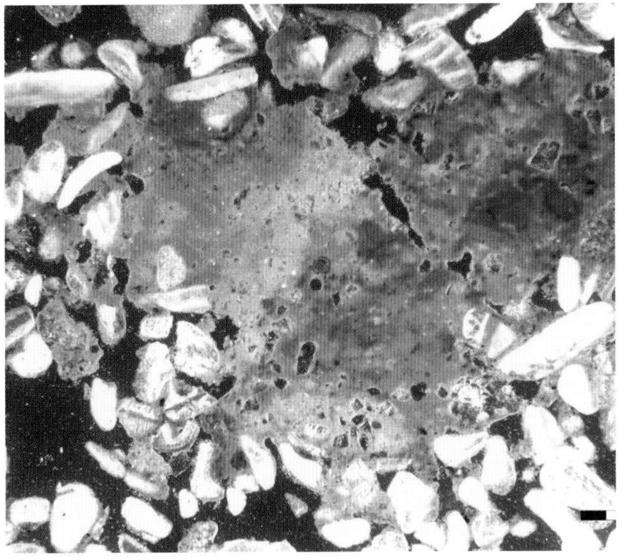

87: Pottery fragment (LON07, C, OIL)

88: Bone fragment (LON07, B, XPL)

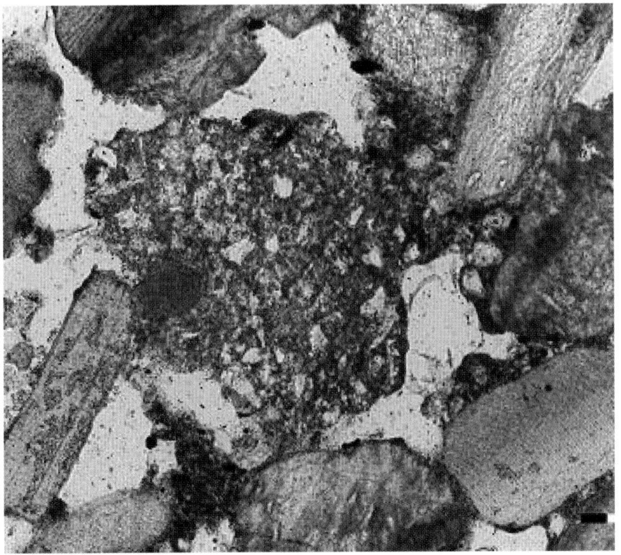

89: Turf ash present in LON07, B, PPL)

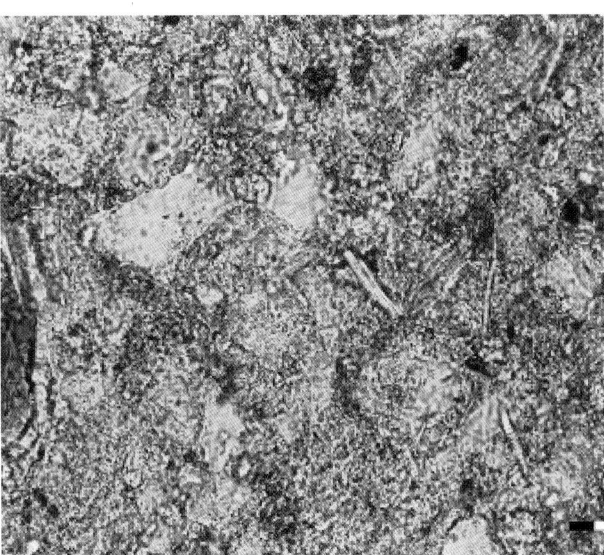

90: Detail of 89 showing phytoliths present in turf ash (PPL)

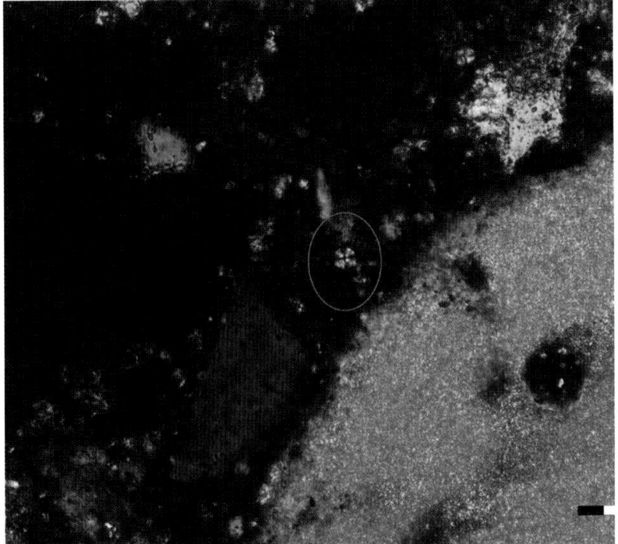

91: Calcium spherulite, indicative of herbivore dung (LON07, B, XPL)

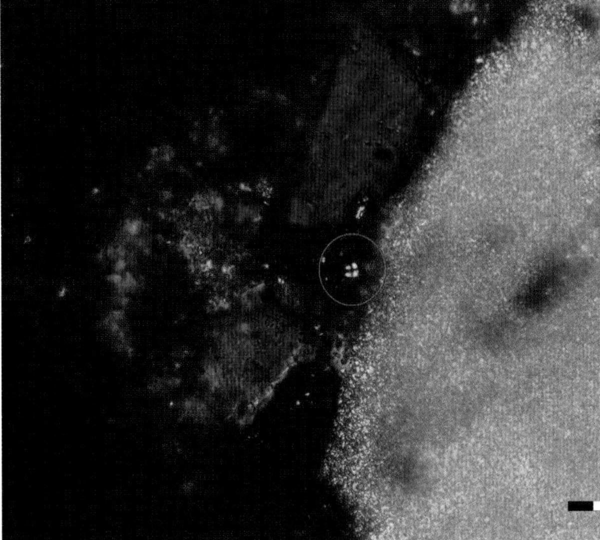

92: Calcium spherulite (LON) and B, XPL)

13 THE WORKED BONE

Sean Rice

Introduction

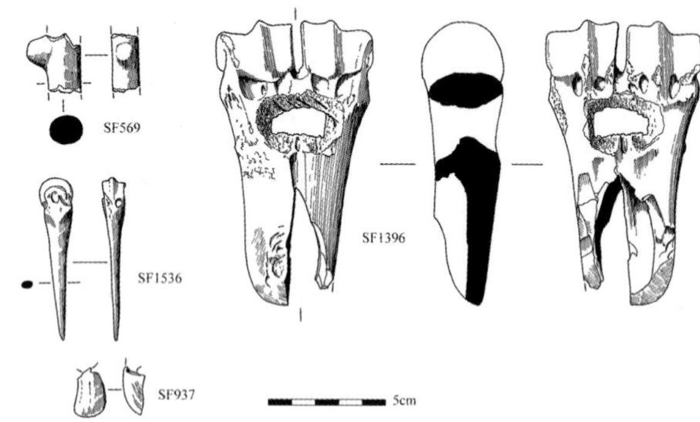

93: Worked bone objects: mattock SF1396; pin fragment SF569; point SF1536; bead-making debris SF937, cut tooth

The recent work at Links of Noltand 2007–9 has produced a considerable amount of worked bone. The assemblage currently consists of 302 small find entries, accounting for some 335 individual items of skeletal material that have been purposefully modified in some way, be it as implements, beads, or as manufacturing debris. The assemblage has been well-preserved and includes some 141 complete or near-complete artefacts in remarkably good condition. Employing criteria used on the bone assemblage from Tofts Ness (Davies 2007, 325), Illus 94 classifies the assemblage within four states of completeness; complete, near-complete (small fragment broken off), broken (broken into a large piece), and fragment (small fragment).

complete	91	27%
near complete	50	15%
broken	59	17.50%
fragment	135	40.50%

94: Condition of worked bone

Illus 95 shows the animal species utilised for the production of bone artefacts. While identification is not possible for many finely worked, worn or fragmented finds, it is clear that the bulk of the assemblage consists of domesticates: sheep/goat and cattle.

sheep/goat	126	37.60%
cattle	106	31.60%
not identified	92	27.50%
whale	5	1.50%
seal	2	0.60%
deer	2	0.60%
bird	2	0.60%

95: Worked bone: sources of bone used

The vast majority of sheep/goat bones utilised are metapodials which have been split to make points or notched to make beads. While cattle metapodials have also been utilised in the manufacture of mattocks and slices, a wider range of cattle bones have been utilised, such as scapulae for shovels, astragali for polishers and mandibles and teeth in the manufacture of blunts and beads respectively. Illus 96 gives a breakdown of worked bone artefacts.

astragalus polishers	21	6.30%
awls	11	3.30%
beads/bead making debris	63	18.80%
bevel ended tools	4	1.20%
blunts	22	6.60%
indented or perforated calcaneum	8	2.40%
mattocks	9	2.70%
pins	6	1.80%
point pins	8	2.40%
points	112	33.50%
scapula tools	5	1.50%
slices/spatulae	10	3%
splinter points	27	8%
whalebone/marine mammal	6	1.80%
other perforated objects	9	2.70%
miscellaneous bone objects	14	4%

96: Worked bone by category

As Illus 96 shows, points are by far the most abundant class of bone artefact in the assemblage. This is also true of Skara Brae (Childe 1931, 115), and as with Skara Brae, one particular form of point (Skara Brae form A1a) made from a split sheep/goat metapodial with part of the articular end left to form the head of the implement is the most common (ibid). While this point type has been recovered from both Neolithic and Bronze Age contexts, it has been found in much smaller numbers in the latter. Very thin, very fine splinter points have also been recovered at Links of Noltland. These points, which have so far only been found in Bronze Age contexts, including two caches, are far less robust than type A1a and were perhaps produced to perform a specific function, not carried out in the Neolithic settlement.

While a high proportion of the worked bone assemblage was identified during excavation, significant quantities of worked bone have also been recovered as a direct result of the extensive sampling and sieving programme.

excavation	196	58.50%
1cm dry sieve	17	5%
retent from sampling	11	3.30%
unstratified	3	0.9%
post excavation	108	32%

97: Table showing sources of all worked bone recovered

The benefits of this strategy are most significant in the recovery of smaller finds such as beads and bead manufacturing debris. Some of the beads recovered measure only a few millimetres and are easily missed during excavation, indeed of the 11 finished beads so far recovered, only 3 have been discovered while excavating.

bone bead	1	1	3	1
tooth bead	2	1	1	1
cut tooth bead making debris	20	4	1	8
cut bone bead making debris	10	2	2	3
stripped/polished tooth	2	0	0	0

98: Breakdown of beads and bead-making debris by source

dry sieving	8	13%
excavation	35	55%
post excavation	13	21%
retent	7	11%

99: Beads and bead-making debris, percentage recovery by source

Perhaps most surprising is the quantity of worked bone material identified during post-excavation processing. No astragalus polishers, for example, were identified as a result of either excavation or sieving. However, close examination after cleaning revealed that 21 cattle astragali, 50 per cent of those recovered as general finds showed signs of wear or polishing on the four raised condyles of the posterior surface. Foxton's (1991, 158) analysis of astragali with similar wear from Skara Brae (Skara Brae 862–82) suggests this type of wear is consistent with use in the rubbing of hide or plant material (ibid).

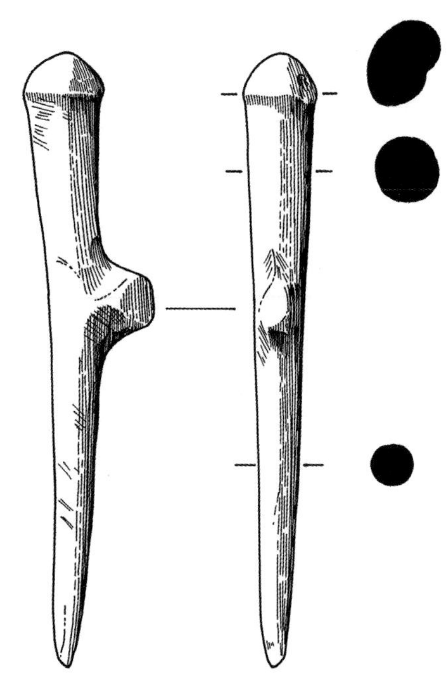

100: Antler pin, SF1750

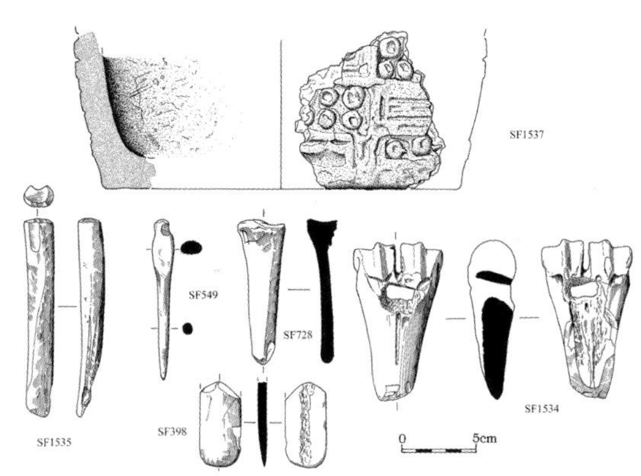

101: Worked bone objects: bevel-ended tool SF1535; pin SF549; blunt SF728; mattock SF1534; spatula/slice SF398. Pottery: SF1537

14 THE POTTERY

Alison Sheridan

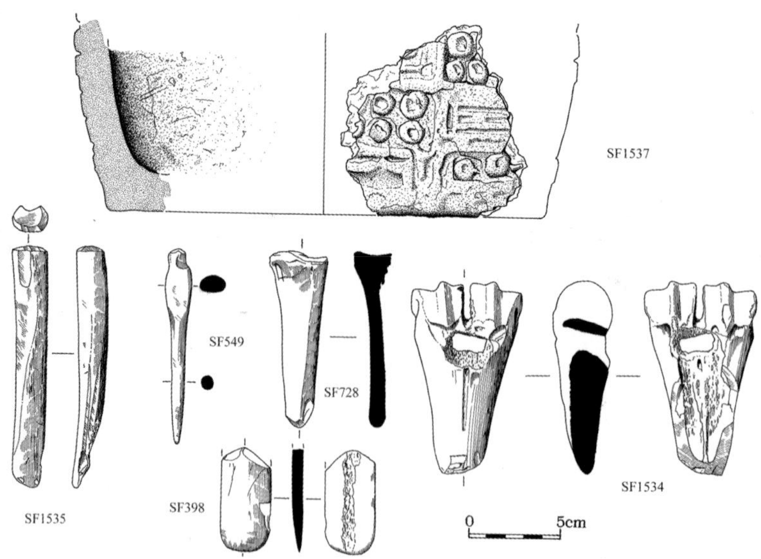

101: Worked bone objects: bevel-ended tool SF1535; pin SF549; blunt SF728; mattock SF1534; spatula/slice SF398. Pottery: SF1537

Introduction

Over 5000 sherds were recovered, representing a large but indeterminate number of individual vessels, but the limited time available for assessment meant that it was only possible to 'eyeball' around half of them and to form an overall, generalised impression of the assemblage. During the assessment, the boxes were opened and their contents examined by eye, basic notes were taken (and rim and base diameters and some wall thicknesses measured), a selection of sherds for illustration was made and 50 sherds were collected for lipid analysis. The small amount of pottery recovered from the Bronze Age contexts was not examined and no pottery that was not obviously Grooved Ware was encountered. With but a very few exceptions, the assemblage matches very closely the material found during the Links of Noltland 1979–81 excavations.

Vessel Shape and Size

The range of vessel shapes basically accords with that encountered in the earlier excavations (Sheridan 1999, Illus 12.3, 12.4), with most pots taking the form of roughly cylindrical or bucket-shaped vessels of various sizes and wall thicknesses (with all the pots being flat-based). The smallest of these (with the exception of the miniature vessels – see below) are vessels such as the thin-walled cylindrical cup, SF2671 (context 9017) with an estimated rim diameter of c 100mm and wall thickness of c 7mm. Some cooking pots (identified by the burnt-on encrusted organic material on their interior and/or exterior) are not much larger than this. At the other end, the largest vessels are well over 300mm in rim and/or base diameter, with one – from SF2539 (context 9021) – possibly being as wide as 400mm. While the larger vessels tend to have thicker walls, there is no consistent thickening with increasing size.

No example of the low, trunconic vessel form as featured in Sheridan 1999, Illus 12.3 c, has yet been encountered – this was a rare shape in the previous excavations – but there are two clear examples of miniature vessels, analogous with the hollow-cube form (a very rare form) as seen in Illus 12.3d of that publication. One, which is complete but for part of its wall and whose interior is nearly full of midden sediment, has a thin (c 4.5mm), gently splaying wall and rim and base diameters of 50.5mm and 45mm respectively; it is around 50mm tall (SF632, from context 7302 spit 3). The other (from among SF1537, from context 7307) has a wall, around 8mm thick, that splays irregularly from the base; the estimated rim and base diameters are c 80mm and c 50mm respectively. Both vessels are undecorated. Neither has a 'convenient' sherd that could be sampled for lipid analysis, although the question of the function of these miniature pots is an important one. The SF1537 example, the interior surface of which is clearly visible, has no sign of ochre; a probable use in grinding ochre has been noted for small stone vessels from Skara Brae.

Manufacture

Once more, the assemblage closely matches the material found in the earlier excavations. No example of the use of shell filler was seen amongst the assessed material (although some sherds of this type were provisionally identified by David Clarke during a site visit in 2007). Shell-tempered pottery was in the minority in the 1979–81 assemblage. Instead, angular fragments of crushed (and almost certainly local) stone has been used. Many vessels, especially the thin-walled pots, appear to contain very little filler (and the two miniature pots seem to be inclusion-free), while the larger and thicker-walled pots tend to contain the most filler. Walls are often uneven, and most pots have been slipped. Numerous sherds have 'false rims' where the sherd has come apart along a coil joint plane, a natural plane of weakness – and the crispness and smoothness of the narrow, inverted U ridge of clay suggests that the pot had been allowed to dry to a considerable extent before the next coil was added.

Decoration

Again, the assemblage closely matches the 1979–81 assemblage. In the overwhelming majority of cases it is restricted to the upper part of the pot, and features applied, 'plastic' decoration; where incision is present, it is almost always used just to help define horizontal cordons. By far the most common decoration is the use of multiple horizontal applied cordons just below the rim, very often with an additional one (or two) applied cordons on the rim's interior, making a seating for a pot lid. The cordons come in a range of shapes, but often they have been smoothed down on application, leaving a slightly triangular profile. One possible example of a wavy cordon has been noted (SF663 from context 7302 spit 3, box 5).

More elaborate decoration is rarer. A few pots have scalloped rims – in one case clearly made by the application of half-moon pellets. Round, hemispherical pellets set between horizontal (or possibly vertical) applied cordons are present on one pot from SF1168 (from context 7302 spit 5) and also on one pot with a scalloped rim (SF2669 from context 9017). A further example (see Illus 101) has a line of such pellets just below the rim, and probably had horizontal cordons beneath (from SF743 from context 7302 spit 4). A fragment of a lozenge-shaped applied cordon was noted on SF8018 from context 1444 and SF743 from context 7302 spit 4.

The most elaborately decorated pots tend to be large – in one case, very large (SF2539 from 9021) – and where lower parts of the pot are present, the decoration seems to extend over much or all of the exterior. The SF2539 pot has narrow diagonal and curving cordons running down from the rim; these are reminiscent of the complex design seen on a large, coarse pot from the earlier excavations (Sheridan 1999, Illus 12.9). Diagonal cordons are also present on a smaller, thinner pot (SF1216 from context 7302 spit 8,). Other notable pots are:

- SF1537 (from context 7307): a large, thick-walled (c 20mm), coarse pot with a row of dimpled pellets above at least one horizontal cordon, its edge defined by an incised groove.
- At least one pot with slashed cordons: a large pot, SF660 from context 7302 spit 3 may have vertical, narrow, slashed cordons, interspersed with vertical plain cordons. Other sherds (for example, SF335, SF401, SF655, SF735 and SF744 from the same context) probably come from the same pot.
- A large pot, SF750 from context 7302 spit 4, seems to have vertical, blobby applied decoration.
- The most elaborately decorated pot is a large pot (estimated base diameter 250mm) with a complex design featuring panels of dimpled pellets interspersed with cordons and with areas of incised decoration (see Illus 101). Parts of this are SF1537 from context 7307. The state of preservation of this pot is highly variable and it is likely that some of it had been burnt. This pot is reminiscent of some of the pots from Skara Brae.

One pot base has 'accidental' decoration on its interior, in the form of multiple finger and/or thumb impressions (SF2573 from context 9022).

Several vessels are undecorated, including some small cylindrical jars, and one large vessel with a bevelled rim-top, SF1416 from context 8008 (estimated rim diameter c 200mm).

No example has yet been seen of the 'fish scale', 'network', 'oval', and 'stud' applied designs as seen on the earlier assemblage.

Non-vessel Ceramics

Several oval or roughly spherical, pellet-shaped lumps of fired clay (for example, SF3258 from context 7306) are almost certainly potter's clay that has accidentally been fired; the same is true of a fragment of a flattish, cake-shaped lump. This adds to previously obtained evidence that pottery was being manufactured at the settlement.

One larger, tennis ball-sized and -shaped piece of fired clay (SF3087 from context 7307) is not, however, potter's clay, but instead is a deliberately made object. It is roughly spherical, with two opposed flattish facets with batter marks, and other slight facets. The fired clay is very hard and almost stony in texture (although the object is clearly not of stone), and it is likely that this object had been used as a ball-shaped pounder, perhaps for dehusking grain.

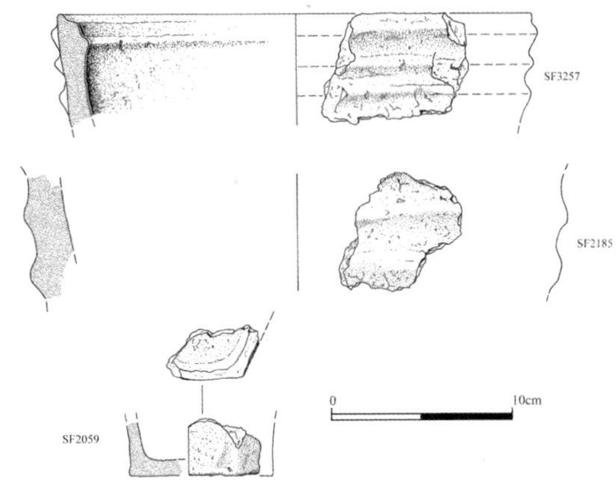

102: Pottery

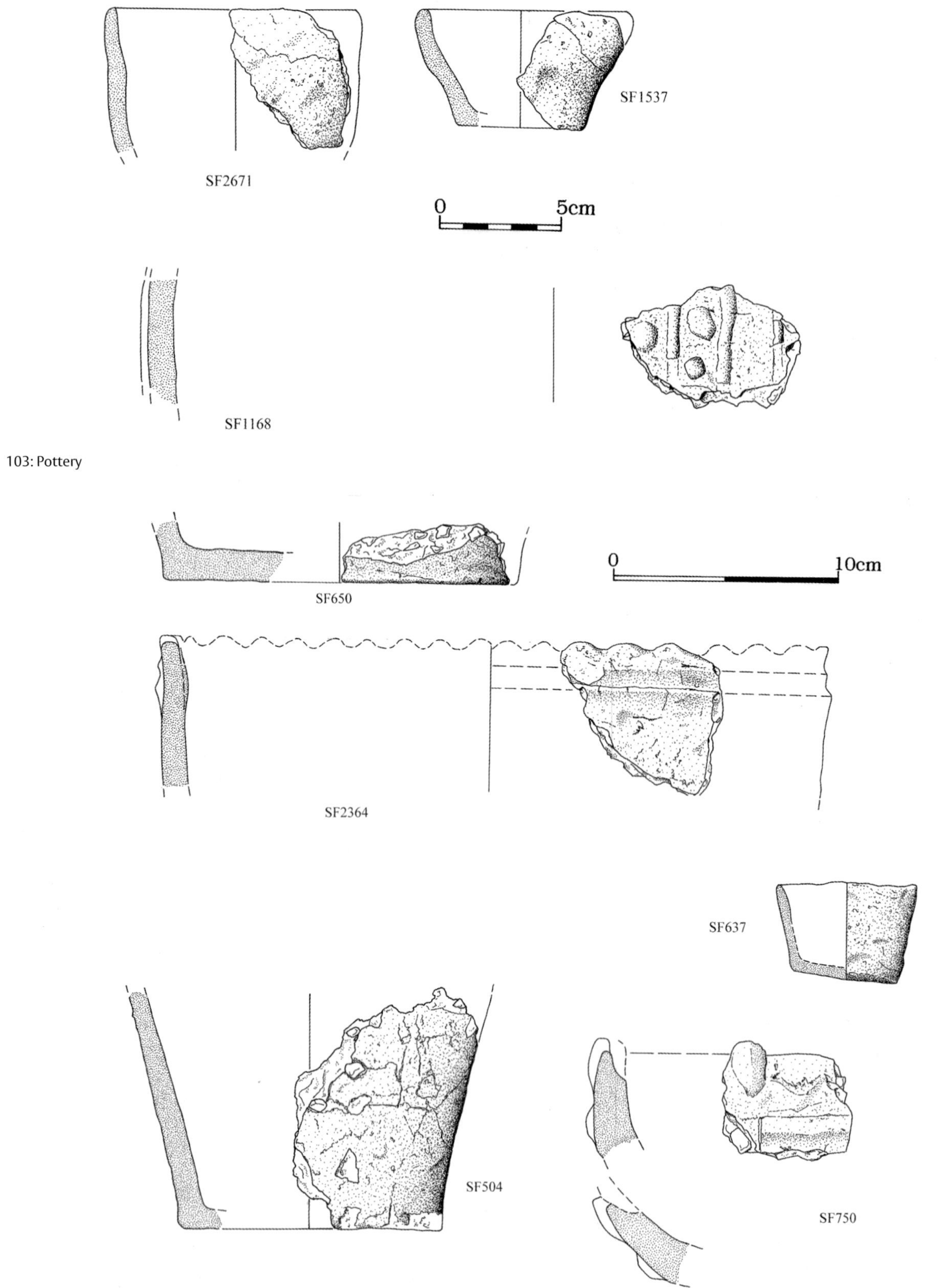

103: Pottery

104: Pottery

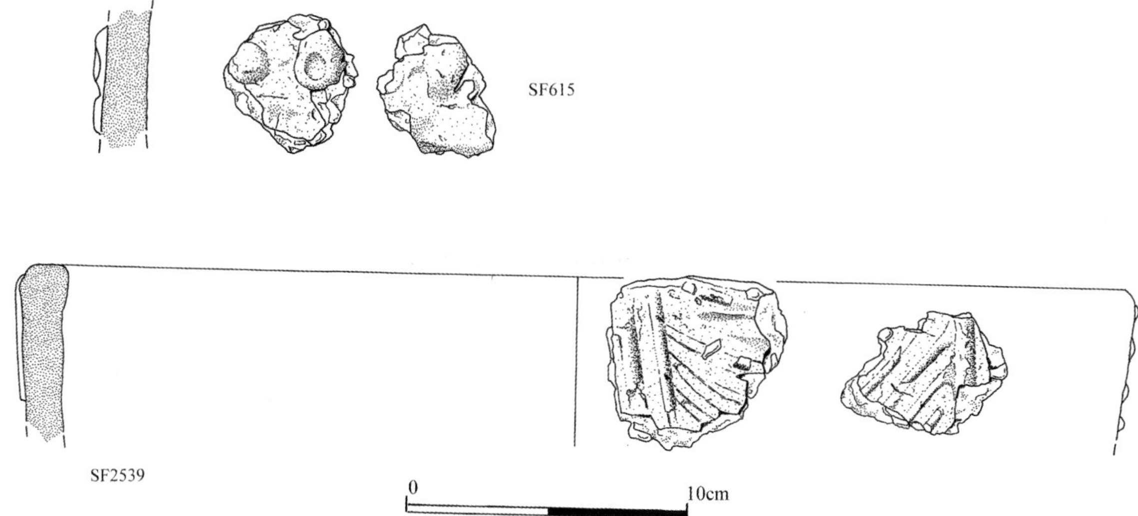

105: Pottery

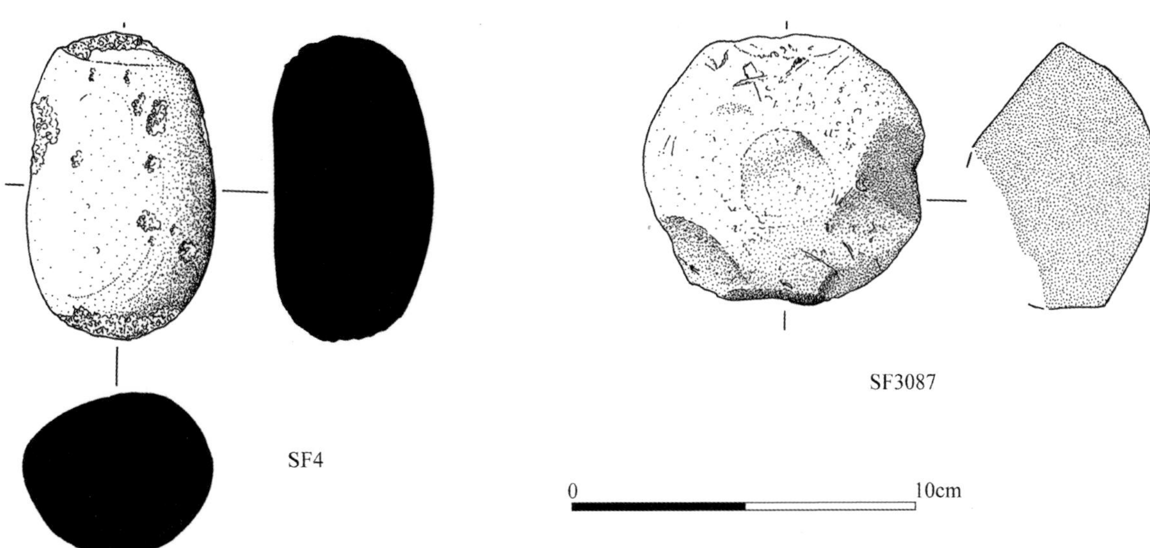

106: Stone tool SF4; Pottery object SF3087

15 THE STRUCK LITHIC ARTEFACTS

Alan Saville

Introduction

Somewhere in excess of 3000 lithic artefacts were recovered. For the purposes of rapid assessment it was only possible to examine a limited number of them in the time available, and because of the unwashed condition all the identifications and descriptions given here must be regarded as provisional. Nevertheless, it was possible to obtain an overview of the technology, raw material, and assemblage composition of the material from the Neolithic contexts, sufficient to indicate that this is an important assemblage which will warrant detailed study and analysis once fieldwork is completed.

General Description

Four hundred and eighty-nine individual bags were examined from the 2009 season, containing artefacts from the following contexts:

- 7300, 7302, 7303, 7312, 7314
- 8003, 8008, 8010, 8013, 8015, 8029
- 9000, 9002, 9003, 9006, 9007, 9009, 9011, 9012, 9013, 9016, 9017, 9020, 9021, 9022, 9023, 9026, 9031

These contexts are all classified as Neolithic and for this assessment the contents of the bags are treated as a single sub-assemblage, although when individual pieces are referred to their find numbers are given to permit context correlation. The basic typological composition of this sub-assemblage is given in Illus 107.

Of the total 681 pieces, 149 (22 per cent) were too dirty to make a proper assessment of their type, but it is considered unlikely that this excluded element would have an undue biasing effect on the proportional representation of types as revealed by those which could be assessed. Among the classified pieces the proportional presence of the major categories is as expected in an Orcadian Later Neolithic assemblage. The number of chips is far lower than should be the case if 100 per cent sieving was practised (for example, chips represent 75 per cent of all struck lithic artefacts recovered from the 1972–3 excavations at Skara Brae; Saville 2004). [*It should be noted, however, that the assessment did not include material recovered from wet sieved fractions of the soil samples. HLM*]. Of itself this is of little consequence, since in general chips have a low information potential other than confirming the presence of on-site knapping and indicating the location of knapping events if they are from in situ deposits. However, it may point to less than total recovery of other artefacts, especially the smaller tool types such as the piercer discussed below.

Type	No.	%
Unretouched flakes, primary	36	
Unretouched flakes, secondary	114	
Unretouched flakes, tertiary	137	
Chips (less than 10mm in length)	114	
Total flakes and chips	401	59
Cores	21	
Core fragments	16	
Total core pieces	37	5
Scrapers	33	
Chisel arrowheads	1	
Flakes/fragments of polished implements	3	
Piercers	1	
Edge-trimmed flakes	8	
Miscellaneous retouched pieces	23	
Total retouched pieces	69	10
Split/tested pebbles	3	
Unstruck pebbles	8	
Unclassified chunks	4	
Unclassified burnt pieces	10	
Pieces too dirty to assess	149	22
Total	**681**	

107: Struck lithics, the basic composition of the sub-assemblage

Raw Material and Condition

Virtually all the sub-assemblage is comprised of artefacts of flint, exploited primarily in the form of small water-rolled pebbles with a thin cortex, which exhibit a wide variety of colours. These pebbles are assumed to derive from a marine beach, although the possibility of derivation from terrestrial diamicton on Westray or elsewhere in Orkney cannot be excluded without targeted fieldwork. The unstruck flint pebbles in the sub-assemblage have a mean maximum dimension of only 21.7mm and probably do not represent unused raw material, being present in the deposits for purposes unrelated to knapping or for entirely natural reasons.

The flint is very variable in terms of colour and condition. The colour of the interior flint surfaces was recorded for 450 of the artefacts, with the results shown in Illus 108. From this it is clear that red-brown is the dominant colour type of the locally available raw material. This is even clearer when it is appreciated that cream, and combination colours red-cream, red-cream-brown, and cream-pink, are corticated versions of the red-brown flint, the exposed surfaces having discoloured as a result of weathering and soil conditions. In some of the cream-coloured examples cortication has progressed to the extent that areas of the artefacts, mainly the edges, have become crumbly (cf Henshall 1983, 86). Grey flint is the other main type, but this appears less homogenous than the red-brown variety and is likely to reflect flints derived from a variety of sources, in a few instances probably reflecting imported artefacts rather than imported raw materials.

A few of the grey or grey-brown pieces (SF1680, SF2831, SF3527, SF3539) exhibited a more matt surface appearance and could be chert, possibly of the *Rhaxella* variety. Otherwise there was no exploitation of other knappable siliceous raw materials, such as the pitchstone at Barnhouse (Middleton 2005) or the black chert at Skara Brae (Saville 2005).

Most of the artefacts in the sub-assemblage are unburnt. Apart from those listed as unclassified burnt pieces in Illus 107, indications of burning were observed on only four of the classified artefacts (two scrapers, SF1555 and SF2798, and two tertiary flakes, SF1892 and SF3599).

In general the condition of the flints was sharp and uncorticated. Definite 'rolling' was observed on only one artefact (SF1673), though the fact that all the flints are unwashed may obscure this characteristic.

Colour	No.	%
Red-brown	184	41
Grey	81	18
Dark grey	49	11
Cream	49	11
Grey-brown	30	7
Brown	13	3
Red-cream	10	2
Red-cream-brown	6	1
Grey-cream	6	1
Cream-pink	6	1
9 other colour combinations,	16	4
all <3 artefacts each		
Total	450	100

108: Flint colours

Technology

All the cores are of bipolar, anvil-struck type, a technique which maximises the reduction of small-sized raw material. A maximum dimension was recorded for 15 of the cores, giving a mean value of 25.5mm within a range from 36.9mm to 17.6mm. The large number of core fragments is to be expected with anvil technology because the cores frequently split longitudinally during reduction, although it is recognised that discriminating between pieces which are either complete or fragmentary cores (or sometimes flakes) is also complicated with the residues from this type of knapping.

However, the presence in the sub-assemblage of flakes with plain, relatively deep striking platforms, in contrast to those from anvil reduction with their crushed and/or acute platforms, makes it clear that platform core reduction was also practised. The occasional large-sized flakes also indicate that larger cores than those represented by the anvil-struck ones have been exploited. For example, one of the edge-trimmed flakes (SF1550) has dimensions of length 58.9mm x breadth 43.9mm x thickness 15.9mm, and another piece, too dirty to classify (SF2061) has a maximum dimension of 67.6mm. As at other comparable sites (Saville 2004; 2005), it would appear that platform cores were 'finished' by anvil reduction after the initial platform stage(s), resulting in the residual bipolar cores present here.

Retouched Pieces

Scrapers are the dominant tool type in the assemblage and are all of small, 'thumbnail' size, with the convex scraping edge often covering a significant proportion of the available flake edge. Eleven of the scrapers were measured and gave mean dimensions of length 20mm x breadth 18.3mm x thickness 7mm. No attempt was made to further subdivide the scrapers typologically at this stage, though it was noted that at least two have inverse scraping edges (ie the retouch to fashion the scraping edge is made from the dorsal surface of the blank).

The other pieces of particular note are the arrowhead, the piercer, and the fragments from polished flint implements, presumed to be axeheads. The arrowhead (SF2105) is a chisel example, complete save for minor breaks at the base and top left, with dimensions of length 25.7mm x breadth 16.5mm x thickness 3mm. It is in a variety of grey flint which suggests it could be an imported implement rather than one made on the site.

The piercer (SF2806) is a particularly interesting example on a small flake of red-brown flint. It is extremely small with dimensions of only length 10.2mm x breadth 6mm x thickness 2.2mm. The blank is an intact bulbar flake which has been retouched on both lateral edges to form a point. It has no overtly Mesolithic qualities and is presumed to be part of the Later Neolithic sub-assemblage.

Little can be said about the three small fragments which derive from polished flint implements, probably axeheads (SF1644, SF1836, SF1901). They are all small fragments, apparently from three separate implements, and are of various shades of grey flint. They may derive from breakage of the polished implement during use, or from subsequent reworking or cannibalisation of parts of an implement after breakage.

The edge-trimmed flakes are of various kinds, mostly fragmentary, and without extensive working. The miscellaneous retouched pieces are also mostly fragments, and probably include several broken scrapers. One oddity (SF2046) in this group is a small distal flake or blade segment which has blunting edge retouch and could possibly be a residual Mesolithic piece. If so, it would be the only sign so far within the Neolithic assemblage of any residuality from a previous period.

Discussion

This sub-assemblage from the 2009 season indicates the presence of a homogeneous Later Neolithic flint industry at Links of Noltland, and is directly comparable with other Orcadian assemblages of similar date, in particular that from Skara Brae (Saville 2004; 2005). As at Skara Brae and Pool (Finlayson 2007), bipolar anvil-struck cores show that this technology was the norm, at least in the final stages of core reduction. Equally normal is the dominance and small size of scrapers amongst the retouched pieces, a trait which occurs throughout the Orcadian Neolithic. Arrowheads usually occur in only very small numbers at settlement sites (Skara Brae has none) and the presence of a classic Later Neolithic chisel form here is of considerable interest, inviting comparison with the three examples found at Barnhouse (Middleton 2005, fig.13.36). Further discussion should await the opportunity to examine the whole Links of Noltland struck lithic assemblage in detail, but enough has been shown already to demonstrate that it will contribute significantly to enhancing our understanding of the exploitation and use of flint in prehistoric Orkney.

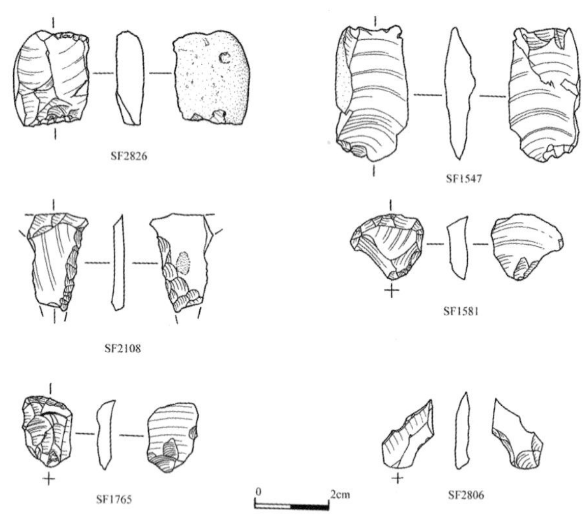

109: Struck lithics

16 THE COARSE STONE

Dawn McLaren

(*See Illus 106, 111–18 and 125*)

Overview

This assessment of the coarse stone was undertaken following a rapid examination of 695 stone artefacts recovered during the 2007–9 excavations of Neolithic and Bronze Age structures in the PIC area at Links of Noltland, Westray (LON 07–09). A further 73 stone tools from the 2007 excavation of Bronze Age structures in the Scheduled Area (SLN 07) were examined in depth and fully catalogued. A summary of the assemblage is presented in Illus 110.

The stone from Links of Noltland is dominated by prosaic, everyday tools primarily used for food processing, butchery and agriculture and is consistent in terms of quantity and range of objects present with other early prehistoric stone assemblages in Orkney and the Northern Isles in general. Skaill knives used as butchery tools are the major constituent of the Neolithic phases, whereas flaked stone bars and ard points used in agriculture, and flaked handled implements, the function of which is uncertain, are most numerous within Bronze Age contexts. A stone figurine and decorated stones form the subject of separate reports.

Summary of main artefact types

Skaill Knives

A distinctive Neolithic tool type, skaill knives dominate the assemblage at Links of Noltland (26 per cent) with 199 examples identified, the majority deriving from Neolithic contexts (99 per cent). A further 92 possible examples are present alongside 61 unworked flakes, likely to be debris from skaill knife production. Skaill knives are manufactured from rounded beach cobbles and are produced by throwing the cobble with vigorous physical force against an anvil stone to detach a flake (Clarke 2006, 18). The thin, long, curvilinear blade produced has been shown by experimental work to function efficiently as a butchery tool, although use in processing other materials is clearly a possibility (Clarke 1989).

Forty-eight per cent of the skaill knives from the site display edge damage in the form of dulling or light chipping of the blade. (Note: This figure is likely to be an overestimation. During rapid examination, any chipping, dulling, or abrasion on the blade was noted but not characterised to determine whether this was the result of manufacture, wear or post-depositional damage. In contrast, evidence of retouch may have been underestimated.) Such a percentage is consistent with edge-damaged knives from earlier excavations at the site (Clarke 2006, 19). Very few of the knives (1 per cent) have any evidence of resharpening in the form of secondary retouch. This is typical of other skaill knife assemblages such as those at Pool and Toft's Ness, Sanday (Clarke 2007a, 359–60; Clarke 2007b, 294).

The quantity of skaill knives at Links of Noltland and limited evidence of blade retouching indicates that these tools were rarely curated, being used for a short time, perhaps even for a single use, before being discarded.

CLASSIFICATION	NEO	BA	U/S	PHASE	TOTAL
Abraded (function unclear)	2				2
Ard point (& ?ard points)	3	6	2		11
Ard point roughout?	6	2	1	1	10
Cobble tools	27	23		1	51
Flaked cobbles	8		1		9
Fire-cracked (unworked)	3				3
Flaked Stone Bars	23	28	3		54
Flaked Stone Implements	3				3
Grooved stones (& ?grooved stone)	4				4
Ground-end tool	1				1
Haematite (worked)	3				3
Handled club (& ?club)		2		1	3
Handled club roughout?		1			1
Handled Flaked Stone Implements (inc. fragmentary)	1	35	1	3	40
Hollowed stones		2			2
Natural	30	4			34
Notched stone tool fragment		4			4

110: Summary of coarse stone toll assemblage

CLASSIFICATION	NEO	BA	U/S	PHASE	TOTAL
Notched stone (& ?notched stone)	2	6		2	10
Pumice (unworked)	29	4			33
Pumice (worked & ?worked)	75	13		1	89
Pot lid fragments	18	5			23
Unfinished pot lid		1			1
Saddle quern fragments? (representing only 1 quern)		5			5
Rubbing stones		2			2
Skaill knives	197	1		1	199
Skaill knives?	88	2	2		92
Skaill knife production?	58	3			61
Working surfaces	6	1			7
?worked		4			4
N/T	4	1			5
TOTAL	591	155	10	10	766

110: Summary of coarse stone toll assemblage

Ard Points

Stone ard points are a distinctive class of artefact well-documented and characterised previously by Rees (1979). These were agricultural tools; hafted within a simple wooden crook they were used to till or plough the soil, producing a distinctive U-shaped pattern of abrasive wear on the tool tip (Rees 1979, 7). A total of eight ard points displaying such wear are present, more frequently from Bronze Age contexts. A further three possible ard points and ten roughouts have been identified.

Flaked Stone Bars

Fifty-four flaked stone bar fragments of varying sizes and shapes were identified, including subrectangular flat examples, tapering bars and oval-shaped tools, the majority deriving from Bronze Age contexts (51 per cent). They were made by removing flakes from the edges of block or cobble to produce the desired shape. Wear typically consists of areas of smoothing and abrasion confined to one end and adjacent edges. Use as a mattock or hoe for breaking up soils prior to cultivation is suggested, although the range of sizes and shapes is likely to reflect variations in function (Clarke 2000, 91). Few provide evidence of hafting, but, where present, it is in the form of notches, pecked or flaked into opposing sides, or a band of smoothing towards the middle of the tool caused by contact with a soft binding rubbing against the stone during use (Clarke 2006, 30).

Flaked Stone Discs

Small quantities of bifacially fractured circular or oval discs were recovered (24, including possible and unfinished examples). These are likely to have functioned as pot lids. The variation in diameters reflects the range of sizes of pottery or wooden vessels used on the site. Few display any obvious damage from exposure to heat, suggesting that they were used to seal vessels rather than used in conjunction with a vessel during cooking. The majority of the pot lid fragments (75 per cent) came from Neolithic contexts.

Flaked handled Implements

Unusually large quantities of flaked handled implement fragments (40) were present amongst the assemblage. Although not anomalous within an Orkney context, they are more typically found within Bronze Age assemblages from Shetland. The vast majority (87 per cent) derive from Bronze Age contexts, representing 26 per cent of the Bronze Age stone tool assemblage. This includes a cache of broken fragments. Only one example was recovered from a possible Neolithic context.

These complex flaked stone implements consist of subrectangular or oval blades, with straight or curving edges and projecting rectangular handles, often tapering in width. A range of handle positions are present at Links of Noltland: some are in line with the back of the blade, some are off-centre and others are positioned centrally in relation to the width of the blade, suggesting differences in the way the tool functioned. Those with centrally placed handles also appear to have tapering heads with blunt, fracture-damaged tips, suggesting utilisation of the end rather than one edge. The variations in form and size are also likely to represent differences in function, those from Sumburgh and Kebister, Shetland, being classified as knives or cleavers and distinguished from each other based on size (Clarke 2006, 42).

The function of such tools is uncertain as few display clear evidence of wear, but use as flensing knives for removing blubber from whales or seals has been suggested (Clarke 2006, 42). Edge damage in the form of dulling and abrasion of the blade is apparent in only a small number of tools. The majority of the handled implements from Links of Noltland are fragmentary (80 per cent). Most have broken at the point of juncture between the head and the handle; the weakest point of the tool during use.

Notched Stones

A small quantity of notched stones was recovered, displaying a wide variety in size and shape. Only one (SF43) is complete, making identification of function difficult to confirm, although use as weights or tether pegs is likely. Some possible tool fragments are also present within this category, some likely to be unfinished, including a possible fragment of a perforated heart-shaped piece similar to those from Sumburgh, Shetland (Clarke 2000, 100).

Cobble Tools

Fifty-one cobble tools were identified as part of the assemblage. The range of wear present includes abrasion from grinding, pitting from pounding, smoothing from rubbing and fracture damage from hammering. It is assumed that many of these tools were used for food processing activities yet equally they could have been utilised in a range of domestic tasks such as preparing clay for potting, crushing and grinding pigments as well as manufacturing other tools of a variety of materials. Single function pounders and hammerstones are the most common amongst this group, some of which may be flint knapping hammers. Multifunction cobble tools are also present (45 per cent), of which 87 per cent show two distinct types of wear and 13 per cent have three wear types. Cobble tools are distributed fairly evenly between the two major phases, the majority deriving from Neolithic contexts (53 per cent). Despite this, the cobble tools comprise a much larger percentage of the Bronze Age assemblage (15 per cent) compared to the Neolithic stone (4 per cent).

Pumice

One hundred and twenty-two fragments of pumice are present, representing 16 per cent of the total assemblage. Most came from Neolithic levels (85 per cent) and the majority of these showed evidence of use. Wear is present as flattened, convex and concave abraded faces as well as abraded grooves and notches which are likely to have been used to smooth, shape and finish bone or wooden points or arrowheads.

Other

A small quantity of other tool types are also present which do not fit readily within the classifications summarised above but are worthy of note. These include faceted, abraded and burnished haematite pebbles, hollowed stones which are likely to have functioned as mortars, working surfaces or anvil stones, and a small quantity of saddle quern and rubbing stone fragments.

Some less typical items were recovered, such as one example of a distinctive Neolithic fragmentary ground-end tool (SF570). Similar ground-end tools are known from Barnhouse (Clarke 2005, 331). Three grooved stones (SF2222, SF2481, SF3085a) and a possible fourth example (SF3114) produced from irregular sandstone blocks were used for shaping and smoothing thick wooden or bone points or rods. These are very similar in appearance to grooved stones from the Neolithic site of Crossiecrown (Clarke 2006, 64, Illus 5.17), but at Links of Noltland appear to be functional tools rather than decorative sculpted stones such as those from Pool (Clarke 2007a, 384–5), Quoyness (Henshall 1963) and Skara Brae (Childe 1931, 63).

Three handled clubs were recovered, including one small, finely finished, utilised example (SF88) and a possible roughout (SF75). Typically, these objects have a finely shaped circular-sectioned handle projecting from a large subrectangular or ovoid club-like head produced from a flaked blank which has been carefully pecked and ground to shape (Clarke 2006, 58–9). The function of these objects is unclear, but extensive bifacial fracturing to the head indicates they were utilitarian objects rather than purely decorative as their careful dressing could suggest.

Overview of Stone Assemblage by Phase

Neolithic

As is typical of Later Neolithic stone tool assemblages from Orkney, the assemblage from Links of Noltland is substantial (590) and dominated by skaill knives and debris relating to skaill knife production (58 per cent). The quantities of skaill knives are comparable to those found during Dr Clarke's excavations of Noltland in the 1970s and 1980s (Clarke forthcoming b). Although not currently present in such substantial numbers as found in the later phases at Skara Brae and Pool (Clarke 2006, 69), they may well match, if not exceed, such numbers by the conclusion of this current phase of excavation.

The presence of cobble tools, albeit in small numbers (4 per cent), is also consistent within Orcadian assemblages of this date, as is the suite of pumice (18 per cent) and pot lids (3 per cent) and the single ground-end tool. Ard points and a significant number of flaked stone bars were found within both Neolithic and Bronze Age deposits and may indicate that a far greater degree of stratigraphic mixing has occurred than has hitherto been recognised.

Bronze Age

The composition of the Bronze Age assemblage, which includes flaked stone bars (18 per cent) and cobble tools (15 per cent), as well as small numbers of ard points (5 per cent), notched stones (6 per cent) and pumice (11 per cent), is fairly typical of Orkney stone assemblages of this period. A small quantity of skaill knives are present (5 per cent), contrasting sharply with significant numbers from the preceding phase.

A more unusual aspect to the stone tool assemblage is the presence of 35 fragments of flaked handled implements, comprising 23 per cent of the total Bronze Age assemblage. Eight fragments representing a minimum of five handled implements were found in a cache alongside a flaked stone bar, skaill knife and other worked stone from context 7106. Although a recognised tool type in the Northern Isles and not unexpected within an Orcadian assemblage, they are more commonly a feature of Shetland's Bronze Age stone repertoire and are present at sites such as Bayanne (Clarke 2006, 94), Sumburgh (Clarke 2000, 99) and Kebister (Clarke 1999, 153, 157, Illus 147:2). Similarly the pecked-handled clubs and the very tentatively identified fragment of a perforated heart-shaped object, are both tool types which are more commonly known from Shetland.

Conclusions

The coarse stone from Links of Noltland forms a significant assemblage which, given its recovery under modern excavation conditions, has the potential to enable a more rounded, fuller understanding of everyday life in early prehistoric Orkney and merits full study and publication. In particular, a detailed comparison of aspects of the Neolithic and Bronze Age assemblages will be vital in allowing a full understanding of the subsistence and resource procurement strategies and craft activities taking place during these periods and how these aspects may have changed throughout the life of the settlement.

As with other early prehistoric settlement sites in Orkney, the stone tool assemblage from Links of Noltland is dominated by prosaic, everyday tools used for food processing, butchery and agriculture, the staple activities of daily life within a self-sufficient community. On-site manufacture of objects is represented by the presence of abraded pumice and grooved stones, used to shape and finish bone and wooden objects, and unfinished stone items such as pot lids, ard point blanks and roughouts for handled implements.

Although many aspects of stone tool use remain consistent throughout the life of the settlement, some differences can be identified between the Neolithic and Bronze Age phases which may relate to changes in the way the people of Links of Noltland used the land and utilised local resources. Skaill knives used as butchery tools were easily manufactured and quickly discarded and form the major constituent of the Neolithic phases. In contrast, flaked stone bars and ard points used in agricultural activities, and flaked handled implements whose function is uncertain, are more numerous within Bronze Age contexts.

A further notable aspect of the assemblage is the condition of the stone tools themselves. A sizeable quantity, approximately 5 per cent, has suffered severe post-depositional weathering in the form of wind and sand abrasion, removing much of the surface of the tool and obscuring individual tool or wear marks. This indicates that the same natural erosion that threatens the structural remains at Links of Noltland is also having a similar damaging effect on the material culture of the site.

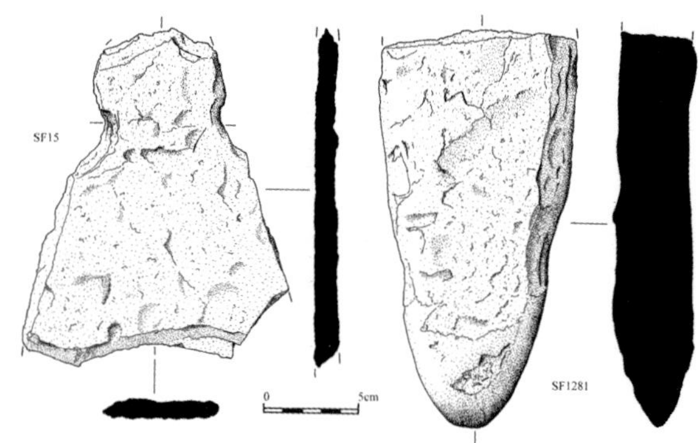

111: Coarse stone tools 15, 1281

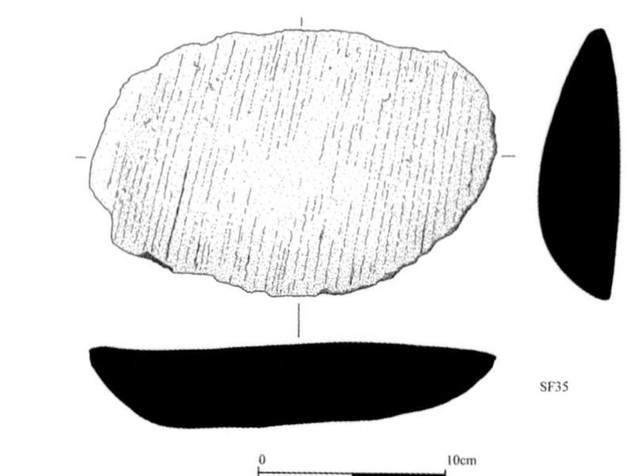

112: Coarse stone tool 35

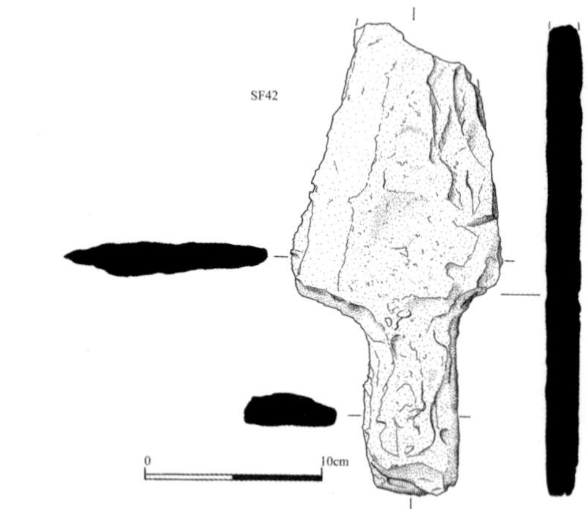

113: Coarse stone tool 42

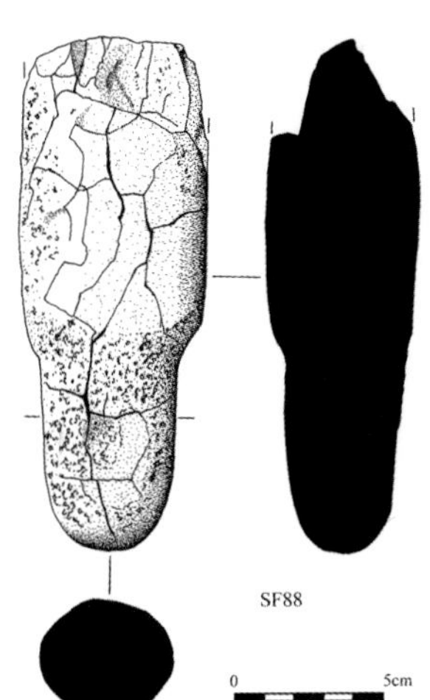

114: Coarse stone tool 88

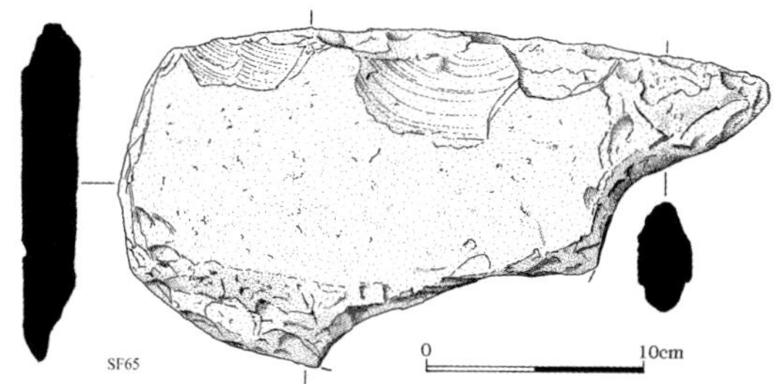

115: Coarse stone tool 65

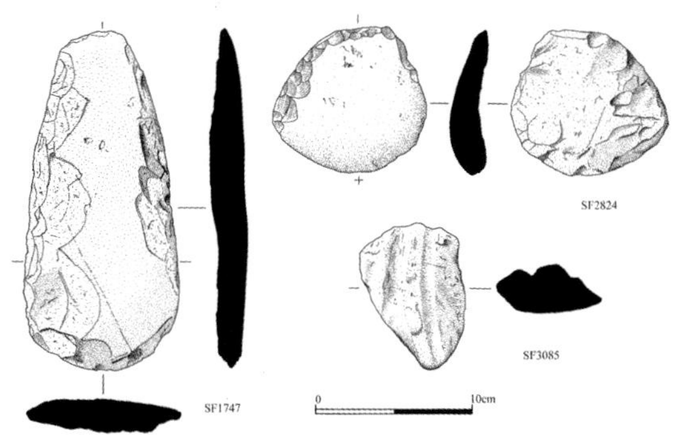

116: Coarse stone tools 1747, 3085, 2824

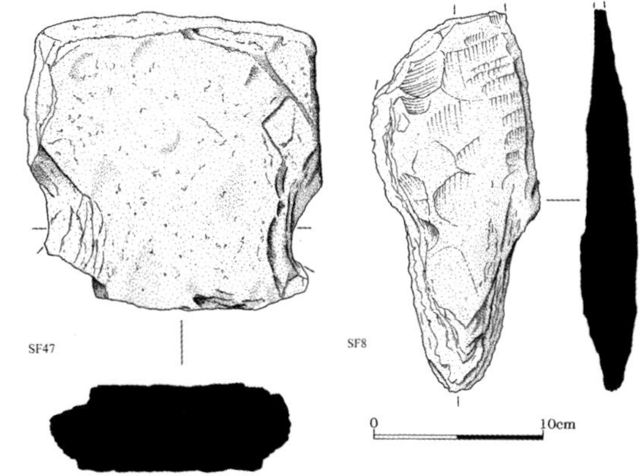

117: Coarse stone tools 47, 8

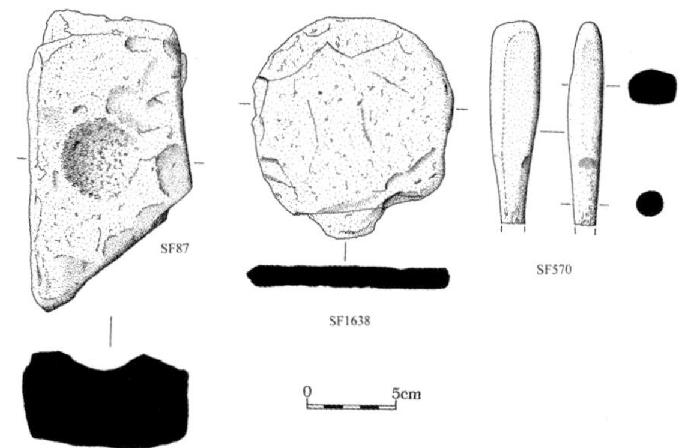

118: Coarse stone tools 87, 1638, 570

17 THE FIGURINE: A PRELIMINARY ASSESSMENT

Elizabeth Goring

Examination

The figurine was examined prior to cleaning and conservation. Its surface was studied under a low-powered stereoscopic microscope using direct and raking fibre-optic lights.

The purpose of the examination was to investigate evidence of pre-depositional wear and damage which might shed light on its function. Similar wear analysis of figurines from the Chalcolithic period in Cyprus have suggested patterns of contemporary handling and treatment which have assisted in developing interpretation.

The examination used established criteria for determining accidental and deliberate damage, and wear resulting from a repetitive form of usage where the resulting impairment is unintentional.[1]

Object Description

Anthropomorphic figurine
Sandstone
Height 41mm Width 31mm Thickness 12mm

(In the following description, left = left side proper; right = right side proper)
The front surface is flat; the back surface is slightly convex. The left side is thicker than the right (12:9mm), and the whole is slightly wedge-shaped.

Head: This is roughly oblong, with its longer edges horizontal. The front surface is flat, the back convex. A finely incised M-shaped line across the front surface can be interpreted as a brow line. Two parallel vertical lines running from the brow to the lower edge of the face can be understood as a nose. Two widely spaced round dots, apparently representing eyes, are simply impressed about 7mm from the top edge of the head. There is no indication

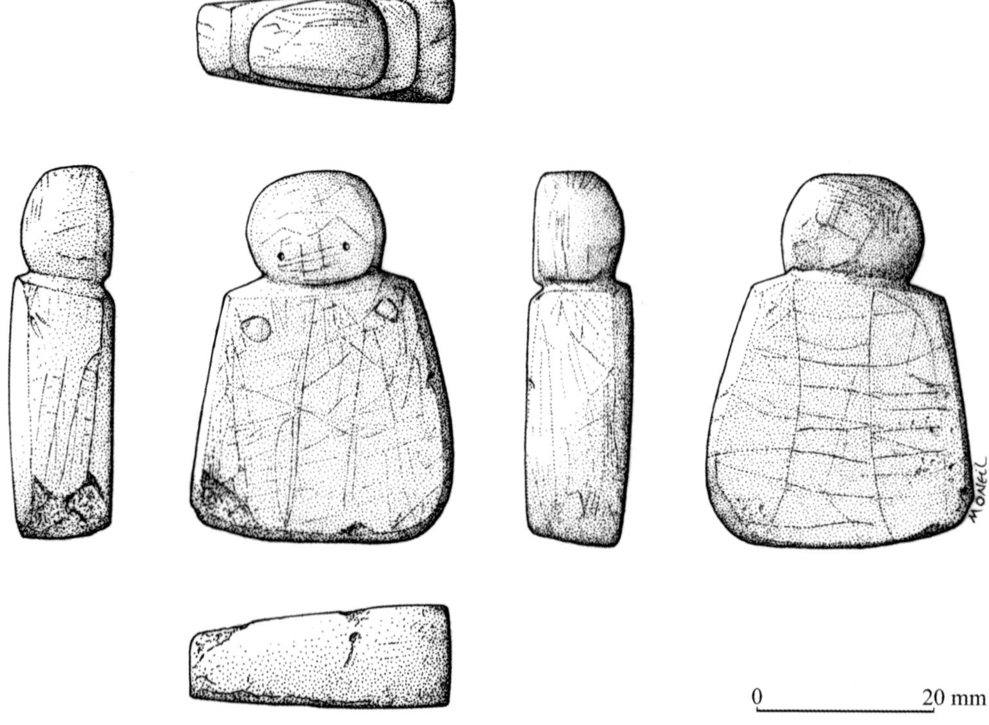

Links of Noltland figurine
Illustration: Marion O'Neil

119: Figurine, SF2289

of a mouth. The head has convex edges. There are shallow parallel striations on the top and back of the head and three horizontal incisions on its right side.

Neck: The head is sharply divided from the shoulder line of the torso by a deep groove. The shoulder line is asymmetric, with the left side higher and slightly more rounded, the right side more angled.

Torso: The asymmetric trapezoidal torso expands from the shoulders to the base. The right edge is straighter and more sharply defined. The left edge is curved. The lower edge is straight, curving up towards the sides. There is no indication of legs or arms. What appear to be breasts are indicated by fine incision. The right 'breast' is squarer and more emphasised than the left, which is diamond-shaped. A fine, apparently interrupted, V-shaped incised line runs from the right edge of the right breast to the mid-torso and up to the top of the left breast, slightly echoing the brow line above. The back surface has a horizontal incised line running across it below the shoulders. Three fine vertical incisions run from this to just above the bottom of the figurine, dividing the back into vertical panels. These are each subdivided by horizontal incised lines, often crossing the verticals.

The right side of the torso bears clear oblique parallel striations and short parallel horizontal striations. A few fine longitudinal striations are also visible on the left side.

The figurine will stand unsupported, though this is not a stable position. The underside has fine striations.

Interpretation of Surface Markings

These conclusions are based on examination of the surfaces in their uncleaned state. Cleaning, conservation and the results of laser scanning may produce additional information.

The capacity to distinguish deliberate decoration from surface wear is affected by the fineness of the incisions and 'drillings', and by the evident softness of the stone. At the time of examination the stone was thought to be a local type of sandstone. It is evidently quite soft, and marks easily. My impression was that it could have been shaped using pecking and grinding, smoothed by abrading with sand, and decorated quickly and easily with materials as soft as bone.

Decoration

There is clear evidence of original decoration. On the head, the M-shaped brow line and nose were lightly and deliberately incised into the surface. Two eyes were lightly impressed into the surface, probably by twisting a simple pointed implement. There were no signs of the concentric striations typical of drilling, and it was probably not necessary to use abrasive. The outlines of the breasts were lightly and rapidly incised into the surface. They may be linked by a deliberately incised V. I could see no other definite traces of decoration on the front of the figurine. This does not exclude the possibility that other decorative details, perhaps in the form of pigment, may have been lost.

Based solely on the surviving traces of deliberate marks on the front surface, emphasis was on the brow and nose line and the upper torso. The eyes are indicated but not emphatic, and there is no evidence of mouth or ears. The two rounded markings on the front of the chest may indicate breasts, but they are not emphatic, and may be open to alternative interpretation. There is no other surviving feature which might be taken as indication of gender.

The back surface was decorated very carefully, again with very fine, quickly executed but quite deliberate incision. The radiating, subdivided lattice pattern on the back is very clear. If intended to be representative rather than purely decorative, it might suggest textile or clothing, such as a cloak, or, less likely, body decoration.

Marks of Working

There are few visible traces of working. There are some peck marks at the top edge of the front surface of the torso, and further slight pecking on the back, especially towards the lower right edge. Most of the striations across the faces and sides of the figurine seem to be shaping marks. The rather more emphatic shallow parallel striations across the head also seem to be shaping marks rather than decoration. Further striations are visible in the groove between the head and torso.

Damage and Wear

There are chips from the right lower front corner and from the lower edge. There is a sharp scratch across the underside of the base which looks recent. There are small chips from the left side edge. All these result from accidental damage. There is no evidence of deliberate damage ('slighting'). The edges and base of the figurine are very smooth. There is slight wear polish on the base, but no signs of wear polish on the front and rear faces, and the edges of the torso are very crisp and sharp. No wear is evident in the groove between head and torso (as might be expected if the figurine had been suspended from this area as a pendant).

Further Comments

If this object was used as a pendant, it was very lightly worn or not worn in life at all. If this object was used as a figurine, there was no evidence that handling was involved in its function. The existence of decoration on both front and back surfaces might suggest it was intended to be viewed in the round. The freshness and smoothness of the surfaces suggest that it could have been made shortly before deposition, or indeed for deposition. The smoothness and polish around the edges of the figurine, and the back of its head, may be natural – for example, if it was adapted from what had been a water-worn pebble. If it had been kept in, for example, a leather bag, more extensive general smoothing might have resulted.

Emphasis on brow line, nose and, to a lesser extent,

eyes, together with the absence of a mouth, and the uneven shaping of breasts, are not in themselves unusual figurine characteristics.2 Superficial resemblances with aspects of schematised anthropomorphic figurines which are more common from distant cultures and places, such as form and features chosen for emphasis, are to be expected: there are only limited ways of recognisably representing a human form. Such resemblances, in themselves, should notbe taken to indicate any form of connection, direct or indirect, or commonality of function or significance.

Notes

1 For criteria for defining accidental and deliberate damage to figurines, see Elizabeth Goring in Peltenburg, E *et al*, *Lemba Archaeological Project II.1A. Excavations at Kissonerga-Mosphilia 1977 –1995* (Studies in Mediterranean Archaeology 70:2, Jonsered, 1998), 162–3; Elizabeth Goring in Peltenburg, E *et al*, *Lemba Archaeological Project II.2. A Ceremonial Area at Kissonerga* (Studies in Mediterranean Archaeology 70:3, Göteborg, 1991), 49–52; and Elizabeth Goring in Peltenburg, E, *et al*, *The Chalcolithic Cemetery of Souskiou-Vathyrkakas, Cyprus. Investigations of Four Missions from 1950 to 1997* (Nicosia, 2006), 76–7.

2 See, for example (and with no implied connection), *Lemba Archaeological Project II.1A*, Fig 83.1, 6 and 9.

18 THE DECORATED STONES

Hazel Moore and Graeme Wilson

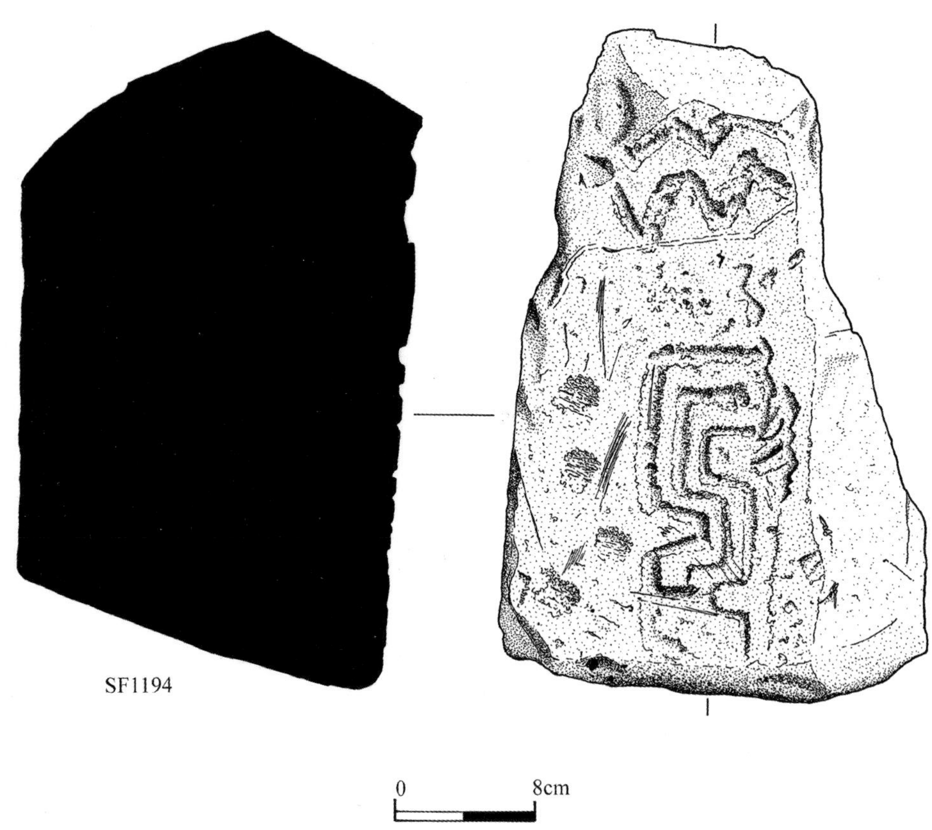

120: Decorated stone

Summary

A total of seven decorated stones have been identified during excavation; only one of which has been lifted so far. Of the remaining stones, at least two bear cup markings; these are built into walls which have not yet been fully exposed. The remainder have lightly incised geometric designs; one has pecked chevrons. Six of the decorated stones are associated with Structure 8 and one (a cupmarked stone) is associated with structural remains located between Structures 8 and 9 which may form part of another building.

The recovered stone (SF1194) is an angular block of sandstone. It measures 24.6cm by 36.4cm by 22cm. Decoration is visible on one face only (Illus 120). The stone has been damaged on two sides and in both instances this has truncated part of the decoration. The decoration is dominated by a double chevron motif and a key-pattern type motif, both of which are roughly pecked . Numerous other incised lines and peck marks are visible on the stone; at least some of which may represent damage or wear rather than part of the original design. Further analysis will be carried out in the future.

19 ASSESSMENT OF POSSIBLE COPROLITES

John Carrott

Introduction

Possible coprolites recovered from contexts within the midden (from 19 context and spit combinations, in 47 separate bags and totalling 70 individual items/fragments) were submitted to Palaeoecology Research Services Limited, Kingston upon Hull, for an assessment of their bioarchaeological potential. All of the remains were from a late Neolithic midden infilling a building (Structure 8).

Methods

Not all of the submitted remains were examined for this assessment, but at least one item was investigated from each context/spit combination and multiple items were examined from the more productive deposits.

The remains were examined using a low-power (x7–x45) binocular microscope and a general description of their composition was made, with additional notes made for any macrofossil or other inclusions.

The material was also examined for the eggs of intestinal parasites and other microfossils using the 'squash' technique of Dainton (1992); although primarily for the detection of parasite eggs, the 'squash' technique routinely reveals other microfossil remains, such as diatoms and pollen grains/ spores, and, where present, these have also been noted. Slides were scanned at x150 magnification, with x600 employed where necessary.

Results

Most of the submitted remains were almost certainly dog coprolites composed largely of heavily degraded bone, with inclusions of individual bone fragments. Many of the remains also had areas of black ash or rotted charcoal on their surfaces, presumably acquired from other waste discarded into the midden.

Three of the items examined were either not dog coprolites or may have been but were of uncertain nature. There was an iron-rich concretion from context 8008 which was probably iron-pan but could conceivably be artefactual, an indeterminate fragment from context 9000, and some material from context 9003 which could perhaps be a burnt dog coprolite, but appeared more likely to be indurated or 'baked' sediment containing burnt bone fragments.

Examination of the material for microfossil remains revealed a predominantly mineral composition likely to be mostly from degraded bone tissue, with traces of charred material (from the charcoal/ash) and only occasional identifiable microfossils. Fungal hyphae were quite frequently recorded in small numbers, but such remains are of no interpretative value. Diatoms were present in three of the items examined (from contexts 8001, 9003 and 9029), but, again, were few in number and were also very poorly preserved and, consequently, could provide no significant information for interpretation; they may have arrived via groundwater entering the deposits, waste water discarded into the midden, or perhaps even from animal or human bodily waste.

No eggs of intestinal parasites were recorded. This is usually the case for dog coprolites composed largely of bone, however; it seems unlikely that this means that the animals did not have worm infestations, but rather that the preservational conditions were such that remains of these have not survived.

Discussion

Most of the submitted items assessed (and on the basis of visual examination only, those not examined in detail also) were almost certainly dog coprolites.

The remains were of little interpretative value, although their presence within the midden implies that this foul matter was deliberately disposed of and presumably therefore it was from domestic animals kept by the inhabitants. The composition of the coprolites suggests that the dogs had a bone-rich diet which probably derived from the remnants of human food.

20 STEATITE ARTEFACTS

Amanda Forster

Summary

The small assemblage of steatite artefacts recovered from Links of Noltland includes worked material in the form of vessel fragments and reworked vessel fragments. The lack of raw material or working debris suggests that the artefacts were not manufactured at the site, and implies that steatite artefacts were introduced as finished objects. Once vessels had broken, at least some examples were repaired or reworked where possible, with a number of burnishing tools being present in the assemblage. On morphological grounds, the assemblage would appear to be of early prehistoric date with clear parallels at sites in Shetland and, to a lesser extent, within Orkney.

Introduction

Steatite is not a natural resource in Orkney and would have been imported from the more northerly archipelago of Shetland. Although not unique to this site, the recovery of a collection of steatite vessels from an early prehistoric and domestic site in Orkney is certainly rare. More commonly, steatite has been recovered from funerary contexts (as cremation urns or accessory vessels) with only a handful of examples from datable domestic contexts (see Forster and Sharman 2009). The recovery of steatite vessels from a domestic setting has been seen as a predominantly Shetland phenomenon during this period, with only occasional imports to Orkney being recorded (Smith 2007, 286). As Smith rightly points out, however, the use-life of the vessels recovered from funerary contexts is unknown, and they may well have functioned as domestic vessels prior to their final deposition (ibid). The large assemblage of steatite vessels recovered from the domestic site of Bayanne included a number of vessel types comparable with those from funerary contexts in Orkney (Forster forthcoming a). Whilst it is impossible to draw too many conclusions from morphology alone, it does seem likely that vessels used at this time in Orkney were certainly performing a range of functions. Despite its relatively small numbers, the material recovered from Links of Noltland is extremely significant in this contextin adding to the slowly growing corpus of clearly domestic steatite vessels.

Assemblage Summary

In total, 118 countable fragments of steatite were recovered from Links of Noltland, including 28 small finds units recorded on-site. The total assemblage weighs just under 4.5kg. The distribution of artefact types is very limited and comprises vessel fragments, reworked vessel fragments and a small number of miscellaneous fragments (Illus 121). Overall the assemblage is not badly preserved, but does include a number of very burnt, worn and/or degraded fragments. Within the assemblage group, there are vessel sherds which could arguably derive from a single vessel, although in the majority of cases these have been excavated as a group and recorded as a single find. There are no apparent cross-joins within the assemblage. With this borne in mind, the assemblage could represent up to 15 vessels. However, without closer petrological examination and due to the inhomogeneity of vessel morphology, it is difficult to estimate this accurately and the true number may be smaller.

	Vessel	Misc (fragments)	Totals
Unit number	19	6	28
Weight (g)	3737g	608g	4345g

121: The steatite assemblage: primary artefact description

	Burnisher	Reworked	Repair
Unit number	3	2	3
Weight (g)	115g	221g	158g

122: The steatite assemblage: secondary reworking (all primary vessel fragments)

Vessels

The vessels recovered from the site are all comparable with finds recovered from Shetland and, to a lesser extent, Orkney. All the vessels are four-sided and probably square in plan, with flared walls and a flat base. There are two recognisable types within the assemblage; Type 1, being a more curved and probably smaller example than Type 2, which is larger and perhaps more angular (Illus 123).

The lack of any large rim, base, or corner fragments from either vessel type precludes detailed reconstruction.

Notwithstanding, based on evidence from Bayanne, Shetland (which has the most complete vessels assemblage from this period), it is likely that Noltland Type 1 is equivalent to the Bayanne small square vessel (see Forster forthcoming a or b?). These pots were found to have a wall thickness of between 4mm (at the rim) and 18mm (at the wall), the majority falling between 8mm and 15mm. The depth of the vessels at Bayanne ranged from 50mm to 90mm and the width at the rim tended to approximate 100mm. The base width was only slightly smaller due to the slightly convex wall profile. This vessel seems to be the most widely distributed of the early prehistoric vessel types, and recovered from the majority of sites in Shetland (including Jarlshof, Sumburgh and Bayanne) and Orkney (Tofts Ness (Sanday), Calf of Eday and Skaill (Deerness)). Noltland Type 2 seems to be equivalent to the large square vessels recorded at Bayanne. This type is not widely recorded elsewhere although some of the vessel fragments recovered from Skaill, Deerness, bear a striking resemblance to the Bayanne Type 2 vessels (personal observation). These pots were found to be c 150–200mm at rim width, although the complete base of vessel with a width of 300mm indicated that they could be somewhat larger. None of the examples recovered from Links of Noltland are likely to be of a particularly large size, although any estimates from such small fragments would be very subjective. The depth of vessels at Bayanne ranged from c 50–150mm, although, again, the height would probably be proportionate to the width at the base. The main characteristic of larger vessels, other than size, is the profile. Whereas the smaller vessels were upright and convex, the larger pots were flared profile with either slightly convex or straight walls (see Illus 123).

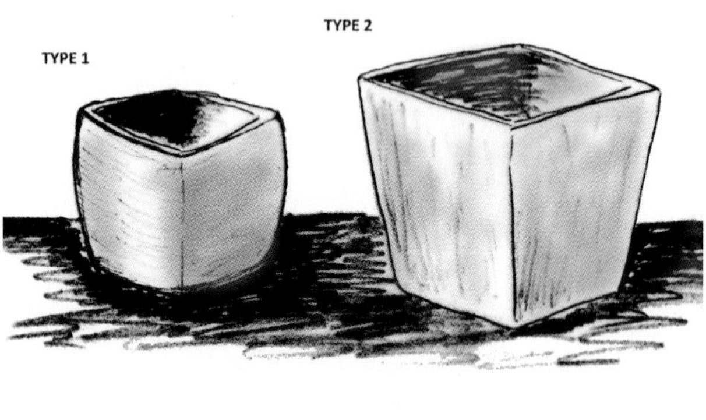

123: Reconstruction of Type 1 and Type 2 vessels at Links of Noltland

One vessel recovered from Links of Noltland (SF76) may be a circular vessel, rather than a four-sided one (SF76). The fragmentary state of this vessel precludes accurate reconstruction of the size and full form of the vessel and, consequently, it has not been classified as a recognisable type. The vessel fragments (SF76) were recovered from context 7117 which also contained both Type 1 and Type 2 vessels. At Bayanne, circular vessels were associated with the earlier phases of the settlement, although they were recovered in fewer numbers than the four-sided examples. Like the Links of Noltland fragments, they were also badly preserved, but it was possible to estimate the diameter of the vessels to between 80mm and 190mm (the depth could not be estimated). Circular and oval vessels have also been recorded from funerary contexts in both Orkney and Shetland.

In addition to the basic form, a couple of the vessels appear to have added accoutrement. One vessel (SF56a) is decorated with an incised line (1.5mm) around the external wall below the rim (which is no longer extant). Originally, there were at least two incised lines, but the vessel seems to have split along the incision of the lower one. A second vessel (SF30) has the very faint impression of an incised line 4mm below the rim. It is extremely worn and only barely visible. This type of decoration was recorded on small square vessels at Bayanne which is consistent with the evidence here, both vessels being of Type 1 form.

Three of the vessel fragments (SF30, SF77, SF3612) displayed signs of having been repaired, or having had a repair attempted. SF3612, the most elaborate of these, has one full perforation with a deep groove leading to it, and one half-perforation to the side of it. At first glance this could represent a small hemispherical Norse vessel of Viking date, showing evidence for a handle. The location of the perforation, however, appears to be at the base angle of the vessel and therefore more likely to be a repair. There is still a possibility that this vessel is Norse *[although it was recovered from a secure Bronze Age context* HLM and GW]. SF77 has a large perforation (10mm diameter) just beneath the rim and the other half in section across the fracture. Reworking is visible on the fracture on two sides. The final example, SF30, has only a small indent on the external wall which may be the first attempts at repairing the vessel. Although this could just as well be accidental, it does seem to have happened pre-deposition.

The vessel assemblage recovered from Links of Noltland was clearly a well-used domestic assemblage. All of the vessel fragments were well worn with smoothed surfaces on the interior wall. Although the vessels were probably finished with a smoothed surface, the use-wear of the vessels often suggests that they have been cleaned with an abrasive substance, such as sand and water. The exterior walls of the vessels had also been smoothed, with faint working only apparent on three examples (SF76, SF56g, SF80) representing the different vessel types. Sooting was present on both internal and external walls, and also in the fractures, providing a further indication that the vessels were well-used. Fracturing probably occurred as a result of extended use, with soot building up in small surface cracks and forcing a more substantial break to occur. Only one large fragment from a base was recovered (SF84), from a Type 2 vessel. It was a flat base with a clear base to wall angle, as would be expected from this vessel type. As with extensive soot recorded on some of the vessels, the oxidation of the external base wall indicated prolonged contact with heat which has caused it to degrade. This leaves a thinner surface across the base, which has been known to wear away and fracture as a result. Extreme cases of this have been

SF No	Context	No of frags	Primary artefact	Secondary working?	Description	Vessel form	Wall thickness (mm)	Weight (g)
0	14	2	Vessel	Burnisher	Vessel fragment reworked as ?burnisher on all sides. Probably a medium sized Type 1 vessel, plain working on both walls.	Type 1	14	46
0	21	1	Vessel		Rim sherd from small, possibly Type 1 vessel although it may be a circular rim rather than a small square one.	unclear	9	20
30	7143	1	Vessel	Repair	Vessel rim sherd from small four-sided vessel. Looks like someone has tried a repair with a small indent on the external surface which is sooted.	Type 1	12	37
31	7143	1	Vessel		Vessel wall/ corner fragment. Too small to see vessel form though working and thickness would suggest Type 1.	Type 1	Aug-13	9
39	7083	16	Vessel		Many fragments from a very burnt and worn vessel. From the profile of the vessel, it looks like it may have been a Type 2 vessel.	unclear	17-20	134
56a	7117	1	Vessel		From large group: 1 x dec wall frag, corner, Probably Type 1. Decorated with an incised line (1.5mm) around the external wall below the rim (rim not extant). Originally there were at least 2 incised lines, looks to have split.	Type 1	17	71
56b	7117	1	Vessel	Burnisher	Reworked vessel wall, Type 1. Reworked into sub rounded oblong, perhaps used as a burnisher.	Type 1	10	37
56c	7117	1	Vessel	Burnisher	Reworked vessel fragment (Type 1) into triangular shape. Probable burnishing tool.	Type 1	16	32

124: Steatite: table of worked fragments

SF No	Context	No of frags	Primary artefact	Secondary working?	Description	Vessel form	Wall thickness (mm)	Weight (g)
56d	7117	1	Vessel	Reworked fractures	Vessel rim/wall from a very worn and well used Type 1 vessel with fracture reworking. Rim to possible wall/ base angle - though would be very shallow.	Type 1	8-Nov	93
56e	7117	9	Vessel		Nine badly burnt and worn wall and base fragments. The group represents fragments from one vessel, but only 2 conjoin and the preservation is so bad they are unlikely to be re-fittable. Form is probably a Type 2, large four sided pot.	Type 2	18	572
56f	7117	9	Vessel		Wall fragments (2 x conjoining) from a Type 1 vessel, thin-walled and quite large four sided vessel. Working on the interior is smoothed, and the exterior is very worn. Has broken at the base angle. Fractured at laminations.	Type 1	11	388
56g	7117	7	Vessel		Fragments from vessel Type 1, including probable base and definite wall corner. Two large fragments conjoin to form what is probably a large base fragment, but without the usual use-wear, just sooting. Slight reworking on a couple of the fractures.	Type 1	15-18	571
63	6	1	Vessel	Reworked fractures	Reworked vessel wall. This vessel may have been a smoothed Type 2 vessel, but could even be Norse and circular but with a straight profile. The fractures have been smoothed, perhaps for refit, but then abandoned.	unclear	17	128

124: Steatite: table of worked fragments

SF No	Context	No of frags	Primary artefact	Secondary working?	Description	Vessel form	Wall thickness (mm)	Weight (g)
76	7117	8	Vessel		Eight conjoining fragments from a very badly burnt and shattered vessel wall/ base fragment. Looks like it could be a large and circular vessel rather than a four-sided one.	Circular	17-20	349
77	7117	1	Vessel	Repair	Vessel rim sherd, very straight walled upright vessel with probable repair perforations, one just beneath rim and the other half in section. Reworking on the fracture on two sides. Very odd geology, looks like temper in steatitic clay but it is steatite.	Type 2	17	99
80	7117	5	Vessel		Vessel rim and wall from Type 2 vessel. 5 sherds all conjoining. There is some wear on one or two of the breaks, others are relatively fresh. Almost full rim to wall profile.	Type 2	15-21	346
84	17	3	Vessel		Partial vessel base from a medium sized Type 1 vessel with wall angle extant. Likes like it has fractured along breaks.	Type 1	May-16	164
106	7159	6	Vessel		Four conjoining and one other from probable Type 1 and relatively shallow vessel.	Type 1	16-20	167
107	7159	5	Vessel		Five conjoining fragments from the base/ wall angle of a very burnt and well used vessel. Steatite is very fibrous and laminar.	unclear	14-24	173
110	7159	18	Vessel		Three large fragments and many small fragments of very badly preserved, burnt and extremely laminar steatite, presumably from a vessel as sooting is present, though the surfaces are imperceptible.	unclear	Oct-26	278

124: Steatite: table of worked fragments

SF No	Context	No of frags	Primary artefact	Secondary working?	Description	Vessel form	Wall thickness (mm)	Weight (g)
3611	7159	1	Vessel		Very small fragment from a vessel wall, 16mm thick	unclear	16	1
3612	7165	0	Vessel	Repair	Very odd vessel sherd, with perforation and groove on external surface, presumably for repair. Strange geology, very dark almost black steatite and very fine grained and smooth. Worn fractures.	unclear	10	22

124: Steatite: table of worked fragments

recorded at both Bayanne and Jarlshof, where the worn base is removed and the basal fracture smoothed to form a 'collar' (see Forster forthcoming a; Forster and Sharman 2009).

Burnishers

The only other artefact type recognised within the assemblage are burnishers or items used as abrasive tools (SF56a, SF56b and SF56c). These artefacts are all reworked from broken vessel fragments and identified purely from the use-wear present on fractures and surfaces. Although the use is entirely interpretable, the material seems to have been a useful addition to the potter's toolkit and similar artefacts have been recovered from Iron Age and later deposits at Old Scatness (Forster forthcoming b) and two from the contemporary site of Bayanne, Shetland (Forster forthcoming a). The largest of the Noltland examples is 42mm by 30mm and 10mm thick – the thickness reflecting that of the original vessel – and the other two are not much smaller. All three fit easily into the hand and have faceted use-wear on the fractured surfaces, perhaps suggesting they have been used to rub against another surface. Steatite is a well-known addition to ceramics as a temper. Sometimes so much is added that the ceramics material can actually appear to be steatite or to be made of steatitic clay. A further consideration would be the use of the material as a burnishing tool, not just to help smooth the surface of the vessel, but perhaps also to add to its aesthetic value and make it appear more like steatite. It has been noted that use of steatite as a temper for pottery enables it to be burnished to a high lustre (Yarrington 2000, 78), and it is possible that use of steatite as a burnishing tool may have had a similar effect on ceramic surfaces. The use of smoothed pebbles has been proposed for the achievement of a high lustre or leathery finish on ceramic vessels (Johnston 1997, 203), and it is reasonable to suggest that the use of broken and smoothed steatite vessel sherds could achieve similar results.

Discussion

The relatively recent recovery of a substantial assemblage of Bronze Age to early Iron Age steatite vessels from Bayanne, Shetland, demands a reappraisal of many of the earlier prehistoric finds from the Northern Isles. It is clear, for example, that morphologically similar vessel types were being used in funerary contexts within Orkney and in a domestic setting in Shetland (see Forster forthcoming a; Forster and Sharman 2009). It is also apparent that steatite vessels were utilised to differing extents across regions of Shetland during prehistoric periods (Forster and Sharman 2009). In Orkney, a lack of vessels from domestic contexts (compared to at least 30 recorded from funerary sites) has led to the conclusion that the import of steatite vessels was rare and costly, and a perfect material to demonstrate the high status and prestige of the dead (Sharman 2007, 26). Whilst it is arguable that the small group of material recovered from Links of Noltland challenges the idea that prehistoric steatite in Orkney was limited to funerary uses, the general lack of material recovered from domestic contexts remains undeniable. At Skaill, Deerness, a few steatite vessel fragments may well date to the Neolithic and Bronze Age phases, but the phasing of the site is unreliable (see Buteux 1996). Tofts Ness and Pool, both in Sanday, Orkney (Dockrill 2007 and Hunter *et al* 2007 respectively), have added to the corpus of early prehistoric and multi-period sites in Orkney, but the picture of early steatite vessel remains confused. At Pool, there were no finds of steatite until the much later Viking period levels and at Tofts Ness only eight fragments of steatite were recovered from late Neolithic to early Iron Age contexts (Smith 2007, 286). The finds discussed here could be seen as an anomaly, although the apparent inconsistency in the utilisation of the material in Shetland – from whence all these Orcadian finds derive – adds some degree of believability to this picture. Perhaps one day we will be able to discuss these trends as true reflections of different alliances and networks operating throughout the prehistoric period across these archipelagos.

The finds from Links of Noltland are of great significance in this context. Despite being relatively few in number, this collection provides an important addition to the corpus of steatite finds recovered from prehistoric Orkney. Furthermore, the slight variation between assemblages dating to this long period in Orkney seems in some way to reiterate similar differences seen between Shetland's domestic assemblages. The picture of prehistoric steatite use, although still blurry, is at least one small step closer to being in focus.

Catalogue of Key Steatite Artefacts

St1 **SF63 [006]** Vessel wall fragment with secondary reworking. This vessel may have been a smoothed Type 2 vessel, but could even be Norse and circular but with a straight profile. Vessels walls are smooth on both faces, cleaned on the internal wall, with sooting visible on the external face. The fractures have been smoothed, perhaps for refit, but then abandoned.
17mm (thick) x 34mm x 95mm

St2 **SF77 [7117]** Vessel rim sherd with repair (Type 2 vessel). Very straight-walled upright vessel with probable repair perforations, one large perforation (10mm diameter) just beneath the rim and the other half in section across the fracture. Reworking is visible on the fracture on two sides. Sooting is visible on the external surface and possible in the fractures. The surfaces are very rough, probably owing to geological features of the stone, which looks like temper in steatitic clay (but it is definitely steatite).
17mm (thick) x 52mm x 68mm

St3 **SF84 [017]** Vessel base fragment (Type 1 vessel). Partial vessel base from a medium-sized Type 1 vessel with wall angle extant. Looks like it has fractured along breaks. Very clear sooting on internal surface and in fractures, with an oxidised basal surface.
5–16mm (thickness at base) x 70mm x 120mm

St4 **SF80 [7117]** Vessel rim and wall fragment (Type 2 vessel), including five conjoining fragments. There is some wear on one or two of the breaks; others are relatively fresh. These conjoining fragments represent the best-preserved vessel from the site, with nearly a full rim to wall profile preserved, suggesting the vessel profile would have been flared and approximately 90mm in depth. The vessel is worn with faint vertical tooling present on the external wall. Both walls have patches of sooting, more so on the external wall.
15–21mm (thick) x 90mm x 140mm

St5 **SF56a [7117]** Vessel wall fragment, decorated (probable Type 1). This is a decorated wall fragment from the corner of a probable Type 1 vessel. It has been decorated with an incised line (1.5mm) around the external wall below the rim (no longer extant). Originally, there were at least two incised lines, but the fragment has fracture along the upper one. Both walls have been well smoothed and both have sooting present. The external wall is blackened all over.
17mm (thick) x 34mm x 72mm

St6 **SF30 [7143]** Vessel rim sherd with repair (Type 1 vessel). Vessel rim sherd from small four-sided vessel with possible repair attempt on external surface. Possible decoration of single incised line, but very worn external rim. Some sooting is present on the internal wall, but it is relatively clean and very smooth. The external wall is also smooth, but with a blackened surface from sooting.
12mm (thick) x 32mm x 50mm

St7 **SF106 [7159]** Vessel fragments (Type 1 vessel). Four conjoining and one other from probable Type 1 and relatively shallow vessel. Smoothed and cleaned internal wall with a very sooted external surface.
16–20mm (thick) x 60mm x 85mm

St8 **SF3612 [7165]** Vessel fragment, handle or repair. Very odd vessel sherd, with perforation and groove on external surface, presumably for repair. Strange geology, very dark almost black steatite and very fine grained and smooth. Looks like it has been present on a surface for a while – very worn on all surfaces and fractures. From morphology this could be a Norwegian, Viking period vessel though it is not inconceivable that it is prehistoric [*found in secure Bronze Age context, however*, HLM and GW].
10mm (thick) x 37mm x 44mm

St9 **NSF [014]** Burnishing tool, reworked vessel fragment (Type 1 vessel). Vessel fragment reworked as ?burnisher on all sides. Probably a medium-sized Type 1 vessel. Plain working on both walls and sooting extant on external wall.
14mm (thick) x 26mm x 60mm

St10 **SF56b [7117]** Burnishing tool, reworked vessel fragment (Type 1 vessel). Reworked vessel wall, Type 1. Reworked into subrounded oblong, probably used as a burnisher, evidenced by faceted abrasions on the fractures.
10mm (thick) x 30mm x 50mm

St11 **SF56c [7117]** Burnishing tool, reworked vessel fragment (Type 1 vessel). Reworked vessel fragment (Type 1) into a triangular shape. Probable burnishing tool.
16mm (thick) x 35mm x 45mm

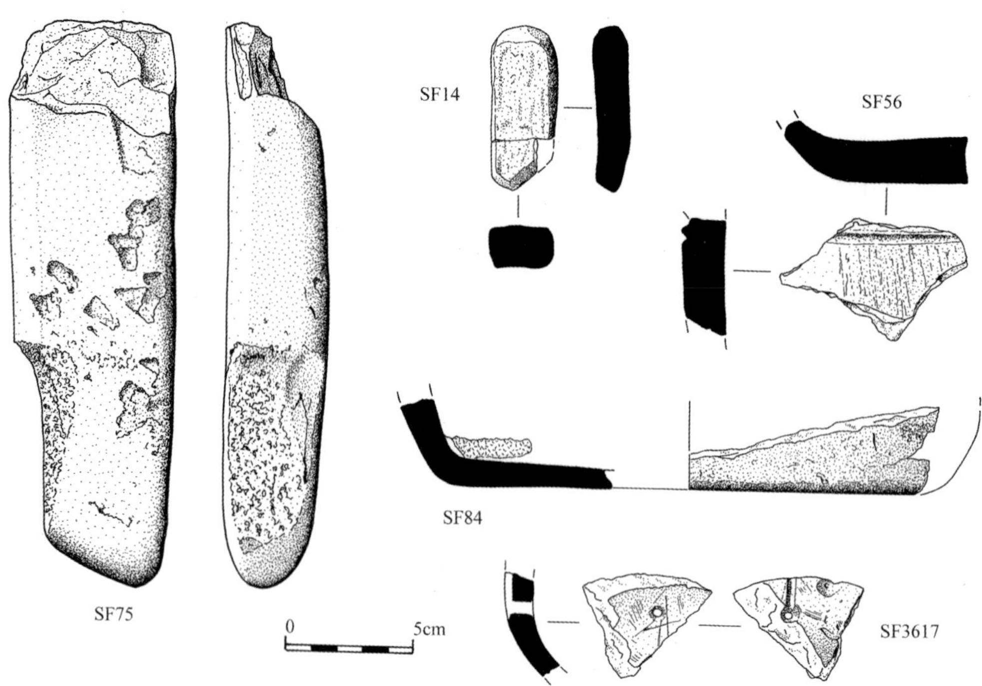

125: Steatite and stone tool (SF75)

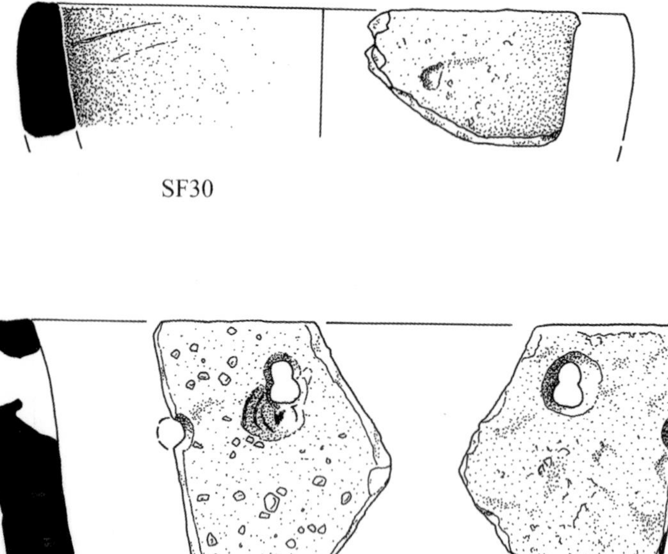

126: Steatite

REFERENCES

Adderley, W P and Simpson, I A 2005 'Early Norse home-field productivity in the Faroe Islands', *Human Ecology* **33**, 711–36.

Albarella, U 2002'"Size matters": how and why biometrics is still important in zooarchaeology', in Dobney, K M and O'Connor, T P *Bones and the Man: Studies in Honour of Don Brothwell*. Oxford, Oxbow Books.

Albarella, U and Serjeantson, D 2002 'A passion for pork: meat consumption at the British Late Neolithic site of Durrington Walls', in Miracle, P and Milner, N *Consuming Passions and Patterns of Consumption*. Cambridge, McDonald Institute Monograph, 33–49.

Amorosi, T 1989 *A Postcranial Guide to Domestic Neo-natal and Juvenile Mammals: The Identification and Aging of Old World Species*. Oxford, BAR.

Ashmore, P J 1998 'Radiocarbon dates for settlements, tombs and ceremonial sites with grooved ware in Scotland', in Gibson, A and Simpson, D (eds) *Prehistoric Ritual and Religion*. Stroud, Sutton Publishing, 139–47.

Anderson, D A, Binney, H A, Smith, M A 1998 'Evidence for abrupt climatic change in northern Scotland between 3900 and 3500 calendar years ago', *Holocene* **8**, 97–105.

Andrews, A H and Noddle, B A 1975 'Absence of premolar teeth in ruminant mandibles found at archaeological sites', *Journal of Archaeological Science* **2**, 137–44.

Ashmore, P J 1999 'Radiocarbon dating: avoiding errors by avoiding mixed samples', *Antiquity* **73** (1999), 124–30.

Ashmore, P J 2000 'Dating the Neolithic', in Ritchie, A (ed) *Neolithic Orkney in its European Context*. Cambridge, McDonald Institute Monograph, 299–308.

Armour-Chelu, M nd The faunal remains from the Links of Noltland site (unpublished).

Baker, J and Brothwell, D R 1980 *Animal Diseases in Archaeology*. Burlington MA, Academic Press Inc.

Balasse, M and Ambrose, S H 2005 'Distinguishing sheep and goats using dental morphology and stable carbon isotopes in C4 grassland environments', *Journal of Archaeological Science* **32**, 691–702.

Balasse, M and Tresset, A 2007 'Environmental constraints on the reproductive activity of domestic sheep and cattle: what latitude the herder?', *Anthropozoologica* **42** (2), 71–88.

Balasse, M, Tresset, A, Ambrose, S H 2006 'Stable isotope evidence (13C, 18C) for winter feeding on seaweed by Neolithic sheep in Scotland', *Journal of Zoology* **270**, 170–6.

Barber, J, Duffy, A, O'Sullivan, J 1996 'The excavation of two Bronze Age burial cairns at Bu Farm, Rapness, Westray, Orkney', *Proceedings of the Society of Antiquaries of Scotland* **126**, 103–20.

Barclay, G J 1997 *State-funded Rescue Archaeology in Scotland, Past, Present and Future*. Edinburgh, Historic Scotland Ancient Monuments Division, Occasional Paper Number 2.

Bartosiewicz, L 2008 'Environment stress in early domestic sheep', in Miklíková, Z and Thomas, R *Current Research in Animal Paleopathology: Proceedings of the Second ICAZ Animal Paleopathology Working Group Conference*. Oxford, BAR International Series **1844**.

Bass, W M 2005 *Human Osteology: A Laboratory and Field Guide Manual*. 5th edition. Springfield, Missouri Archaeological Society.

Binford, L R 1978 *Nunamiut Ethnoarchaeology*. New York, Academic Press.

BOAT 1998 'The Links of Noltland', *Bulletin of The Orkney Archaeological Trust* **2**, 1.

Bocek, B 1986 'Rodent ecology and burrowing behavior: predicted effects on archaeological site formation', *American Antiquity* **51**, 589–603.

Bond, J 2007 'An articulated cattle skeleton' in Dockrill, S J (ed) *Investigations in Sanday, Orkney*, vol 2, *Tofts Ness, Sanday. An island landscape through 3000 years of prehistory*. The Orcadian Ltd/Historic Scotland, 195–201

Bond, J 2007a 'The mammal bone', in Hunter, J *Investigations in Sanday, Orkney*, vol 1, *A Multi-period Settlement from Neolithic to Late Norse Times*. Kirkwall, The Orcadian Press Ltd/Historic Scotland.

Bond, J 2007b 'An articulated cattle skeleton from the late Neolithic midden', in Dockrill, S J *Investigations in Sanday, Orkney*, vol 2, *Tofts Ness, Sanday: An Island Landscape through 3000 Years of Prehistory*. Kirkwall, The Orcadian Ltd/Historic Scotland, 195–202.

Bonnichsen, R, and Sorg, M 1989 *Bone Modification*. Orono, Maine, Center for the Study of the First Americans, University of Maine.

Boyle, K V 2005 'Late Neolithic seal hunting in Southern Brittany: a zooarchaeological study of the site of Er Yoh (Morbihan)', in Monks, G G *The Exploitation and Cultural Importance of Sea Mammals*. Oxford, Oxbow Books.

Brewer, D, Clark, T, Phillips, A A 2002 *Dogs in Antiquity: Anubis to Cerberus: the Origins of the Domestic Dog*. Warminster, Aris & Phillips.

Brickley, M and McKinley, J I (eds) 2004 *Guidelines to the Standards for Recording Human Remains*. IFA Paper no 7, BABAO/IFA.

Brothwell, D 1993 'On the problem of interpreting within-sample variation', in Clason, P, Payne, A S, Uerpmann, H-P (eds) *Skeletons in her Cupboard: Festschrift for Juliet Clutton-Brock*. Monograph **34**, Oxford, Oxbow Books.

Buckley, T E and Harvie-Brown, J A 1891 *A Vertebrate Fauna of the Orkney Islands*. Edinburgh, David Douglas.

Bullock, D and Rackman, J 1982 'Epiphyseal fusion and teeth eruption of feral goats from Moffatdale, Dumfries and Galloway, Scotland', in Wilson, B, Grigson, C, Payne, S *Ageing and Sexing Animal Bones from Archaeological Sites*. BAR British Series **109**, Oxford, British Archaeological Reports.

Bullock, P, Federoff, N, Jongerius, A, Stoops, G, Tursina, T, and Babel, U 1985 *Handbook for Soil Thin Section Description*. Wolverhampton, Waine Research Publications.

Buikstra, J E and Ubelaker, D H (eds) 1994 *Standards for Data Collection from Human Skeletal Remains*. Arkansas Archaeological Survey Research Series no 44, Arkansas, Arkansas Archaeological Survey.

Buteux, S 1997 *Settlements at Skaill, Deerness, Orkney: Excavations by Peter Gelling of the Prehistoric, Pictish, Viking and Later Periods, 1963–81*. BAR British Series **260**, Oxford, British Archaeological Reports, 70–95.

Cachel, S 2000 'The human career: human biological and cultural origins', *Geoarchaeology* 15 (4), 373–5.

Chaplin, R E 1971 *The Study of Animal Bones from Archaeological Sites*. London/New York, Seminar Press Ltd.

Chaplin, R E 1983 'The ecology and behaviour of deer in relation to their impact on the environment of prehistoric Britain', in Bailey, G *Hunter-Gatherer Economy in Prehistory: A European perspective*. Cambridge, Cambridge University Press.

Charleson, M M 1902 'Note of a chambered cairn in the parish of Firth, Orkney', *Proceedings of the Society of Antiquaries of Scotland* **36**, 733–8.

Childe, V G 1931 'Final report on the operations at Skara Brae', *Proceedings of the Society of Antiquaries of Scotland* **65** (1930–1), 27–77.

Childe, V G 1950 *Skara Brae*. Edinburgh.

Childe, V G and Grant, W G 1939 'A Stone Age Settlement at the Braes of Rinyo, Rousay, Orkney', *Proceedings of the Society of Antiquaries of Scotland* **73** (1938–9), 6–31.

Childe, V G and Grant, W G 1947 'A Stone Age Settlement at the Braes of Rinyo, Rousay, Orkney (second report)', *Proceedings of the Society of Antiquaries of Scotland* **81** (1946–7), 16–42.

Clark, G 1952 *Prehistoric Europe: The Economic Basis*. London, Methuen.

Clarke, A 1989 'The skaill knife as a butchering tool', *Lithics* **10**, 16–27.

Clarke, A 1999 'The coarse stone tools', in Owen, O and Lowe, C *Kebister: The Four-thousand-year-old Story of One Shetland Township*. Society of Antiquaries of Scotland Monograph.

Clarke, A 2000 'The coarse stone tool assemblage', in Downes, J and Lamb, R *Prehistoric Houses at Sumburgh in Shetland*. Oxford, Oxbow, 87–104.

Clarke, A 2005 'The stone tool assemblage', in Richards, C (ed) *Dwelling among the Monuments. The Neolithic Village of Barnhouse, Maeshowe Passage Grave and Surrounding Monuments at Stenness, Orkney*. Cambridge, McDonald Institute Monograph, 323–34.

Clarke, A 2006 *Stone Tools and the Prehistory of the Northern Isles*. BAR British Series **406**, Oxford, British Archaeological Reports.

Clarke, A 2007a 'The coarse stone', in Hunter, J *Investigations in Sanday, Orkney*, vol 1, *Excavations at Pool, Sanday, a Multi-period Settlement from Neolithic to Late Norse Times*. Kirkwall, The Orcadian Ltd, 353–8.

Clarke, A 2007b 'The coarse stone', in Dockrill, S J *Investigations in Sanday, Orkney*, vol 2, *Excavations at Tofts Ness, Sanday, an island landscape through 3000 years of prehistory*. Kirkwall, The Orcadian Ltd, 292–316.

Clarke, A forthcoming b 'The coarse stone assemblage', in Clarke, D V and Shepherd, A *Links of Noltland*.

Clarke, D V and Sharples, N 1985 (reprinted 1990) 'Settlements and subsistence in the third millennium BC', in Renfrew, C (ed) *The Prehistory of Orkney*. Edinburgh, Edinburgh University Press, 54–82.

Clarke, D V, Hope, R and Wickham-Jones, C R 1978 'The Links of Noltland', *Current Archaeology* **6**, 2 (1978), no 61, 44–6.

Clutton-Brock, T H 2004 'The causes and consequences of instability', in Clutton-Brock, T H and Pemberton, J *Soay Sheep: Dynamics and Selection in an Island Population* Cambridge, Cambridge University Press.

Clutton-Brock, J 1976 'Animal remains from Stones of Stenness, Orkney', *Proceedings of the Society of Antiquaries of Scotland* **107**, 34–7.

Clutton-Brock, J 1979 'Chapter IX: Report of the mammalian remains other than rodents from Quanterness', in Renfrew, C *Investigations in Orkney*. London, Society of Antiquaries, 112–34.

Clutton-Brock, T H and Albon, S D 1989 *Red Deer in the Highlands*. Oxford, BSP Professional Books.

Clutton-Brock, T, Guinness, F, Albon, S 1982 *Red Deer: Behaviour and Ecology of Two Sexes*. Edinburgh, Edinburgh University Press.

Cooney, G 2000 *Landscapes of Neolithic Ireland*. London, Routledge.

Copley, M S, Berstan, R, Dudd, S N, Dockerty, G, Mukherjee, A J, Straker, V, Payne, S, Evershed, R P 2003 'Direct chemical evidence for widespread dairying in prehistoric Britain', *Proceedings of the National Academy of Sciences USA* **100**, 1524–9.

Courty, M A, Goldberg, P and Macphail, R I 1989 *Soils and Micromorphology in Archaeology*. Cambridge, Cambridge University Press.

Dainton, M 1992 'A quick, semi-quantitative method for recording nematode gut parasite eggs from archaeological deposits', *Circaea, the Journal of the Association for Environmental Archaeology* **9**, 58–63.

Davidson, D A 1979 'The Orcadian environment and cairn location', in Renfrew, C *Investigations in Orkney*. London, Society of Antiquaries, 7–20.

Davidson, D A and Jones, R L 1985 'The environment of Orkney', in Renfrew, C *The Prehistory of Orkney*. Edinburgh, Edinburgh University Press, 10–35.

Davidson, D A and Simpson, I A 2001 'Archaeology and Soil Micromorphology' in Brothwell, D R and Pollard, A M (eds) *Handbook of Archaeological Sciences*. Chichester, Wiley, 167–77.

Davis, S M J 1987 *The Archaeology of Animals*. New Haven, Yale University Press.

Davis, S J M 1996 'Measurements of a group of adult female Shetland sheep skeletons from a single flock: a baseline for zooarchaeologists', *Journal of Archaeological Science* **23**, 593–612.

Davis, S J M 2000 'The effect of castration and age on the development of the Shetland sheep skeleton and a metric comparison between bones of males, females and castrates', *Journal of Archaeological Science* **27**, 373–90.

Diamond, J 2002 'Evolution, consequences and future of plant and animal domestication', *Nature* **418**, 700–7.

Dickson, C 1999 'The plant remains', in Ballin-Smith, B, *Howe: Four Millennia of Orkney Prehistory, Excavations 1978–1982*. Edinburgh, Society of Antiquaries of Scotland Monograph **9**.

Dobney, K, Envynck, A, Albarella, U, Rowley-Conwy, P 2007 'The transition from wild boar to domestic pig in Eurasia, illustrated by a tooth development defect and biometrical data', in Albarella, U, Dobney, K, Envynck, A, Rowley-Conwy, P *Pigs and Humans: 10,000 Years of Interactions*. Oxford, Oxford University Press, 57–82.

Dockrill, S J 2007 *Investigations in Sanday Orkney*, vol 2, *Excavations at Tofts Ness, Sanday, an island landscape through 3000 years of prehistory*. Kirkwall, The Orcadian Ltd.

Downes, J and Lamb, R G 2000 *Prehistoric Houses at Sumburgh in Shetland*. Oxford, Oxbow.

Downes, J and Richards, C 2000 'Excavating the Neolithic and Early Bronze Age of Orkney: Recognition and interpretation in the field', in Ritchie, A (ed) *Neolithic Orkney in its European Context*. Cambridge, McDonald Institute Monograph.

Downes, J, Foster, S M, Wickham-Jones C R and Callister, J (eds) 2005 *The Heart of Neolithic Orkney World Heritage Site Research Agenda*. Edinburgh, Historic Scotland.

Driesch, von den, A 1976 *A Guide to the Measurement of Animal Bones*. Peabody Museum Bulletin **1**.

Dunwell, A 1995 *Links of Noltland, Westray, Orkney: Topographic Survey 1980–81 and 1994*. CFA Report no **193**.

Edwards, C J, Bollongino R, Scheu, A, Chamberlain, C, Tresset, A, Vigne, J-D, Baird, J F, Larson, G, Ho, S Y W, Heupink, T H, Shapiro, B, Freeman, A R, Thomas, M G, Arbogast, R-M, Arndt, B, Bartosiewicz, L, Benecke, N, Budja, M, Chaix, L, Choyke, A M, Coqueugniot, E, Döhle, H-J, Göldner, H, Hartz, S, Helmer, D, Herzig, B, Hongo, H, Mashkour, M, Özdogan, M, Pucher, E, Roth, G, Schade-Lindig, S, Schmölcke, U, Schulting, R J, Elisabeth Stephan, E, Uerpmann, H-P, I Vörös, I, Voytek, B, Bradley, D G, Burger, J 2007 'Mitochondrial DNA analysis shows a Near Eastern Neolithic origin for domestic cattle and no indication of domestication of European aurochs', *Proceedings of the Royal Society*, Series B, *Biological Sciences* **274**, 1377–85.

Ervynck, A 2005 'Detecting the seasonal slaughtering of domestic mammals: Inferences from the detailed recording of tooth eruption and wear', *Environmental Archaeology* **10**, 153–69.

Fabis, M 2005 'Pathological alteration of cattle skeletons – evidence for the draught exploitation of animals? Diet and health in past animal populations : current research and future directions', International Council for Archaeozoology. 9th Conference 2002, Durham England.

Fenton, A 1978 *The Northern Isles: Orkney and Shetland*. East Linton, Tuckwell Press.

Finlay, J 2006 'Faunal remains', in Simpson, D, Murphy, E, Gregory, R *Excavations at Northton, Isle of Harris*, BAR. British Series **408**, Oxford, British Archaeological Reports, 75–7.

Finlayson, B 2007 ' Flint', in Hunter, J *Investigations in Sanday, Orkney*, vol 1, *Excavations at Pool, Sanday: A Multi-period Settlement from Neolithic to Late Norse Times*. Kirkwall, The Orcadian Ltd/Historic Scotland, 389–403.

First Statistical Account of Scotland 1795.

Fisher, J W 1995 'Bone surface modifications in zooarchaeology', *Journal of Archaeological Method and Theory* **2**, 7–68.

FitzPatrick, E A 1993 *Soil Microscopy and Micromorphology*. Chichester, Wiley.

Forster, A and Sharman, P 2009 'Use in early prehistoric Shetland: from the Neolithic to the early Iron Age', in Forster, A, K and Turner, V E (eds) *Kleber: Shetland's First Industry. The Archaeology of Steatite in Shetland*. Lerwick, Shetland Amenity Trust.

Forster, A K forthcoming a 'Steatite vessels and other objects', in Moore, H and Wilson, G *Excavations at Bayanne, Yell, Shetland*.

Forster, A K forthcoming b, 'The steatite assemblage', in Dockrill, S, J and Bond, J M *Old Scatness Broch: The Iron Age*. To be published as a Shetland Amenity Trust Monograph.

Fowler, K, Greenfield, H, van Schalkwyk, L 2004 'The effects of burrowing activity on archaeological sites: Ndondondwane, South Africa', *Geoarchaeology* **19**, 411–70.

Fraser, D 1981 Results reported in Dunwell, A 1995 *Links of Noltland, Westray, Orkney: Topographic Survey, 1980–81 and 1994*. CFA Report no **193**.

Geigl, E-M and Pruvost, M 2004 'Plea for a multidisciplinary approach to the study of Neolithic migrations: the analysis of biological witness and the input of palaeogenetics', in Mondini, M, Munoz, S, Wicker, S *Colonisation, Migration and Marginal Areas*. Oxford, Oxbow Books.

Goss, R 1983 *Deer Antlers: Regeneration, Function and Evolution*. London, Academic Press Inc.

Graham-Campbell, J, and Batey, C E 1998 *Vikings in Scotland: An Archaeological Survey*. Edinburgh, Edinburgh University Press.

Grant, A 1982 'The use of tooth wear as a guide to the age of domestic ungulates', in Wilson, B, Grigson, C, Payne, S *Ageing and Sexing Animal Bones from Archaeological Sites*. BAR British Series **109**, Oxford, British Archaeological Reports.

Grogan, E 2004 'The implications of Irish Neolithic houses', in Shepherd, I A and Barclay, G J (eds) *Scotland in Ancient Europe*. Edinburgh, Society of Antiquaries of Scotland Monograph, 103–14.

Grubb, P 1974 'Population dynamics of the Soay sheep', in Jewell, P, Milner, C, Morton Boyd, J *Island Survivors*. London, Athlone Press

Guttmann, E B, Simpson, I A, Davidson, D A, and Dockrill, S J 2006 'The management of arable land from prehistory to the present: case studies from the Northern Isles of Scotland', *Geoarchaeology* **21** (1), 61–92.

Gwynne, D and Boyd, J M 1970 'Relationships between numbers of Soay sheep and pastures at St Kilda', in *Animal Populations in Relation to their Food Sources*. A Watson. Edinburgh, Blackwell Scientific Publications, 289–99.

Haber, A 2007 'A statistical method for dealing with isolated teeth: aging pig teeth from Hagoshrim, Israel', in *Pigs and Humans: 10,000 Years of Interactions*. Albarella, U, Dobney, K, Envynck, A, Rowley-Conwy, P . Oxford, Oxford University Press, 218–27.

Hastie, M forthcoming a, 'The carbonised plant remains from a multi-phase site at Bayanne, Yell', in Moore, H and Wilson, G *Excavations at Bayanne, Yell, Shetland*.

Hastie, M forthcoming b, 'Langskaill, Westray, Orkney: the carbonised plant remains', in Moore, H and Wilson, G *Excavations at Langskaill, Westray, Orkney*.

Hedges, J W 1975 'Excavation of two Orcadian burnt mounds at Liddle and Beaquoy', *Proceedings of the Society of Antiquaries of Scotland* **106** (1974–5), 39–99.

Hinton, P 2005 'The charred plant remains from Barnhouse and Maeshowe', in Richards, C *Dwelling among the Monuments: The Neolithic Village of Barnhouse, Maeshowe Passage Grave and Surrounding Monuments at Stenness, Orkney*. Cambridge, McDonald Institute of Archaeological Research.

Historic Scotland 1998 *Heart of Neolithic Orkney: Nomination for World Heritage Status*. 5, (ii), Edinburgh, Historic Scotland.

Henshall, A S, 1983 'Flint and chert', in Ritchie, A 'Excavation of a Neolithic farmstead at Knap of Howar, Papa Westray, Orkney'. *Proceedings of the Society of Antiquaries of Scotland* **113**, 84–7.

Henshall, A S 1963 *The Chambered Tombs of Scotland*. Edinburgh, Edinburgh University Press.

Hull, R 2007 *Scottish Mammals*. Edinburgh, Birlinn.

Hunter, J R 2007 *Investigations in Sanday, Orkney*, vol 1, *Excavations at Pool, Sanday: A Multi-period Settlement from Neolithic to Late Norse Times*. Kirkwall, The Orcadian Ltd.

Johnston, D A 1997 'Biggar Common, 1987–93: an early prehistoric funerary and domestic landscape in Clydesdale, South Lanarkshire', *Proceedings of the Society of Antiquaries of Scotland* **127**, 185–225.

Jones, A, Cole, W J, Jones, R E 2005 'Organic residue analysis of Grooved ware from Barnhouse', in Richards, C *Dwelling among the Monuments: The Neolithic village of Barnhouse, Maeshowe Passage Grave and Surrounding Monuments at Stenness, Orkney*. Cambridge, McDonald Institute of Archaeological Research.

Jones, K T and Metcalfe, D 1988 'Bare bones archaeology: bone marrow indices and efficiency', *Journal of Archaeological Science* **15**, 415–23.

King, S E 2005 'Barnhouse faunal remains, in Richards, C *Dwelling among the Monuments: The Neolithic Village of Barnhouse, Maeshowe Passage Grave and Surrounding Monuments at Stenness, Orkney*. Cambridge, McDonald Institute of Archaeological Research.

King, S and Barrett, J, 2002 'Appendix 1: Human bone', in Moore, H, Wilson, G and Barrett, J *Report on an Assessment at The Links of Noltland 2001*. EASE/University of York Report, 54–5.

Kitchener, A C and Bonsall, C 1997 'AMS radiocarbon dates for some extinct Scottish mammals', *Quaternary Newsletter* **83**, 1–11.

Lamb, R G 1983 *The Archaeological Sites and Monuments of Papa Westray and Westray: Orkney Islands Area*. Edinburgh, The Royal Commission on the Ancient and Historic Monuments of Scotland.

Larson, G, Dobney, K, Albarella, U, Fang, M, Matisoo-Smith, E, Robins, J, Lowden, S, Finlayson, H, Brand, T, Willerslev, E, Rowley-Conwy, P, Anderson, L, Cooper, A 2005 'Worldwide phylogeography of wild boar reveals multiple centers of pig domestication' *Science* **307**, 1618–21.

Legge, T 2005 'Milk use in prehistory, the osteological evidence' in Outram, A K and Mulville, J *The Zooarchaeology of Fats, Oils, Milk and Dairying*. Oxford, Oxbow Books, 8–13.

Loftus, R T, MacHugh, D E, Bradley, D G, Sharp, P M, Cunningham, P 1994 'Evidence for two independent domestications of cattle', *Proceedings of the National Academy of Sciences, US* **91**, 2757–61.

Lyman, R L 1994 *Vertebrate Taphonomy*. Cambridge, Cambridge University Press.

Lyman, R L 1987 'On the analysis of vertebrate mortality profiles: sample size, mortality type and hunting pressure', *American Antiquity* **52**, 125–42.

Lynn, D and Bell, B 1990 'Links of Noltland, Westray, Orkney', *Discovery and Excavation in Scotland*, 45.

MacGregor, A 1985 *Bone, Antler, Ivory and Horn: The Technology of Skeletal Materials since the Roman Period*. London, Croom Helm.

MacKenzie, W S and Adams, A E 1994 *A Colour Atlas of Rocks and Minerals in Thin Section*. London, Manson Publishing.

Mather, A S, Smith, J S, Ritchie, W 1974 *Beaches of Orkney*. Countryside Commission for Scotland, 116–19.

McCormick, F and Buckland, P C 2003 'Faunal change: the vertebrate fauna', in Edwards, K and Ralston, I *Scotland after the Ice Age: Environment, Archaeology and History, 8000 BC–AD 1000*. Edinburgh, Edinburgh University Press.

McGovern, T 1985 'Contributions to the paleoeconomy of Norse Greenland', *Acta Archaeologica* **54**, 73–122.

McGrail, S 1998 *Ancient Boats in N.W. Europe: The Archaeology of Water Transport to AD 1500*. London, Longman.

Meadows, R 1999 'The use of size index scaling techniques for research on archaeozooloical collections from the Middle East', in Becker, C, Manhart, H, Peters, J, Schibler, J, *Historia Animalium ex Ossibus: Festschrift fur Angela von den Driesch*. Rahden, Verlag Marie Leidorf, 285–300.

Middleton, R, 2005 'The Barnhouse lithic assemblage', in Richards, C (ed) *Dwelling among the Monuments: The Neolithic Village of Barnhouse, Maeshowe Passage Grave and Surrounding Monuments at Stenness, Orkney*. Cambridge, McDonald Institute Monograph, 293–321.

Moore, H and Wilson, G 1997 'Food for thought: burnt mound survey and excavations at Tangwick, Eshaness, Shetland', *Proceedings of the Society of Antiquaries of Scotland* **129**.

Moore, H and Wilson, G 1998 *Orkney Coastal Zone Assessment 1998: Westray, Papa Westray, Holm of Papa Westray and West Mainland*. EASE/Historic Scotland Report.

Moore, H and Wilson, G, 2000 *Report on Rescue Investigations at Links of Noltland, Westray, Orkney*. EASE/Historic Scotland Report.

Moore, H, Wilson, G and Barrett, J 2002 *Report on an Assessment at the Links of Noltland, 2001*. EASE/University of York Report.

Moore, H and Wilson, G 2006 *Report on Assessment in PIC Area at Links of Noltland, Westray, Orkney, 2006*. EASE/ Historic Scotland Report.

Moore, H and Wilson, G 2007a *Report on Excavations at Links of Noltland, Westray, Orkney, 2007*. EASE/Historic Scotland Report.

Moore, H and Wilson, G 2007b *Data Structure Report: Excavation and Assessment at The Links of Noltland, Westray, Orkney, September–November 2007*. EASE/Historic Scotland Report.

Moore, H and Wilson, G 2007c *Excavation of a Second Bronze Age Settlement at Links of Noltland (Scheduled Area), Westray, Orkney, October 2007*. EASE/Historic Scotland Report.

Moore, H and Wilson, G 2009 *Landscape and Settlement at Links of Noltland, Westray: Recent Work Reviewed*. Ease Archaeology/ScARF Neolithic Research Framework [accessed through http://www.socantscot.org March 2010].

Mulville, J 2002 'The role of Cetacea in prehistoric and historic Atlantic Scotland', *International Journal of Osteoarchaeology* **12**, 34–48.

National Park Service 2006 'Common Plants of Lake Clarke Area', US Department of the Interior [accessed through http://www.nps.gov/lacl/naturescience/common-plants.htm 17/12/09].

Needham, S and Spence, T 1997 'Refuse and the formation of middens', *Antiquity* **71**, 77–90.

Nicholson, R A and Davies, G 2007 'Mammal bones', in Dockrill, S J *Investigations in Sanday, Orkney*, vol 2, *Tofts Ness, Sanday: An island landscape through 3000 years of prehistory*. Kirkwall, The Orcadian Ltd/Historic Scotlan, 169–95.

Noddle, B 1984 'Exact chronology of epiphyseal closure in domestic animals of the past: an

Noddle, B 'The animal bone', in Ritchie, A 1983 'Excavation of a Neolithic farmstead at Knap of Howar, Papa Westray, Orkney', *Proceedings of the Society of Antiquaries of Scotland* **113**, 40–121.

Noe-Nygaard 1977 'Butchering and marrow fracturing as a taphonomic factor in archaeological deposits', *Paleobiology* **3**, 218–37.

O'Conner, T 2000 *The Archaeology of Animal Bones*. Stroud, Sutton Publishing.

Outram, A K 2004 'Identifying dietary stress in marginal environments: bone fats, optimal foraging theory and the seasonal round', in Mondini, M, Munoz, S, Wicker, S *Colonisation, Migration and Marginal Areas*. Oxford, Oxbow Books.

Outram, A K 2002 'Bone fracture and within-bone nutrients: an experimentally based method for investigating levels of marrow extraction', in Miracle, P, Milner and N *Consuming Passions and Patterns of Consumption*. Cambridge, McDonald Institute Monograph, 51–63.

Outram, A K 2001 'A new approach to identifying bone marrow and grease exploitation: why the "intermediate" fragments should not be ignored', *Journal of Archaeological Science* **28**, 401–10.

Outram, A K and Mulville, J 2005 'The zooarchaeology of fats, oils, milk and dairying, an introduction and overview', in Mulville, J and Outram, A K *The Zooarchaeology of Fats, Oils, Milk and Dairying* Oxford, Oxbow Books, 1–6.

Ovrevik, S 1985 'The second millennium and after', in Renfrew, C (ed) *The Prehistory of Orkney*. Edinburgh, Edinburgh University Press, 131–49.

Owen, O 1986 *Report on the Archaeological Watching Brief Undertaken during Stabilisation Programme of the Links of Noltland, Westray, Orkney*. Edinburgh, Historic Scotland.

Payne, S 1987 'Reference codes for wear stages in the mandibular cheek teeth of sheep and goats', *Journal of Archaeological Science* **14**, 609–14.

Petrie, G 1868 'Notice of ruins of ancient dwellings at Skara, Bay of Skaill, in the parish of Sandwick, Orkney, recently excavated', *Proceedings of the Society of Antiquaries of Scotland* **7**, 201–19.

Petrie, G nd Notebook no 9, 26–9.

Platt, M 1956 'Animal remains' in Hamilton, J *Excavations at Jarlshof, Shetland*. Edinburgh, HMSO, xiv, 227.

Rackman, D J and Young, R 1989 'Overall assessment: excavations at the Point of Buckquoy', in Morris, C *The Birsay Bay Project: Brough Road Excavations 1976–1982*. Durham, University of Durham. Department of Archaeology, 102.

Reitz, E J and Wing, E S 1999 *Zooarchaeology*. Cambridge, Cambridge University Press.

Rees, S E 1979 *Agricultural Implements in Prehistoric and Roman Britain*. BAR British Series **69**, Oxford, British Archaeological Reports

Richards, C (ed) 2005 *Dwelling Among the Monuments: The Neolithic Village of Barnhouse, Maeshowe Passage Grave and Surrounding Monuments at Stenness, Orkney*. Cambridge, McDonald Institute Monograph.

Richards, M P 2004 'The early Neolithic in Britain: new insights from bimolecular biology', in Shepherd, I A G and Barclay, G J *Scotland in Ancient Europe: The Neolithic and Early Bronze Age in Scotland in their European Context*. Edinburgh, Society of Antiquaries of Scotland.

Richards, M P and Hedges, R E M 1999 'A Neolithic revolution? New evidence of diet in the British Neolithic, *Antiquity* **73**, 891–7.

Reitz, E A and Wing, E S 1999 *Zooarchaeology*. Cambridge, Cambridge University Press.

Ritchie, J 1920 *The Influence of Man on Animal Life in Scotland: A Study in Faunal Evolution*. Cambridge, Cambridge University Press.

Ritchie, A 1995 *Prehistoric Orkney*. Batsford, London.

Roberts, C and Cox, M 2003 *Health and Disease in Britain: From Prehistory to the Present Day*. Stroud, Sutton Publishing.

Saville, A 2000 'Orkney and Scotland before the Neolithic period', in Ritchie, A (ed) *Neolithic Orkney in its European Context*. Cambridge, McDonald Institute Monograph, 91–100.

Saville, A 2004 Skara Brae 1972–73: Struck lithic artefacts. Unpublished specialist report, Archaeology Department, National Museums Scotland.

Saville, A, 2005 Skara Brae: Struck lithic artefacts from the 1927–1930 excavations. Unpublished specialist report, Archaeology Department, National Museums Scotland.

Schiffer, M 1976 *Behavioral Archaeology*. New York, Academic Press.

Schulting, R J 2004 'An Irish sea change: some implications for the Mesolithic–Neolithic transition', in Cummings, V and Fowler, C *The Neolithic of the Irish Sea*. Oxford, Oxbow Books.

Scottish Natural Heritage (Agency) and Great Britain Forestry Authority Scotland 1996 *Red Deer*. Edinburgh, Scottish Natural Heritage.

Serjeantson, D 1990 'The introduction of mammals to the Outer Hebrides and the role of boats in stock management', *Anthropozoologica* **13**, 7–18.

Serjeantson, D and Bond, J 2007a. 'Cattle and sheep husbandry at Pool: Evidence from toothwear analyses', in Hunter, J *Investigations in Sanday, Orkney*, vol 1, *Excavations at Pool, Sanday: A Multi-period Settlement from Neolithic to Late Norse Times*. Kirkwall, The Orcadian Ltd/Historic Scotland.

Serjeantson, D and Bond, J 2007b 'Cattle and sheep husbandry: evidence of dairying from analysis of tooth eruption and wear', in Dockrill, S J *Investigations in Sanday, Orkney*, vol 2, *Tofts Ness, Sanday. An Island Landscape through 3000 Years of Prehistory*. Kirkwall, The Orcadian Press Ltd/Historic Scotland, 195–202.

Sharman, P M 2000b 'Steatite and other fine stone objects', in Lamb, R and Downes, J (eds) *Excavations at Sumburgh, Shetland*. Oxford, Oxbow, 82–7.

Sharman, P M 2007 'Excavation of a Bronze Age funerary site at Loth Road, Sanday, Orkney', *Scottish Archaeological Internet Report* **25** [accessed through http://www.sair.org.uk June 2010].

Sharples, N 1992 *Links of Noltland: Report on Erosion*. Edinburgh, Historic Scotland.

Sharples, N 2000 'Antlers and Orcadian Rituals: An ambiguous role for red deer in the Neolithic', in Ritchie, A (ed) *Neolithic Orkney in its European Context*. Cambridge, McDonald Institute Monograph, 107–16.

Sheridan, A, Brophy, K 2008 ScARF *Neolithic Research Framework: Suggested Themes*. [accessed through: http://www.socantscot.org March 2009]

Sheridan, A 1999 'Grooved ware from the Links of Noltland, Westray, Orkney', in Cleal, R and MacSween, A (eds) *Grooved Ware in Britain and Ireland*. Oxford, Oxbow, 112–24.

Shipman, P, Foster, G, Schoeninger, M 1984 'Burnt bones and teeth: an experimental study of colour, morphology, crystal structure and shrinkage', *Journal of Archaeological Science* **11**, 307–25.

Silver, I 1969 'The ageing of domestic animals', in Brothwell, D and Higgs, E *Science and Archaeology* London, Thames and Hudson, 283–302.

Simonds, J 1854 *The Age of the Ox, Sheep and Pig*. London, W S Orr and Co.

Simpson, I A 1997 'Relict properties of anthropogenic deep top soils as indicators of infield management in Marwick, West Mainland, Orkney', *Journal of Archaeological Science* **24**, 365–80.

Simpson, I A, Barrett, J H and Milek, K B 2005 'Interpreting the Viking Age to medieval period transition in Norse Orkney through cultural soil and sediment analyses', *Geoarchaeology* **20**, 355–77.

Simpson, I A, Dockrill, S J Bull, I D and Evershed, R P 1998 'Early anthropogenic soil formation at Tofts Ness, Sanday, Orkney', *Journal of Archaeological Science* **25**, 729–46.

Simpson, I A, Dockrill, S J, Guttmann, E, Bull, I D and Evershed, R P 2007 'Soils and the early cultural landscape' in Dockrill, S J (ed) *Investigations in Sanday, Orkney*, vol 2, *Tofts Ness, Sanday. An Island Landscape through 3,000 Years of Prehistory*. The Orcadian Ltd/Historic Scotland, 239–52.

Simpson, I A , Guttmann, E B, Cluett, J and Shepherd, A 2006 'Characterising anthropic sediments in north European

Neolithic settlements: an assessment from Skara Brae, Orkney', *Geoarchaeology* **21**, 221–35.

Simpson, I A, Adderley, W P, Guðmundsson, G, Hallsdóttir, M, Sigurgeirsson, M and Snæsdóttir, M 2002 'Soil limitations to agrarian land production in pre-modern Iceland', *Human Ecology* **30**, 423–43.

Simpson, I A, van Bergen, P F, Elhmmali, M, Roberts, D J and Evershed, R P 1999 'Lipid biomarkers of manuring practice in relict anthropogenic soils', *The Holocene* **9**, 223–9.

Simpson, I A, Kirkpatrick, A H, Scott, L, Gill, J P, Hanley, N and MacDonald, A J 1998 'Application of a grazing model to predict moorland utilisation and implications for nature conservation', *Journal of Environmental Management* **54**, 215–31.

Smith, A 2007 'The steatite', in Dockrill, S J *Investigations in Sanday Orkney*, vol 2, *Tofts Ness, Sanday: An Island Landscape through 3,000 Years of Prehistory* The Orcadian Ltd/Historic Scotland, 285–8.

Smith, C 1994 'Animal bone', in Ballin Smith, *Howe: Four Millennia of Orkney Prehistory* Edinburgh, Society of Antiquaries of Scotland, 139–53.

Sommerville, A A, Sanderson, D C W, Hansom, J D and Housley, R A 2001 'Luminescence dating of Aeolian sands from archaeological sites in Northern Britain', *Quaternary Science Reviews* **20**, 913–19.

Stiner M C and Kuhn, S L 1995 'Differential burning, recrystallisation, and fragmentation of archaeological bone', *Journal of Archaeological Science* **22**, 223–37.

Stoops, G 2003 *Guidelines for the Analysis and Description of Soil and Regolith Thin Sections.* Fitchburg, Wisconsin, Madison, WI, Soil Science Society of America.

Studer, J and Pillonel, D 2007 'Traditional pig butchering by the Yali people of West Papua (Irian Jaya): an ethnographic and archaeozoological example', in Albarella, U, Dobney, K, Envynck, A, Rowley-Conwy, P *Pigs and Humans: 10,000 Years of Interaction*. Oxford, Oxford University Press, 308–29.

Svensson, E M, Gotherstrom, A, Vretemark, M 2008 'A DNA test for sex identification in cattle confirms osteometric results', *Journal of Archaeological Science* **35**, 942–6.

Thomson, A M and Simpson, I A 2007 'Modelling historic rangeland management and grazing pressures in landscapes of settlement', *Human Ecology* **35**, 151–68.

Tipping, R and Tisdall, E 2004 'Continuity, crisis and climate change in the Neolithic and Early Bronze Age periods of north-west Europe', in Shepherd, I A G and Barclay, G J *Scotland in Ancient Europe: The Neolithic and Early Bronze Age in Scotland in their European Context*. Edinburgh, Society of Antiquaries of Scotland.

Tresset, A 2003 'French connections II: of cows and men', in Armit, I, Murphy, E, Nelis, E, Simpson, D *Neolithic Settlement in Ireland and Western Britain*. Oxford, Oxbow Books, 224.

Troy, C S, MacHugh, D E, Bailley, J F, Magee, D A, Loftus, R T, Cunningham, P, Chamberlain, A T, Sykes, B C, Bradley, D G 2001 'Genetic evidence for near-eastern origins of European cattle', *Nature* **410**, 1088–91.

Watson, D M S 1931 'The Animal Bones from Skara Brae' in Childe, G. V *Skara Brae: A Pictish Village in Orkney*. London, Kegan Paul, Trench, Trubner and Co Ltd.

Watson, J P N 1978 'The interpretation of epiphyseal fusion data', in Brothwell, D R, Thomas, K D, Clutton-Brock, J *Research Problems in Zooarchaeology.* London, Institute of Archaeology – Occasional Publication **3**, 97–101.

Wickham-Jones, C 2006 *Between the Wind and the Water: World Heritage Orkney.* Macclesfield: Windgather Press Ltd.

World Reference Base 2006. World Reference Base for Soil Resources. ISSS Working Group RB. ISSS, ISRIC, FAO.

Yarrington, C, 2000 'Fabric groups', in Downes, J and Lamb, R *Prehistoric Houses at Sumburgh in Shetland: Excavations at Sumburgh Airport 1967–74.* Oxford, Oxbow, 38–9.